The Door of No Return

Michael E. Sawyer

The Door of ~~No~~ Return

Being-as-Black

TEMPLE UNIVERSITY PRESS
Philadelphia • Rome • Tokyo

TEMPLE UNIVERSITY PRESS
Philadelphia, Pennsylvania 19122
tupress.temple.edu

Published 2026

Library of Congress Cataloging-in-Publication Data

Names: Sawyer, Michael E., 1967– author
Title: The door of no return : Being-as-Black / Michael E. Sawyer.
Other titles: Door of return
Description: Philadelphia : Temple University Press, 2026. | In the title the word 'no' is presented with a strikethrough. | Includes bibliographical references and index. | Summary: "This book offers a new system of speculative theory and philosophy that proposes the manner in which Black people bring into being a Black future that is not predicated on a dialectical relationship to whiteness"— Provided by publisher.
Identifiers: LCCN 2025052259 (print) | LCCN 2025052260 (ebook) | ISBN 9781439925560 cloth | ISBN 9781439925577 paperback | ISBN 9781439925584 pdf
Subjects: LCSH: Philosophy, Black | Black people—Race identity—Philosophy | Black people—Intellectual life—Philosophy | Arts, Black—Philosophy | Aesthetics, Black—Philosophy
Classification: LCC B808.8 .S29 2026 (print) | LCC B808.8 (ebook)
LC record available at https://lccn.loc.gov/2025052259
LC ebook record available at https://lccn.loc.gov/2025052260

The manufacturer's authorized representative in the EU for product safety is Temple University Rome, Via di San Sebastianello, 16, 00187 Rome RM, Italy (https://rome.temple.edu/).
tempress@temple.edu

♾ The paper used in this publication meets the requirements of the American National Standard for Information Sciences—Permanence of Paper for Printed Library Materials, ANSI Z39.48-1992

Printed in the United States of America

9 8 7 6 5 4 3 2 1

Contents

Prefatory Note

This book arrives having already moved through a series of intense and sometimes discordant conversations about the boundaries of Black Studies, the limits of philosophy, and the authority of aesthetic production. At its core, *The Door of ~~No~~ Return: Being-as-Black* is not offered as a literature review of anti-Blackness discourse nor as a synthetic engagement with the canon of Africana philosophy. Rather, it is a speculative philosophical intervention grounded in the conviction that the Black Aesthetic—music, fiction, performance, visual art—constitutes a domain of cognition in its own right. It is from this terrain that I draw a theory of consciousness and being that insists on the capacity to imagine beyond the foreclosure of Black life.

This project emerges from a felt and conceptual impasse. If the dominant formulations of Black subjectivity conclude with Blackness being defined as the lack of, as abjection, or as the negative limit of the Human, then what remains for us beyond that understanding? What possibilities lie on the other side of the conceptual foreclosure that frames the Middle Passage as the death of history, the end of subjectivity, or the proof of ontological exclusion?

This book wagers that another theoretical path exists—not one of recovery or nostalgia but of invention. Drawing from Toni Morrison's evocative suggestion that we imagine a "*third, if you will pardon the expression, world*," I begin not from philosophy as a disciplinary inheritance but from the speculative richness of Black artistic expression as a form of cognition. When Bob Marley performs "War / No More Trouble," when Morrison stages rememory in *Beloved*, or when Ellison writes through the break, they are not merely describing Black life—they are modeling temporal ruptures, affective reordering, and cognitive innovations that cannot be separated from theory. These are not analogies to thought; they are thought.

This method will not satisfy those seeking philosophical rigor solely within the conventions of Eurocontinental metaphysics. It will also frustrate those who wish to preserve Afropessimism as the only legitimate mode of accounting for anti-Black violence. But I believe there is value in neither repeating the closure of despair nor retreating into the citadel of dialectical form. Instead, this book stages a speculative movement: from cognition (as distorted under white supremacy) to consciousness (as reorganized through aesthetic practice) and, finally, to Being-as-Black—a mode of existence that defines itself not through negation but through generative world making.

Some readers have challenged the philosophical legitimacy of such a move. They ask: Can aesthetic works do theory? Is Morrison's invocation of a "third world" a philosophical proposition or a narrative gesture? Does Blackness precede its ontological subjection, or is that idea itself a fiction born of longing?

These are valid questions. I do not pretend to resolve them definitively. I offer instead a map—provisional, diagrammatic, and, at times, elliptical—through which the speculative force of the Black Aesthetic might become legible as a theory of consciousness, time, and world. The diagrams included are not illustrations but arguments: visual architectures modeling spatial and temporal relations, which the text seeks to elaborate.

This is not a book that surveys the landscape of Black thought; it is one that attempts to alter it. Its primary referents—Morrison, Ellison, Marley, Walker—are not used to ornament theory but to instantiate it. The speculative turn enacted here may challenge familiar protocols of philosophical argumentation, but that is precisely the point. To imagine a future beyond the anti-Black world requires a radical reorganization of the tools we use to think, feel, and know. That reorganization begins with a revision of cognition itself.

In that spirit, *The Door of ~~No~~ Return: Being-as-Black* offers itself as one possible passage. It is neither a final word nor a totalizing claim but a speculative philosophy of Blackness grounded in the belief that another world is not only imaginable but *already emergent*.

Michael E. Sawyer
Pittsburgh, PA
Cripple Creek, CO
2025

Acknowledgments

This project began during the externally imposed pause on the world caused by the global pandemic. It started as a form of self-imposed penance involving a close rereading of Hegel that became a critical part of this project dedicated to finding and maintaining the hope that the German philosopher is dedicated to denying. Like any book project, this one would have been impossible without the kind attention, guidance, and care of many people and institutions.

First, I thank the Department of English at the University of Pittsburgh for the posting I enjoy and the variety of colleagues who have been such generous supporters of my work. I am particularly grateful for Pitt allowing me to spend the 2022–2023 academic year as a visiting scholar at the Humanities Institute at the Pennsylvania State University. Special gratitude is due to the director, John Christman, and associate director, Lauren Kooistra.

This project benefited immeasurably from the opportunity to present portions of the work in a variety of forums over the years of writing. Early vibrations of what would become the mediations on Melville here were worked out during the Carl J. Worrell Annual Lecture on Literature at St. John's College, Santa Fe, New Mexico. My friend and colleague, Kwabena Opoku-Agyemang aided in internationalizing the discourse through his kind invitation to the University of Ghana. My Colorado College colleague Professor Christian Sorace was kind enough to allow me to participate in the "On Fugitive Aesthetics" seminar with Fred Moten and Stefano Harney. I was welcomed back "home" to Brown University, where I gave a talk titled "The Threshold of the Door of No Return." This talk was at the Ruth J. Simmons Center for the Study of Slavery and Justice's Advanced Knowledges Group. This was by the invitation of Professor J. L. Feldman, a scholar whose work I hold in great regard. My dissertation chair, Professor Anthony Bogues, has supported my career and this project without limits and none of my work would be possible without his mentorship and the guidance of the Simmons Center. Additionally, some material in this volume draws on previous publications in *Duquesne Studies in Phenomenology* and the *Journal of French and Francophone Philosophy.* I thank both journals for confirming permission for their use in this book.

I am not a philosopher by training but have enjoyed the attention of those who are in support of this project. The Department of Philosophy at Texas A&M University hosted my talk "Elements of *A Door of No Return: A Phenomenology of Black(ness)*" at their Philosophy Colloquium. I am grateful for the invitation from Professor Amir Jaima and the useful discourse on Hegel with Professor José Louis Bermúdez. New York University's Department of Comparative Literature hosted a two-day seminar on this project around a talk I gave there called "Ishmael, Jack-the-Bear, and Beloved at the Threshold of the Door of No Return." The visit was ably hosted by Professor Jay Garcia and featured deep engagement with Professors Rich Blint and Sybil Cooksey. The project was given space at Stanford University's Humanities Center, where I was able to finally meet a scholar I have admired, Professor Ato Quayson. As I was pulling together the final draft, Professor Anita Chari was kind enough to host me at the University of Oregon's colloquium in the Department of Political Science. Finally, through the kind invitation of Professor Paul Eiss, I presented the last moments of the text at the Humanities Center at Carnegie Mellon University just before I hit send.

I am grateful to all and hope to return the favor.

Writing is never a singular activity, and, in addition to these formal interactions, I have had countless conversations with colleagues who I consider friends who have been kind enough to hear me out even when this project wasn't clear to me. Professors R. A. Judy and Tony Bogues represent the superstructure of my little corner of the "life of the mind." Professor Maya Kronfeld and I have had a running conversation since we met at the School of Criticism and Theory more than a decade ago and having her as an interlocutor is nothing short of miraculous. Andrés Henao Castro read the very first musings of this project, and I cannot express how generative our friendship has been. I am so grateful to have you in my life. Professor Tendayi Sithole is a scholar and friend who gave commentary that was critical to the completion of this project. Professor Judith Butler has offered important mentorship and guidance regarding how to consider my work in the larger context of critical thinking.

The same goes for friends and colleagues like Sora Han, Wellington Bowler, Erin Graff Zivin, Margot Crawford, John Drabinski, Timothy Bewes, Jonathan Lee, Felix Germain, Adi Ophir, Richard Benson, Clyde Pickett, Ariella Azoulay, Nicole Fleetwood, Abou Farman, Achille Mbembe, Michael Berube, Tommy Curry, Fumi Okiji, Janine Jones, Percival Everett, Fred Moten, Tamara Payne, Paul Bove, Robyn Marasco, Illya Davis, Paul Harper, Rocio Zambrana, William Scott, Angie Cruz, Gayle Rogers, Melina Abdullah, Marcus Rediker, Dominic Taylor, Sohail Daulatzai, Calvin Warren, Peniel Joseph, Anwar Uhuru, Joy Priest, Joy James, Rashid Johnson, Piotr Gwiazda, and all of the students who I am constantly asking for input on these ideas.

Pat Cruz, Andre Wright, Flores Forbes, Courtney Henderson, Douglass Wilson, Awwal Gbadamosi, Maurice Brown, and Faith Childs are friends who smooth out bumpy roads along this journey.

My parents, Ernest and Theresa continue to be my biggest supporters in every area of my life along with Ashley and Ellis who offer direction even when they don't know I'm asking for it. My little brother, Mark Sawyer, is missed, and this book suffers from not having him to ask for help. I miss you. Our precious dogs Einstein, Oleo, and Mingus give us more than we could ever give them. We lost Einstein and Oleo during the long years of writing this book and Mingus dutifully remained at his workstation until the 27th of September of 2025 when he finally joined his pack. We miss you all daily.

Manya Whitaker has made every aspect of my life a celebration, and this book is dedicated to you.

Note on Language and Terms

There are some conventions of language that are worth underlining before the project in chief. First, there are places in the text where the racial epithet also known as the "n-word" will appear in full. Some readers may be jarred by this, and they should be. When artists like Toni Morrison employ the term, it is not used for shock value but to invite the reader into the linguistic realm of harm that is a constant feature of the world we live in. When I employ the term, it is not meant to cause additional harm but to memorialize the event as it occurred.

Second, throughout the text, there are conventions of capitalization that need to be marked. For instance, the term "World" does a great deal of work in the book. The capitalized term, "World," is meant to index the concept, while the lowercase term, "world," denotes a specific instantiation of the phenomenon. The same goes for the terms "Space" and "Event." The capitalized version is the concept, and the lowercase version is a specific phenomenon.

The Door of ~~No~~ Return

Introduction

A Black Future

Acceptance of the World as it stands is a luxury that Black people can ill afford.

This book presents, as its central ambition, a work of speculative theory and philosophy as it proposes both the manner in which Black people bring into being that future and what the world that serves as the spatiotemporal context for that existence looks like.

This means that an important component of Africana Thought, and here that term is meant to encompass both theory and philosophy specifically as well as other modalities of inquiry, is to describe the past and present and reach beyond the horizon of the foreseeable to propose a future where Black people do not merely exist as a result of the negative imagination of white supremacist logic that needs a foil for its notion of superiority.

To that end, this work of speculative theory and philosophy endeavors to render inoperative the traditional boundaries around those disciplines. With that in mind, the next move is to trace the implication for thinking about the future of Black people through a musical performance from the late twentieth century.

We Don't Need No More Trouble

In 1977, Bob Marley and the Wailers performed live at the Rainbow Theatre in London during their Exodus Tour. The video of the performance of the medley, *War / No More Trouble*, which is available online, is the text that serves as the point of departure for this effort to think beyond the seemingly inescapable subjective paralysis of Anti-Black Racism. This is substantively due to what I understand to be this performance's significance for the theory and practice of Africana Philosophy, the Black Radical Tradition, and the future of Blackness as we have and will come to understand it. This performance by Bob Marley and the Wailers traces the sweep of Black Radical or Black Revolutionary Thought from the slave coffle to the present moment and beyond, just as this text aspires to do.

I propose that this tracing itself reveals the answers to questions central to Africana thought: (1) What do people of African Descent (Black People) find themselves facing? (2) What is the proper response to the situation? (3) What is the telos or logic of that response? (4) What is the overarching ethos that will be the guide to a beneficial resolution? This same performance by Bob Marley and the Wailers effectively addresses each of these concerns through the musical interpretation of Haile Selassie's 1963 speech at the United Nations, which clearly states the situation at hand, asks and answers the first and second concerns enumerated above, and unequivocally asserts:

> Until the philosophy which holds one race superior and another inferior is finally and permanently discredited and abandoned, everywhere is war. And until there are no longer first-class and second-class citizens of any nation, until the color of a man's skin is of no more significance than the color of his eyes. And until the basic human rights are equally guaranteed to all without regard to race, there is war. And until that day, the dream of lasting peace, world citizenship, rule of international morality, will remain but a fleeting illusion to be pursued but never attained . . . now everywhere is war.[1]

I want to spend a bit of time interrogating the first lines of this quote, which require that the philosophy of white supremacy be first discredited and then, in the aftermath of that exercise, abandoned. For this project, this means several things from a methodological perspective. First, to discredit a philosophical system, it must be thoroughly interrogated; we do that in this book. Second, that system is then abandoned, which is substantively different from being opposed. Africana Philosophy and Theory, as a necessary component of their viability for the project of seeking freedom for the aggrieved, have been necessarily oppositional practices. As this proceeds, the endeavor to construct a philosophical system that speculates on a future untethered from a dialectical relationship to white supremacy must, after the fulfillment of this ambition, also be left behind but never discredited. What Emperor Selassie and Marley understand as "war" is just the physical manifestation of the force of the thorough interrogation that discredits and facilitates abandonment. These moments ought not to be confused.

This performance of Emperor Selassie's text opens with the band's distinctive drum figure from Carlton Barrett, which, in the context we are exploring, must be understood as a call to radical action and, ultimately, war. As mentioned, the text of Emperor Selassie's speech serves as the stuff from which Marley and the Wailers weave this complex engagement with the metaphysics of Blackness in the process of the revolutionary reconstruction of identity. By the beginning of the verse, when Marley begins to press home his indictment of white supremacy via Selassie, the seemingly synchronous relationship between the pace of Marley's lyrics and the methodical vamp of Tyrone Downie, leading the rhythm section on keys, is discernibly shattered. By this I mean that the pace of the rhythm section quickens, and Marley both resists the urge to flee and remains steady in his methodical pursuit of the argument. After exploring this performance and listening closely, it appears to me that the rhythm section is running *forward* to the place of resolution and away from the chaos and mayhem of the war Bob Marley, at this stage of things, is insisting on. They cannot wait, but there is still work, both physical and metaphysical, to be done.

This is indicative of a primary methodological question that arises out of the need to discredit and then abandon white supremacy. This proposes that a systemic replacement happens as the result of a process: an intellectual journey rather than a sudden revelation. Although the moment of the collapse of white supremacy may very well appear as revelatory, it actually results from working through a process that seems to be what Marley insists on with and against the impatience of the rhythm section. Process. It is a journey versus a sudden revelatory alteration, which recognizes the importance of not rushing while, at the same time, resisting the impulse to become comfortable in that exercise.

Here, my attention is immediately drawn to the backing vocals and movements of Rita Marley, Marcia Griffiths, and Judy Mowatt: the I-Threes. Far from existing as the mere background to the lead vocals of Marley, the I-Threes serve here as the disciplining force that dissipates the unresolvable tension between Marley and the rhythmic fugitivity of Aston "Familyman" Barrett and the aforementioned drummer and keyboardist. The I-Threes are at once a Greek Chorus, the three Weird Sisters that foretold the tragedy that would befall Macbeth, and the prime meridian against which this musical and philosophical chaos operates. The metaphoric relationship to Macbeth is important here. In this sense, as with the Weird Sisters, Macbeth, here Marley who is visiting these soothsayers, must, contra the Scot, not seek sovereignty within the context of the system as it stands. That project is doomed to fail. In my reading of this milieu, I found it is the I-Threes who mark, verify, and demand the parameters of the liminal space between the stages that Bob Marley is traversing. At the three minute and twenty-six second mark in the performance, Marley is driven from the mic and joins the I-Threes to exhort them to redouble their metronomic repetition of the consequences and corrective to this form of oppression: "War." The I-Threes are unfazed. Their facial expressions belie the gravity of this argument and, in their failure to react, drive Marley back to his microphone to continue his narrative. At three minutes and fifty-seven seconds, the band, the I-Threes, and Marley reach a point of transition when he voices the next phase of the conflict, uttering "we don't need . . ." and is frozen between war and the desire for the absence of trouble, for twelve seconds, in Moten's Break, the Cut, where Ellison's Jack-the-Bear explains:

> Sometimes you're ahead and sometimes behind. Instead of the swift and imperceptible flowing of time, you are aware of its nodes, those points where time stands still or from which it leaps ahead. And you slip into the breaks and look around.[2]

Here, in this space, we can begin to tease out several things about the pause, halting, rest, or, in Ellisonian terms, hibernation that we witness. Motion is of critical importance here, both in the performance and in the forward momentum of Black Study, but, in at least two senses, motion is necessarily relative. The first sense is macromovement, which can appear immobile because of its vast nature. An oversimplification of this is that, as I am writing, my desk appears to be stable but is only relatively so when, in fact, the Earth is rotating, as is the solar system, as is the galaxy, and so on. Therefore, even in segments of temporal examination where motion appears to be static, it may only be so relative to larger movements, or it may be in steady motion without acceleration, which gives the appearance of immobility. Marley has halted his individual motion forward, but the machine of transportation they have constructed together has grown in mass to accommodate the appearance of a lack of movement.

This is revelatory. Thinking here of Ellison through Marley, who is ahead of the band, in that he is all too aware of where this argument leads but behind their flight to safety: Now. Resonant with our own "Now," the front man is jarred from his space of nodal existence by the reappearance of the opening drum figure and is thrown back to the circularity of reprising the problematic; however accurate the cul-de-sac of pessimism happens to be with respect to its taxonomy of the problem at hand, it does not provide forward momentum. I want to linger here in the fulsome nature of the break and ensure that we understand, far from a node characterized by absence, it is rather a space-time that portends possibility. Mark this as a space of vertical temporal movement rather than the horizontal movement from the past through the fleeting present to the always arriving future. This dis(re)orientation is explored in this book in great detail. Suffice it to say, at this point, as time halts in the common experience of horizontal orientation, Marley has conjured for this exploration/journey a space that facilitates this temporal shift, and it requires patience to explore, with the depth of the node, before revisiting its breadth.

He literally begins again: the band has moved on to the next phase, while he pulls the I-Threes back to the point of departure. It is important to note that this recurring sameness is necessarily different, because, as Marley has traversed this territory, he has learned, and this learning allows for the possibility of a retracing of this space, which has the potential to yield a new result. This, returning to Ellison, cannot be the boomerang that Jack-the-Bear cautions against. ("Beware . . ." Ellison writes, "of those who speak of the *spiral* of history; they are preparing a boomerang. Keep a steel helmet handy.")[3] Marley will have none of it. He has found the path forward where he left it and leaves the I-Threes repeating "War" as he (re)establishes the point of transition, returning to the threshold of the node singing again "We don't need . . ." and the I-Threes drop the repetition of "War!" and describe the need to be without trouble. In the next verses, which serve as the bridge, Marley addresses the wages of pessimism after attesting that "what we need is love sweet love," as he exhorts the listener to "Speak happiness. We're sad enough without our woes (or wars or both). Come on and speak of love, we're sad enough without your wars." I hear this lyric variously as the requirement to "Speak" and/or "Seek" happiness. In the case of Marley's exploration and the project here, to seek is to speak and vice versa. At this moment of crossing, forward motion requires both naming and, in the production of that sonic object, having found, in seeking through speaking, the way forward. Toward this end, Marley is both in preparation and beyond the threshold: between war and love, between discrediting and abandoning, with the middle term being the speaking and seeking of Happiness.

This formulation is complicated, in that it can be read as Marley shifting the territory of what constitutes seemingly irreconcilable states of being. What may be useful here is to imagine that the speaking of happiness into existence facilitates the introduction of the type of euphoria needed to progress to a position of agency under conditions of threat. Agency in this case requires a termination of the state of being warred upon to enter a state of war against just that condition. The human condition under the threat of racialized coercion is a sadness of sufficient depth and breadth to be sufficiently articulated net of additive woes beyond that reality. Further, by resolving the imperative of conflict with the palliating force of Love, the articulation of happiness overwhelms that same condition of sadness that arrives along with woes and foes just as the silencing of woes alone accomplishes in some measure.

Marley, with this journey both backward and forward from the point of *now*, is indicative of the current moment in Black Radical Theory and Philosophical practice that struggles to find a way forward without forgetting the point of departure. The title of this book, *The Door of ~~No~~ Return*, which leaves the negation of the possibility of return in place to be refuted, is written to propose that the metaphysical obstruction represented by the Door of No Return can be penetrated. To do so is to imagine a World different from the one that confounds something like the positive formation of Black Self-Consciousness under the coercive regime of white supremacy and Anti-Black Racism. This project is speculative in its vision and convinced that there is a way of Being-as-Black that is available to us that exceeds the seemingly impenetrable and irreducible nature of Anti-Blackness as the dominant discourse of the world as we know it. The notion of Imagination is a constant companion here, and it is important to take a moment to articulate its power for a radical political project. The term bears the bulk of the weight of this effort to think about the futurity of Blackness beyond the boundary of Anti-Blackness. This means that the Black Aesthetic, as the manifestation or product of the machine of the imagination, is simultaneously the way backward, a way to linger in the fullness of the break/present, and a way to see, manifest, and secure the future. With this in mind, the project has reached a point of oscillation from the practice of Marley's sonic philosophizing to literature.

The Black Aesthetic as Guide

It may be useful to make some foray into articulating how the world we currently live in is a manifestation of the imagined racist, sexist, homophobic, and so on, world that did not exist prior to it being conjured into existence. As a practical matter, the notion of Manifest Destiny serves as a negative instantiation of the power of imagination. The nineteenth-century belief on the part of white settlers that they would inhabit and completely dominate the land (of which they had no actual awareness) between the Atlantic and Pacific Oceans was an act of imagination that now is all too true. Imagination in this book introduces into our current culture the notion that there can be a kenosis of the logic that renders our world a debased place for the existence of Black people that will then allow for a new way of Being, which can only be properly described as the existence of a New World and is expressed clearly in the imagination of thinker Toni Morrison.

This project is deeply indebted to the work of Toni Morrison, an artist whose oeuvre exemplifies what I am situating as the fact that the Black Aesthetic has the "answer" to this dilemma. It is the primary challenge of Black Radical Thought to piece together the terms and conditions of what is a "new" manner of Black Being that is the result of rethought and reimagined modalities of cognition and consciousness. What is meant here by the "Black Aesthetic" is in some sense obvious: art, music, literature, and so on. With that in mind, I also expand the elements of the Black Aesthetic tradition to include theory, philosophy, athletics, and other forms of engagement that are dedicated to telling Black stories and displaying beauty under conditions of threat. Morrison's contributions to this tradition provide the road map to that place in her masterful essay "Race Matters" in the collection *The Source of Self-Regard*, where she frames the depth and breadth of the possibilities, writing:

> The distrust that race studies receives from the authenticating off-campus community is legitimate only when the scholars themselves have not imagined their own homes; have not unapologetically realized and recognized that the valuable work they do can be done no other place; have not envisioned academic life as neither straddling opposing worlds nor as a flight from any. . . . W.E.B. Du Bois's observation is a strategy, not a prophecy or a cure. Beyond the outside/inside double consciousness, this new space postulates the inwardness of the outside; imagines safety without walls where we can conceive of a third, if you will pardon the expression, world, "already made for me, both snug and wide open, with a doorway never needing to be closed." Home.[4]

I want to trouble the account of Home that Morrison granted us in that it is dependent on memory but literally the same as memory. Home, then, in the absence of memory, is not home and is devoid of peace and shelter. Both the sinister technology of the Middle Passage and the appearance of the Door that seems to resist return are made of the absence of memory or, following this logic, are themselves the absence of memory. The durability of Blackness before, after, and in excess of the world of Anti-Black Racism is obscured by the technology introduced through the horror of the Passage, the opening of the Door that will be shut and blocked with a void that persists in resisting knowing.

The telos here, Home, is a progression from Morrison's essay titled "Home" also in *The Source of Self-Regard*. Morrison's argument is a response to a colleague's curiosity about her upbringing, and she writes the following answer to the query:

> This region (Lorain, Elyria, Oberlin) is not like it was when I lived here, but in a way it doesn't matter because home is memory and compan-

ions and/or friends who share the memory. But equally important as the memory and place of one's personal home is the very idea of home. What do we mean when we say "home"?[5]

We see later that the implications of finding ways to deal with the complex barriers to the home-sustaining power of memory, erected by white supremacy, is the prime mover in this project. I am using the term "prime mover" here carefully and mean for it to work in the way it does in the realm of ontology. It is necessary to ensure that the catastrophe of the Middle Passage and its associated tidal waves be divested of the power to be understood as the cause to the effect of Black Memory, in response to its destruction of unfettered access to that archive. The conceptualization of Black Memory intended to be developed here through Morrison locates its origination in the ontological existence of Blackness that, by its fundamental nature, survives points of transition both coercive and validating. The understanding we trace here, which reaches beyond the Middle Passage and its echoes to ground subjectivity, is necessitated by that coercive reality, but the memories themselves are self-referential objects restored through the kinetic power of durable Blackness: Morrison refers to this as Home. This means, through a series of mechanical relations, that Morrison's notion of Home, which equals or is constructed of Memory, is Blackness that is coexistent and productively understood as Home.

This leads to a position that allows one to consider the implication of Blackness in the perceived absence of Memory, being forced into deriving an understanding of Home under the duress of this negativity. This product of the illogical and coercive dystopia of white supremacy and anti-Blackness can lead to the debilitating notion that Blackness does not, did not, and will not exist in the absence of coercive and dialogically oppositional whiteness. The dominant cognitive lens that refracts reality in the world that has come into being at and through the Middle Passage, which exists as both a physical and metaphysical object, both fleeting and durable, is designed to render the durability of Blackness as, at best, idiosyncratic, if not an empirical impossibility.

This project intends to take seriously Morrison's proposal to search for a new world that allows us to understand what, indeed, we need to be meaning when we use the term "Home." Morrison's quote is generative for this text but, more importantly, places an explicit challenge before the Black Radical Tradition: to think and act beyond the binary proposition of positive Black subjectivity indexed against Anti-Black Racism. The fact that she immediately, in explicit and implicit terms, summons W.E.B. Du Bois and his canonical thinking from *The Souls of Black Folk* to this discourse is positively destabilizing to the state of Black Thought, which, in many ways, proceeds from the thinking in *Souls*. There is the obvious reference to what I have called Tripartite Subaltern Consciousness,[6] which is examined in some detail in this book, but, at the outset, it is the reference to "space" and then "world" that requires our immediate attention before we can get to the point of defining "Home."

Space- and Place-iality

All of these terms have, in some sense, become ossified in a variety of disciplinary formations. Understanding that, it is important here to gesture at a threshold feature of the methodological argument of this book that first wants to strenuously resist the notion that Black Aesthetic practices, broadly considered, are not doing philosophical work. That is not true. This is in large measure a linguistic claim. It is an argument that states speculative philosophical projects need to be about the business of defining and redefining terms in order to make arguments, when that discipline has framed itself to deny such a possibility. The Black Aesthetic, broadly understood, is philosophy and philosophical in ways that philosophy should recognize but chooses not to. In fact, in many ways philosophy, as currently constructed, is generally incapable of recognizing Black Thought. This statement is, in some ways, a response to recent and important scholarship that provides an opening for this discussion even while it argues the opposite in some sense.

Note that Morrison first marks the existence and cognitive relevance of a "new space [that] postulates the inwardness of the outside: imagines safety without walls where we can conceive of a third world."[7] This book is dedicated to making some progress in defining a liminal space, described here as both the position of and space for observation of the "*third, if you will pardon the expression, world*," which is itself explored and appears as the Threshold of the Door of ~~No~~ Return. In dealing with what I call the liminal space *of* and *for* observation, it is necessary to map a series of interrelated and interconnected spaces and to designate both those spaces of relative stability and those of relative or constant instability, as they are deeply implicated in the generative stuff of the imaginary. To accomplish this, a thorough exploration of the abstract nature of both "space" and "world," and the relationship between the two, is imperative.

It is important, at this point, to give an account of the relationship that I develop here between the concepts of Space, World, Memory, Home, as well as, ultimately, an account of Blackness that is predicated, along with each of these elements, on cognition. First, this section develops a series of diagrams, substantively "maps" or a "mapping" in the sense that Sylvia Wynter employs the term, of the Spaces and Worlds that are the operating context explored here. This argument, in its initial instantiation, proceeds in linear fashion along a predictable and generally accepted timeline, progressing from the past to the future. We may encounter instances and phenomena that require us to abandon our notions of the linearity and horizontal nature of time for other ways of indexing events, and they will be noted. Because of the current context of our being, we exist in a world brought into kinetic reality through what we understand as the Middle Passage. With that in mind, we must give some account of the world prior to that event.

In the details presented by the diagrams included, I show that Worlds contain and are somewhat made up of Spaces. Spaces are made of memory in the sense that the boundaries of an individual event/space are bracketed by memory; the philosopher Alain Badiou describes this as "The Event." These spaces, or "Memory Boxes," can be displaced, misplaced, disoriented, forgotten, reordered, remembered, misremembered, and/or recalled. What I mean here is that a memory, space, or memory space that is established by the awareness of a threshold condition that situates it as an event means there is necessarily a sense of before, after, and during. In the most benign sense, one might understand this with respect to one's own life, which is oriented and composed of a series of befores, afters, and durings that become the type of memory spaces described here. The life of a human subject is generally understood to be an object that begins with the event of birth and ends with the event of death. Within this totality, there are phenomena that achieve the status of events for individuals or collectivities that are understood as pillars for which there is always a before and after. In our contemporary context, most of us have an event-driven understanding of the world in which we exist as it relates to our way of being before and after the global pandemic, COVID-19.

A brief thought experiment here allows us to think about the concepts of World, Space, Memory, and Blackness in thorough fashion. Recall for a moment what it was like at the height of the pandemic to be in public spaces where most people presented themselves wearing masks. Observing this behavior or perhaps the space that it created and not being "aware" of the event of the pandemic would be disorienting. To approach this thinking from another direction, assuming that the condition of a global viral catastrophe represents the mode of being at that time and space, it would be disorienting to witness modes of living that are *not* under the conditions of a pandemic in that same time and space. What this demonstrates is that an event, in this case the pandemic, has the power to force the creation of public spaces that are of such size, durability, and ubiquity to be coterminous with world. Following this logic, viewing the condition of Black Subjectivity under the conditions/event of anti-Blackness is a snapshot of a particular cultural context. That apparition as a knowable and a known event does not mean that the same subject was not in existence prior to or after the phenomenon or that the subject is only understood to exist as a result of that event. Using our example, there were obviously people before the pandemic. During it, people were understood to exist in a particular manner with an unstable relationship to life. If one were to allow oneself to imagine that people, outside the condition of the pandemic, did not exist as a form of foundational being, it would result in a state of abjection instituted from this confusion.

All of this is to facilitate being more careful in understanding the way in which Event(s), and their knowability and knowledge, prove to establish, via the technology of Memory, a space that contains *all* of the formative elements of world and space. An assemblage of these spaces can be perceived in the aggregate and based on some criteria to be worlds. What is important for this book is the relationship between memory, space, and world under the conditions of remembering, forgetting, or what we will come to understand as re-membering.

Questions proceed from this that complicate matters. If we accept that the erasure of memory from knowledge or the possibility of knowing fractures or renders inactive those spaces, then the components of a world are necessarily rendered unstable in their incompleteness. What we are dealing with here is the erasure of a coherent relationship to the memory-space-world triad of the world before the Middle Passage. What results from that exercise is the construction of a world that requires essential elements of it, memory spaces, to be relegated to the bin of established versus actual nonexistence. To re-create or re-collect these memory-space-worlds would then fracture the world that depends on this disappearance.

In tracing the journey toward Morrison's *third, if you will pardon the expression, world*, the first figure represents the base condition we are examining, which proceeds along a linear timeline and lays out the foundational structure of the worlds and spaces being discussed and further developed in this book. Figure 1 diagrams the first layer of this mapping.

The overarching contemporary context, which I have called the Anti-Black World or World_1, in the reckoning of linear time, comes into existence at the

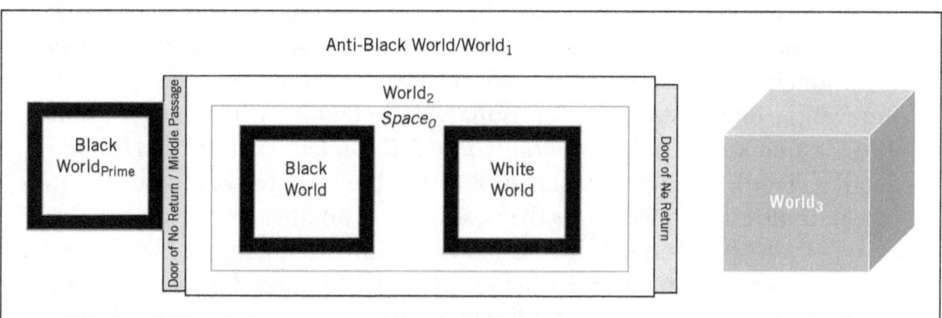

Figure 1 Anti-Black World/World_1 static state.

moment of the encounter of Black World$_{\text{Prime}}$ with Europe. The context that precedes the existence of the Anti-Black World or World$_1$ must be understood as nonexistent in the consciousness or world that I have labeled as Black World$_{\text{Prime.}}$ The transatlantic slave trade and its physical and metaphysical entrepôt to the Anti-Black World, the Middle Passage, forms the boundary of that system, in the present moment, which is characterized most accurately as a type of infinite return that seems to offer no coherent escape from its logic. This project, in summary, proposes that one method for achieving a form of Black Subjectivity that is stable, self-referential, and recognized as such is to *return* to the point of entry and recover, through that phenomenological experience, the necessary consciousness to destabilize and marginalize Anti-Blackness. It is important to note that this return is found through *forward* rather than backward motion and does not portend a physical or metaphysical retracing of the space and time we have traversed.

It is further necessary at this stage to give an additional accounting of the distinction between the terms "space" and "world." In Figure 1, five areas are designated as "world." Black World$_{\text{Prime}}$ precedes the existence of the overarching category of our contemporary way of being, the Anti-Black World or World$_1$, which contains World$_2$. World$_2$ is the repository of *Space*$_0$ (the nomenclature here is meant to assert the existence of other related Spaces that will be exposed in due time), where we find the Black and White Worlds (worlds 3 and 4) that Du Bois, among others, understands to be separated by the Color Line or veil. Finally, at some required disconnect from World$_2$, we find World$_3$ (Morrison's "*third, if you will pardon the expression, world*"), which is the "location" of Home and the fifth of the "world" formations.

Note that there are three Spaces designated in Figure 1. The "space" between the Black World$_{\text{Prime}}$ and the Anti-Black World or World$_1$ is the Door of No Return and the Middle Passage. We have already noted the existence of *Space*$_0$, which is related to the liminal space that is the preoccupation of this book the Door of ~~No~~ Return. There are liminal spaces leading to the threshold of the Door of ~~No~~ Return that will be revealed as we approach them. Developing a theory of the subject by beginning at the level of World requires deeper engagement with the thinkers who have pointed us in this direction, in that it is clearly the preoccupation of Du Bois and the response/innovation/intervention by Morrison. Nahum Dimitri Chandler's *"Beyond This Narrow Now": Or, Delimitations of W.E.B. Du Bois* explores this in some detail. Chandler lays out the stakes of this in the thinking of Du Bois, writing, "His ultimate concern was the possibility of another world, not one that existed in the past and not the present in the future, but another world, one that has not yet been and remains yet to come."[8] In broad gauge, this conceptualization mirrors the thinking of Morrison that serves as the point of departure for this project. The generative intervention by Morrison is in the novelist's resistance to the dialectical nature of Du Bois's formulation. Chandler details this complexity, which Morrison deepens in turn, and he is quoted here expansively:

> Du Bois outlines contrasting experiences of the sense of world. For the "European child" and "white American child," the world consists of horizontal distinctions or social grades, forming a stratified social order. While experienced as a whole or "sphere," it's marked by class distinctions. . . . The "Afro-American" child's experience differs radically. A vertical "fissure" divides the horizontal layers into "white" and "black" hemispheres. Thus, their world, while experienced as a whole, is explicitly marked as categorically divided. . . . The sense of whole here is always already that of the originary nonsimple. Even if only as an infrastructural organization of its possibility, the nonsimple world remains as the sense of "world" in this situation. The sense of world will always have been already phenomenological. . . . Du Bois presents a complicated sense of world, always one of worlds in the plural. The world is experienced differently based on racial identity, with white children perceiving horizontal social stratification, while Black children encounter an additional vertical divide. This creates a fundamentally different worldview, where the sense of a whole world is always already marked by division and complexity.[9]

Chandler's articulation of Du Bois's "sense of world" is of great importance for the arguments in this project. As a matter of translation, I want to gloss the term employed by Chandler, "sense," as another way of pronouncing the fact, here, that forms of cognition grant or implicate forms of consciousness that are derived through sensory engagement. This means that the manner in which a phenomenon is encountered (seen, heard, tasted, felt, etc.) in many ways presupposes the manner in which a subject is conscious of an object/phenomenon. What Chandler exposes here is that Du Bois is referencing the sensory experience of world, which he finds to be "already phenomenological."[10] What Du Bois exposes through Chandler is what I call the "Racist Architecture" of white supremacy. The reality of the series of divisions and thresholds, substantively the "Events" referenced here aggregate themselves into an assemblage that replicates the reality of world that may or may not be world in and of itself. This is an important distinction.

By misunderstanding what I label as "Architecture" as world, one can be led to believe that nothing can be done about it without destroying everything, including the aggrieved subject. If it is architecture, it can be torn down at one extreme or perhaps "re-modeled" at the other without an existential threat to being as the cost of the destruction.

Conversely, misapprehending world for architecture is also catastrophic. What this requires is that we endeavor to develop technologies of cognition that are sensitive enough to facilitate the accurate differentiation of Space, World, and Architecture in order to determine whether an object is as it appears or is posing as something that it is not.

Figure 1, specifically the element of the diagram that depicts the separation between the Black and White Worlds within *Space*$_0$, inside the Anti-Black World, demonstrates the manner in which Du Bois understands this Racist Architecture. The argument here is that Morrison and Du Bois agree about the structure of the world we currently inhabit but disagree when it comes to the manner in which Du Bois's world yet to come and Morrison's "*third, if you will pardon the expression, world*" exist with respect to the Anti-Black World. Again, Chandler's careful examination of Du Bois presents an argument as to how this world yet to come is brought into being or, at the very least, thought by thinking through the relationship of his ambition to temporality:

> There are three primary temporalities of *istoria* for Du Bois: past, present, future. Of those three, the most decisive is the futural aspect, that is, with regard to the temporality that attends to "a people." This is also, then, to say that "a people" is a temporal reference; that is to say, the key matter is the group's relationship to that which is not yet, has not yet been, remains yet to come, becoming; this is the decisive matter for thought and action. This aspect of temporality, precisely as the terms of *istoria* for Du Bois, can be affirmed as—in principle—illimitable. It cannot be limited by prejudgment or predetermination. If telos, it remains open. This we can think of in contemporary thought as a delimitation within and of the thought of Du Bois with regard to his sense of an African American collectivity.[11]

The notion of *istoria* examined here by Chandler requires close attention, in that it is relevant for effectively dealing with the shifts in temporality that I have referenced here. Chandler proposes that what is "most decisive" for Du Bois is that "a people" are referent to that which is to come while necessarily doing so from a presence in the present that may or may not have a concrete or coherent relationship to the past. Chandler indexes this as the fact of Du Bois's "sense" (there is that term again; I want to replace it with the couplet of Cognition and Consciousness) of "an African American collectivity."[12]

This is necessarily an argument for the durability of Blackness across realms of subjective existence/perception. What I mean to take up with that claim is the question, stated simply: Were there Black people or perhaps, more carefully, something that looks a lot like Blackness before the encounter or the catastrophe of the Middle Passage, which stands in here as a cipher for global Anti-Blackness whenever or wherever it appears or appeared?

Recall that Morrison's notion of World specifically rejects, as a strategy, existence between (straddling) oppositional worlds as well as being in flight from one to the other. Morrison indexes the complexity that Chandler exposes against Du Bois's notion of double consciousness that is demoted in her system from telos to almost agential possibility, which she elects to reject. This project is necessarily interested in proposing a way of situating notions of *Was*, *Is*, and *Will Be*, concepts that roughly take up the manner in which Chandler understands that Du Bois's futurity is delimited but also the manner in which Morrison's world to come reshuffles the terms and conditions of the way *Was* and *Is* are perceived as a threshold condition of this *Will Be*.

Figure 1 here demands further attention. Recall that this diagram proceeds from left to right, from the past through the present into the future in roughly linear fashion. As a practical matter, the diagram that would precede this one would necessarily, from the perception of those existing in that context, situate Black World$_{\text{Prime}}$ as World in the absence of any awareness of other prior modes of existence or ones to come. This is the linchpin in understanding the way in which cognition and consciousness require durable referents in order to be grounded. Blackness is established here as just such a point of durable and continuous reference by mapping that claim on top of Chandler's exposing that Du Bois proposes "'a people' is a temporal reference."

What Is at Stake?

Prior to the existence of the Anti-Black World we have mapped here, as conditioned on the event of the Middle Passage, one cannot argue that there were no people. To argue more insightfully that there were no Black People prior to the encounter with white people is compelling in the sense that the notion of Blackness as a distinction from whiteness did not exist. The Afropessimist Frank Wilderson unpacks this point in his September 14, 2022, interview with philosopher George Yancy, published on the truthout online platform. Wilderson proposes the following:

> Paradoxically, Blackness embodies the absence of capacity. This absence vouchsafes the presence that is the relational capacity for the

> human. That's hard to endure and contemplate every waking moment. Before 626 CE, there were no Black people. There were Masai, Kikuyu, the Buganda, etc. They became Black through the imposition of social death, but Blackness did not have a prior plenitude of subjectivity and relationship. Blackness is elaborated simultaneously with social death. When the anti-Black world is destroyed, there will still be people like you and me, just as there were prior to 625, but they will not be Black. There will be a new epistemological order. Just like there were not working-class people all the time. A worker is a paradigmatic position that is no more than 400-years old. Workers did not exist before that.[13]

This foundational claim of Afropessimism is the primary place of distinction between this project and that discourse. Wilderson, in this same discussion, insists on understanding that "in Afropessimism there exists only a descriptive intervention, not a prescriptive intervention. Afropessimism doesn't answer Vladimir Lenin's question, 'What is to be done?' That is because Blackness is the site of destruction of cosmological proportions."[14] As a practical matter, the axiomatic assertion that there is nothing to be done eliminates the necessity of worrying about what is to be done. This project departs from a different space and perhaps an approach that endeavors to derive the paradigmatic structure from the limit case will be useful.

Following Wilderson's insightful requirement that we recognize the diversity of those whom he takes to become Black at the point of coercive force—the Maasai, Kikuyu, Buganda, and so on—is not the point of departure of the thinking I am proposing here that is invited by this opening. I would propose that the cohesion of people that enabled diasporic Black people to find a point of common reference in the hold of the slave ship is not the coercive force of whiteness and social death but the foundational and life-giving force of Blackness and social life even under the direst of circumstances. This project refuses to grant white racists the ability to define the terms and conditions of Black Being then, now, or in the future as being called into existence by their hatred.

This project is speculative and, therefore, necessarily "prescriptive" in its aspirations. It proceeds from a different understanding, as articulated here, of Blackness as it expresses itself prior to what Wilderson cites as the emergence of the Black subject in 625 C.E., post the Middle Passage, and in the world beyond the Door of ~~No~~ Return.

Stated simply, Blackness as a referent provided by people who understand themselves as non-Black, and generally white, does not appear because of the gaze of the non-Black Other. Accepting that the Maasai, Kikuyu, the Buganda, and so on, existed with respect to themselves before what we will call "Wilderson's Encounter" circa 635 C.E., I argue that those ethnicities/cultural formations are typologies of Blackness rather than the reductive (mis)understanding of that existence on the part of Anti-Black racists. This means that the discourse of Patterson's social death in this understanding does not institute Blackness but rather is the accurate description of a technology of existential threat to the idea of sovereign and ontological Blackness, a mission central to the devastating goal of white supremacy and Anti-Blackness.

Returning to Figure 1, it is apparent that there was a point in the common reckoning of linear time when Black $\text{World}_{\text{Prime}}$ did not exist in the system of knowing of Anti-Black racists whomever, wherever, and whenever they might be. This does not mean that Blackness as a positive self-referent did not exist and serve as the primary feature of the contrived animosity of non-Black people to those who become Black, in their reckoning, as a negative way to serve their manifold malevolent interests. At the point in time when Black $\text{World}_{\text{Prime}}$ did not exist in point of reference to the Anti-Black World or World_1, it is "just" World without modifiers and exists without referent to other systems of Being.

Here, the distinction between architecture and world resurges. Architecture, as we have noted, can be abandoned leaving world intact. The opposite is not the case. Blackness in the understanding of this project is not an architectural feature of the white world. Conversely, the durability, scale, and omnipresence of the brand of vampiric whiteness on display in the Anti-Black World poses as world and causes the existential crisis that necessitates its dismantling.

This confusion, understanding that the Black subject as a self-referent is only manifest through the activity of anti-Black racists, allows that technology of erasure to succeed without reference to the temporality of "person" as developed by Du Bois. This is in important and disorienting ways tantamount to understanding "today" to exist without the unbreakable relation to the ontological yesterdays that are mechanically related to tomorrows.

The question of futurity for this project and the thinking on this matter by both Du Bois and Morrison come down to the survivability of subjects through the points of radical transformation that institute new Worlds. For instance, a subject formed in Black $\text{World}_{\text{Prime}}$ suffers the loss of subjective context as a result of crossing from that world through the Door of No Return and across the Middle Passage to the interior of the Anti-Black World or World_1. If we imagine that there are fundamental alterations to the subjects that are ontologically related to Black $\text{World}_{\text{Prime}}$, who find themselves in the Anti-Black World, the notion of the impossibility of returning to that system of Being is related to this problematic. The challenge for this question of futurity is fundamentally a question of what survives in the crossing that is necessary for realizing Du Bois's world to come and Morrison's "*third, if you will pardon the expression, world.*" The operative frameworks of space and world require a complex understanding of geography that serves as the context for the appearance, alteration, and relative stability of subjects.

Katherine McKittrick's 2006 text *Demonic Grounds: Black Women and the Cartographies of Struggle* is canonical in exposing this phenomenon. McKittrick proposes the following in its introduction:

> Indeed, black matters are spatial matters. The displacement of difference, geographic domination, transatlantic slavery, and the black Atlantic Ocean differentially contribute to the mapping of the real and imaginative geographies of black women; they are understood here as social processes that *made* geography a racial-sexual terrain. Hence, black women's lives and experiences become especially visible through these concepts and moments because they clarify that blackness is integral to the production of space. To put it another way, social practices create landscapes and contribute to how we organize, build, and imagine our surroundings.[15]

McKittrick's essential intervention, which recalls for us the manner in which Blackness asserts itself in the "production" of space, assists us in thinking through the durability of Black subjectivity across differential contexts of Being. In some sense, the nomenclature employed here to label the various worlds and spaces reifies the primacy of Blackness for their existence. As a practical matter, it is not *possible* for Black $\text{World}_{\text{Prime}}$ as World to exist without the presence of the Black subject. The same goes for the Anti-Black World or $\text{World}_{1.}$ In the absence of Black subjects against whom the Anti-Black World is designed to render subjects inert in some respect and dynamic in others, that world would not and could not exist. What Morrison is understood to be proposing is what our philosophizing and theorizing (for want of better terms to describe this work) are meant to accomplish, which, in McKittrick's view, is to render a world, in some respects like Black $\text{World}_{\text{Prime}}$, that is legible as itself and not in an imperative dialectical existence to whiteness. It is of critical importance that what had been World and became Black $\text{World}_{\text{Prime}}$, through its encounter with the Anti-Black World, be understood as a world that simultaneously preexists and does not exist prior to the appearance of this oppositional context of whiteness. Meaning, what we understand as a "Black World," from this cognitive perch in the Anti-Black World, existed as itself but not in opposition to whiteness. We thus can misapprehend it as nonexistent prior to this cognitive regime.

The challenge for this book is to describe the manner in which a Black Futurity is configured from the catastrophe of the Anti-Black World and has lines of reference to predicate systems of Being without dependence. This is an act of imagination that this project locates in the Black Aesthetic, generally, and in literature, specifically. It is important here to be as clear as possible with respect to the work that "imagination," or perhaps something that may be best described as "re-imagination" (to map onto Morrison's Rememory), does here. This is the bridge to an understanding of the Black Aesthetic as the prime technology of altering the world.

To (re)imagine a Black World that erupts because of new and renewed forms of Black Being is to be involved in the speculative project represented by this book that refuses the limitation of Black Imagination by the imagination and domination of the language and symbols of white supremacy and Anti-Blackness. This means that the (re)imagination, or rethinking of the terms and conditions, of Blackness, finds itself expressed or, better yet, realized in the materiality of Black aesthetic practice, which also necessarily dismantles standard/European notions of time.

For its part, Pheng Cheah's 2016 *What Is a World? On Postcolonial Literature as World Literature* gestures at this possibility that rejects the prevailing manner in which world is a result of a relationship to European notions of time:

> The mapping of the world by temporal calculations is premised on a conceptualization of the world as a spatial category, namely, an object of the greatest possible spatial extension that can be divided into zones of quantitatively measurable time. World, however, is originally a temporal category. Before the world can appear as an object it must first be.[16]

Cheah endeavors to approach the notion of world, or even perhaps "worlding," by understanding "[t]he theory of world literature [he] propose[s]" suggests that the world is a normative temporal category and not the spatial whole made by globalization.[17] This project, in many ways, synchronizes the thinking of McKittrick and Cheah and proposes that the world to come, Morrison's *third, if you will pardon the expression, world*, is called into being within and through the Black Aesthetic. Further, we are already at the threshold of crossing into the system of Being that has always and already rendered the past and present both essential and anachronistic at the same time, and, in that moment, through a recalibrated system of cognition, full consciousness will be the order of things and establish an altered system of Being-as-Black.

The Literary Imagination

In many ways, this effort is led by the chart provided by Farah Jasmine Griffin's recent text, *Read until You Understand: The Profound Wisdom of Black*

Life and Literature. Griffin asserts that she is guided, as is this text under the protection of her work, "by the following questions: What might an engagement with literature written by Black Americans teach us about the United States and its quest for democracy? What might it teach us about the fullest blooming of our own humanity?"[18] It is perhaps worth being clear here that the full bloom of Black Humanity will be realized in the futurity that has served as the point of departure for this project. In solidarity with Griffin, Kevin Quashie's *Black Aliveness, or a Poetics of Being* has pointed in this direction with this recent text quoted here for its clear articulation of this telos:

> This work begins with a single premise, an instruction, really: imagine a black world. Such a directive acknowledges that the New World plunder of modernity and coloniality enacts a destruction of the world as it was and might have become, that the New World unorders the relationship of the human to place, time, other humans. Or we might say there never was a world, that imperialism's destructiveness *is* that it imposed a world logic. Either case describes world-failure that, among other horrors, mobilizes blackness as an antithesis to human life.
>
> In the face of failure that is so unspeakably broad, I use "imagine" as a turn toward the small, an opportunity to understand black worldness as what black texts do . . . as the aesthetics of black art. . . . "Imagine" postpones the logics of address, dominance, and misrecognition—the terms of an antiblack world—that interferes with beholding black aliveness and a black ethic of relation. This study of aliveness rests on the inclination to imagine that the black text speaks to and in a black world, subjunctive and imaginary as that is, away from the false and damaging expectations that black texts have to speak universally, which means that they speak to the larger racial project or conversation—that is, to people who are black . . . which indeed they do.[19]

The point of departure, here, that allows this project to engage with that of Quashie is explicitly in the world prior to the world/architecture instituted by the Middle Passage, which exceeds its spatiotemporal limits through the subterfuge of white supremacy.

I am drawn to the final lines of the quote rendered here that asserts the existence of Black Aliveness, which is, in at least some preliminary register, in excess of Patterson's theorizing of the Social Death that serves as the ordering principle for the seemingly impenetrable walled in territory of Anti-Blackness that Afropessimism has so effectively mapped: a territory that is roughly coextensive with the Atlantic World and its reverberations. The

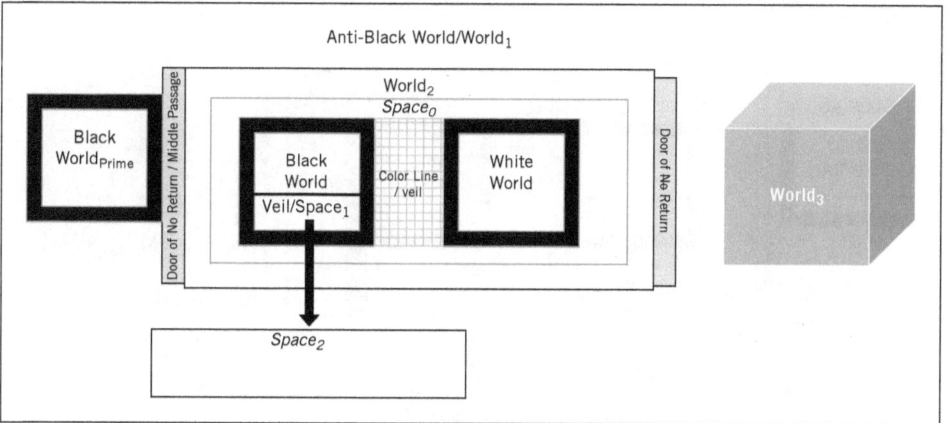

Figure 2 Anti-Black World/World$_1$ destabilized.

existence of this "*third, if you will pardon the expression, world*," in excess of the Black/white World Binary that serves as the dialectical imperative of the thinking of canonical scholars like Du Bois and Fanon, is the telos of the philosophical project of Morrison. This means that the phenomenological system I expose in this book establishes the point of departure as well as the goal for the Black Radical Tradition, which is, in some sense, reimagined, to, in fact, think beyond the limitations of Anti-Black Racism and its subject-dys-forming logic to a world that provides a space for stability for self-referentially formed Black subjectivity. In substance, the philosophical system I explore begins with the identification of the architecture that locates and requires Morrison's "*third, if you will pardon the expression, world*."

This requires a journey, and, as I noted earlier, there are liminal spaces that are appended to the foundational architecture that must be traversed and are illustrated in Figure 1. Figure 2 depicts the next layer of this understanding.

This illustrates an elaboration of Chandler's gloss on Du Bois's exposure of horizontal gradation within the White world, which I am arguing the thinker also locates within the Black World. That space contains the sanctum sanctorum of what we might call his Talented Tenth, where complex thinking leads to *Space$_2$* (fleshed out in Figure 3), and is concealed from the view by what Du Bois designates as another "Veil."

Much more will be said about this as the argument in this book unfolds, but this space, *Space$_2$*, is indexed to what I understand Frantz Fanon to be elaborating in *Black Skin, White Masks* as the generative space for the evolution of the work of thinkers like Ellison, Morrison, and, perhaps surprisingly, Herman Melville. That space, *Space$_3$*, is the threshold of the Door of ~~No~~ Return, where these artists have revealed and presented a portal to the return that will allow cognition, consciousness, and, ultimately, access to World$_3$ or the *third,*

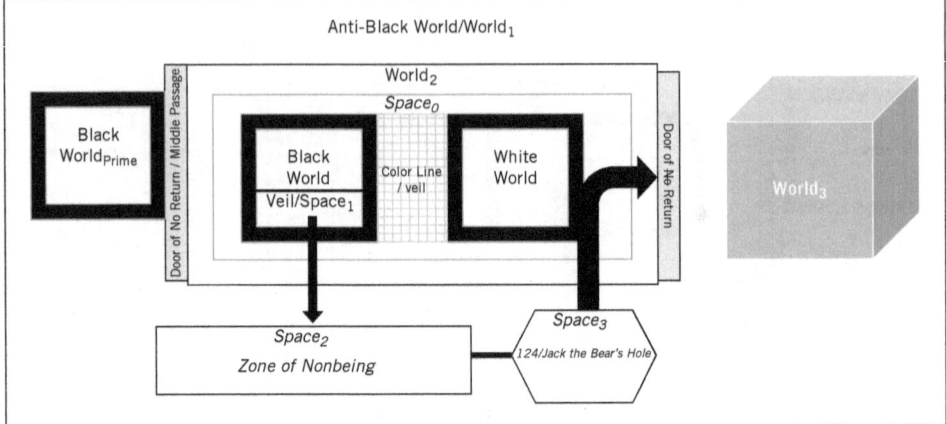

Figure 3 Anti-Black World/World$_1$ map to World$_3$.

if you will pardon the expression, world. The way to World$_3$ requires an exit from the crushing and coercive spatiality of World$_2$, where the prevailing logic prevents forward progress.

Cognition—Consciousness—Being

This movement is hardly meant to propose that racism as such will disappear but rather to provide for a cognitive positionality, pace Morrison, that renders the nature of Du Boisian consciousness "a strategy, not a prophecy or cure."[20] This is in excess of the three elements of Du Bois's formulation that begins with second sight, which I understand as the form of cognition that leads to double consciousness: the system of consciousness, here, that, in some sense, is accessed through Du Bois's Veiled Space$_1$ and, predictably, leads to the form of being, twoness, which forms an irreconcilable binary subjectivity. Morrison, to advance beyond this simultaneously rigid and dialectical system provided by Du Bois and the exemplar of the cul-de-sac that Afropessimism describes, exposes that there must necessarily be, what we call here, for lack of a better term, a "Third-sight," which she names Rememory. This fits with the cause-and-effect relationship proposed by Du Bois: cognition leading to consciousness that resolves itself in a way of Being. Morrison's destination, a "*third, if you will pardon the expression, world*" is only possible from a foundation of nonbinary Cognition and Consciousness.

The architecture that poses as "world" presented in these maps or schematics illustrates a pathway/journey that facilitates the abandonment of architecture posing as world and represents a way *back* by going forward. The architecture presented maps a way *back* to the door that has been understood to be closed forever and protected by walls too thick to breach, too wide to go around, too high to get over, and too low to go under. The system of cognition that is revealed here, again following Morrison, dispenses with the notion that Diasporic Black Subjectivity exists "outside" of the Black World and, therefore, "inside" the world of white supremacy and Anti-Blackness. Recall that Morrison's formulation "postulates the inwardness of the outside." This means that the walls of the slave castle and the portal that seems to allow motion in only one direction is a physical manifestation of a metaphysical fiction. The barrier is not real.

The philosophical project here, after fleshing out an alternative cognitive system, defines the system of Consciousness required for accessing the "*third, if you will pardon the expression, world*," which depends on the threshold condition of access to an altered cognitive state, "Third-sight" and facilitates engagement with the truth of Black subjectivity, or Du Bois's "true self-consciousness," which is hidden, in some sense, despite its presence. It is perhaps useful to defy convention here and first lay out what this book is *not* meant to be before giving some idea of what it *is* meant to accomplish. This speculative philosophical effort to define the futurity of Black Subjectivity is not a book *about* Toni Morrison, though that thinker's work establishes the point of departure and the destiny of this project, and the middle portion of the book wades into the portal that I believe both Ellison and Morrison have granted us. Readers may find elements of Part I pedantic in its careful hermeneutics of Hegel's relevant thinking. Just as this book is not *about* Morrison, it is also not *about* Hegel. That thicket, whether we like it or not, exists, and the disciplining of this effort requires that we execute a comprehensive rereading of that philosopher's work for at least these four reasons: (1) the omnipresence of the master/slave dialectic in Africana theory and philosophy, (2) I argue that Hegel's work is the most comprehensive map that we have of the Anti-Black World from the perspective of whiteness, (3) a careful examination of this thinking will reveal the point of weakness that allows for separation from its crushing logic, and (4), as mentioned earlier, this is a work of speculative philosophy and theory that endeavors to avoid leaning the system on a "Magic Black Box," out of which appears a Theory of the (New) Black Subject. Others should be able to follow the path and agree, disagree depart, enhance, or wholesale reject it based on this detailed work. It also may seem that Hegel is situated to be dismissed only to reappear. That is the fact until the logic of the Anti-Black World that Hegel explicates is left behind across thresholds that can only be crossed after their understanding. This is the detailed work Marley's path requires that leads to the possibility of discrediting and abandoning white supremacy.

Finally, this book is not meant to be a critique of Afropessimism, and here I acknowledge that the assemblage has provided an effective tool for the articulation of the terms and conditions of Anti-Blackness. But, similarly, the fact that an electron microscope is the most accurate tool for examining suitably sized objects means it is probably not what you want to employ to observe a nebula. This text is assembling a tool for looking at a different world, not this one, and is, therefore, talking about something related to, though different from, the preoccupations of that framework.

Structure

This text is divided into three parts that mirror the theory of the subject operating here, which I believe Du Bois has granted this intellectual tradition: Cognition, Consciousness, and, finally, Being.

"Cognition," Part I, proceeds from this opening by further elaborating on the architecture and "laws of motion" that are arrayed against positively formed Black Subjectivity. This, in many ways, is the effect to the cause of a careful analysis of the philosophical system descriptive of the mechanics of white supremacy and Anti-Black Racism, which is in opposition to the system of cognition required to advance to the "*third, if you will pardon the expression, world.*" Here is where Hegel is explored in some detail, in service of the necessity to break the relationship to dialectics and death as the way to knowing and explicate in some detail the functioning of Morrison's "Third Sight" or "Rememory."

Part II, "Consciousness," focuses on elements of the Black Aesthetic, which this project understands to be pointing to the positive resolution of Black Subjectivity not only exemplified by the importance of the work of Toni Morrison but also present in music, other literature, visual art, and a variety of physical disciplines. This section delivers us to the Threshold of the Door of ~~No~~ Return, where the meticulously assembled cognitive tool necessary for the system of consciousness that allows a view of the telos of this argument, a new way of Being-as-Black, is employed. This is an act of the Imagination that allows for consciousness of this way of Being-as-Black prior to the experience of its subjective logic. Part III, "Being," aspires to rescue ontology in the terms Fanon grants us from *Black Skin, White Masks*, in that the Black Subject, at this stage Being-as-Black, presents a thorough and sustainable resistance to coercive force.

The form of the book is reflective of the method of inquiry and multidisciplinary approach necessary to describe an Africana Philosophy of Being. Where we have begun here with Morrison signals the critical importance that African American literature specifically and the Black Aesthetic more broadly plays in this effort. The project presupposes that the Black Aesthetic represents a mode of inquiry, a system of cognition, and an object of analysis. I say the Black Aesthetic "more broadly," in that the assumption here is that the boundaries of what are considered aesthetic practices in this project have been removed or rendered more porous or accommodating, depending on the perspective of the reader. This means that literature, visual art, music, and film are considered alongside philosophy, theory, sports, biography, and anecdote as essential objects and units of analysis. These objects appear as necessary in the text, often as the point of inquiry or the method of analysis but also as exemplars of the ecology of the ways of seeing and expression that serve to describe ways of Being-as-Black. Additionally, it is important that the nonlinear nature of Black existence be allowed to inform the process, which cannot effectively grapple with this complexity by insisting on notions of the sequentiality and predictability of the spatial and the "place-ial" that are deleterious to properly engaging Black Existence. Periodically in the text, there are sections called "Notice to Mariners." In resonance with the utility of this vital information provided to sailors navigating difficult and often unpredictable waters, these provide locational data and descriptions that assist in locating the Black Subject in relation to the Door of No Return, the Door of ~~No~~ Return, and other spaces and places.

Notes on Method

In contradistinctive improvisation on Fanon's assertion in the opening moments of *Black Skin, White Masks*, that he will *not* articulate a method (while doing so), I am explicit about the necessity to do just that. As context, the methodological approach of this project proceeds from the necessity to articulate the utility of philosophy and theory for the Black Radical Tradition. In *Black Minded: The Political Philosophy of Malcolm X*, I dealt with this question in order to elevate the limitation of the discipline of political philosophy and theory to meet the challenge of Malcolm's system of thinking. There is the troubling praxis of Western philosophical thought that espouses the notion that Black people are incapable of such intellectual complexity. This means that the corpus of objects that either are of philosophical significance or present themselves as philosophical in and of themselves must be expanded. Therefore, this project employs material that has been recognized as philosophy and theory as well as objects that seem beyond the boundary of those disciplinary formations. The point of departure here, the performance of Bob Marley, exemplifies this.

In December 1964, Malcolm X insists that the type of philosophy he is providing will "give them something to think about and start them thinking in a way that they should think."[21] In my book on the thinking of Malcolm X, I viewed this as a unisubjective notion, in that it applied to Black people, generally, and Black Radical Thinkers, in particular. That is not the case. The radical nature of Black Radical Philosophy and Theory, in altering the system of awareness of those who identify as Black and/or are affected as if they are, also destabilizes the terms and conditions of the system of harm that is the condition for the existence of Black Radical Thought in the first place and is to the benefit of all humankind dedicated to justice and freedom.

This means that the purpose of Black Radical Philosophy and Theory is at least threefold. First, it erupts as the necessary response to a system of coercive threat. Second, it must rescue the aggrieved Black Subject from a condition of self-hatred as an important condition that renders Blackness always and already a problem. Third, it must look to a futurity and propose a companion to the elegance and profundity of Black Imagining.

As Ralph Ellison writes in the early moments of *Invisible Man*, on the long and oftentimes convoluted journey toward what we can understand as personal and collective freedom, patience is required, so, "Bear with me."[22]

PART I

COGNITION

God didn't mean for man to wear this world like it was a loose garment.

—LEON FORREST, *THERE IS A TREE MORE ANCIENT THAN EDEN*

Preliminary Matters: In the Shadow of David or the Child of the Renaissance

Slugs, I am certain, think they are smart too. What I mean is that the sensory realm in which the slug exists, including the tools available to the animal to witness or sense the world around it, is limited to what they happen to be, and a wise slug will have explored every single millimeter of the world it is able to witness and becomes conscious in its own way of that realm. Obviously, and at least from the perspective of the human animal, we would imagine the slug's sensory realm to be fairly limited, but we also have to realize that perception from our place of cognition, using the tools we have at our disposal, does not speak for the slug or the richness and in-depth knowledge that this creature could possess.

This is the impetus of the utilization here of the introductory quote from Forrest's novel. As the title implies, Forrest argues that there is a world that exceeds the temporal perception of the world that is apparent to our sensory realm. I think here of cognition as a "garment," in the terms proposed by Forrest, and push what we have available to us to its very limit, to the point that it ultimately finds itself bumping up against, if not overlapping, the world that is shaded by the trees that grew from seeds planted before those in Eden.

Like the slug, the human animal, as we have tirelessly endeavored to stretch the horizon of our sensory world and the understanding of the information we receive, may believe that we also are "smart" but, in reality, are likely operating within a tragically limited cognitive realm. The effort to take up the technology of cognition in its existence and to probe its possibilities not only is the first step toward a new form of Being but also is designed to presuppose that the way we have been witnessing the world is encumbered by the logic of a coercive force designed to limit the potentiality of certain subjects. This means the system of cognition that has been imposed upon the subjects, effected by the terms and conditions of the Middle Passage, is designed to deliver several understandings:

1. The Black subject is subhuman.
2. The subhuman condition is by nature not by "nurture."
3. The imposition of the rupture of the Middle Passage slams shut the door of access to the human condition imagined prior to its (il)logic.
4. Right reason reifies this thinking, and any other way of thinking that tends to deny this is irrational.

The presupposition of the marginal nature of the Black subject and the void of Blackness are both the product of a relationship to the world that is limited by a rigged system of cognition, which, therefore, limits the sensory realm. Du Bois canonically refers to this as second sight: seeing oneself through the eyes of another who is dedicated to your subjective marginalization in perpetuity. This creates a notion of both physical and metaphysical crisis expressed in the reverberations of the logic of the Middle Passage and the subsequent bondage that serves as the limiting agent in the proposition of a self-referential Sovereign Black Being.

Returning to Chandler's book, we find this phenomenon exposed in Du Bois's essay "The Development of the People." Chandler glosses the essay, writing, "The provided terms of the narrative and the essay may now be understood as expressed in one sentence: 'The African slave trade was the child of the Renaissance.'"[1] Slavery, as an object of inquiry, finds itself expressed in the visual art of the era and work on display at La Galleria dell'Accademia di Firenze. The main attraction at this venue is obviously Michelangelo's iconic sculpture of David, but what labors in the shadows of that work are representatives of the enslaved who speak to both the notion of bondage and the understanding of the conditions of ineluctable bondage. With that argument in mind, it is productive to visit the center of the Renaissance to witness the manner in which the imaginary of the enslaved condition is made real in the form of visual representation, which was called in the Introduction the *physical manifestation of a metaphysical fiction*.

I am referencing the display of Michelangelo's studies of the enslaved, which are introduced to visitors of the Galleria with the following signage: *Statua Incompiuta di un «Prigione»*. The scare quotes around the Italian term "*prigione*" are important for several reasons, the first of which is the possibility of grammatical confusion. We might, though, initially endeavor to account for the failure of grammar here: the "a" that should be attached to the "*un*" to mark the gender of the noun *prigione* is absent. Further research reveals that this is a premodern formation presented without an explanation of its refutation of modern grammar, leaving open the possibility for linguistic confusion for those who are unfamiliar with the evolution of the language.

Being aware of that slippage, it is perhaps not surprising, after bearing witness to this grammatical artifact, that the description itself is similarly incoherent. It is at best paradoxical in that, in modern Italian, it can be read to mean that the curators are proposing there are incomplete statues of a prison rather than incomplete statues of a prisoner: *statua incompiuta di un «prigioniero»* or perhaps even something like *statua incompiuta di una «prigionia»*, meaning "incomplete statue of imprisonment." The description of these pieces seems unsure as to whether the subject of Michelangelo's work is the body or the context in which the body is presented. Either way, the pieces themselves are, in my mind "completed" in full recognition of the notion of the *incomplete* in this aesthetic tradition. It is the journey to freedom, to partake of the sovereignty of the dominating image of David, that is, in fact, incomplete, and the artist has captured that effort, and that preoccupies my thinking here. This thinking is in concert with the imperative guiding this project that, like these statues, we are witness to a process of movement that is frozen in space and time, but, like the evolution of the language here, they should not be understood to be representative of a permanent condition. Through a series of transpositions, Michelangelo's masterwork can be understood to be a visual representation of the dilemma that faces the reality of Black life, buffeted by the aftershocks of slavery and at the same time indicative of the primary responsibility of Black Radical Thought in this moment. That responsibility, or, perhaps more accurately formulated, "challenge," is to realize that the spectacle of Anti-Blackness as both formative of the contemporary Black Subject and the stuff that, like the marble here, holds the struggling subject in place is finalized or completed in the sense that it depicts a moment in time. Meaning that Africana Thought, perhaps more accurately rendered as Black Radical Thought, must develop the metaphoric hammer and chisel required to free these seemingly unfreeable subjects. We have the "completed" statues of the enslaved on display at the Louvre, but we are not able to witness the work that both went into their completion and the struggle to resolve this stasis. This is the challenge that presents itself with respect to the forward progress of Black Being toward Morrison's "*third, if you will pardon the expression, world.*"

I want to make clear that the linkage between the Italian Renaissance and its child and Atlantic World Slavery is about language, according to Du

Bois through Chandler, and it is what they have to do with this project. There is a way in which the grammar of our language in and around diasporic Black Being, as a result of the condition of slavery, is mistranslated or, more to the point, insufficiently representative of the facts of the matter. Perhaps, like the language presented by the gallerists in Florence, these terms, slave, Black, and so on, are required to be surrounded by scare quotes to alert the careful observer that the "words" are in motion just like the subjects they describe.

Opening Matters

To contemplate the nature of Black Being or, perhaps more appropriately, "*Being-as-Black*" is to first be forced to negotiate the negative formation of Blackness as a product of white supremacist systems of knowing, which, like the bodies of the statues in Florence, Italy, seem locked in an impossible circumstance. Perhaps another way of reading this dilemma is that the prison, as in this circumstance the ironclad (il)logic of Anti-Black Racism, must be rendered inoperative, or, in the language of the Galleria, incomplete, in that even to view the form struggling for freedom is to bear witness to the possibility of the potential for release. This thinking or contemplation has two interlocking goals that at a critical juncture, to be successful, must separate themselves completely. The first is to articulate the nature of phenomenological Blackness as it exists under the subject-(dys)forming pressure of white supremacy. The second is to describe in clear terms *a* phenomenology of Black(ness) existing beyond the boundary of white supremacy, as if the former way of being never existed and becomes a sustainable way of *Being-as-Black*. As a practical matter, it is the break between the two goals, the point of inflection and departure from Blackness under conditions of threat and Blackness as a self-referential way of Being that will be the key to successfully navigating this journey. As the title of this project implies, it is the place of transition, the Door of ~~No~~ Return, that serves as motivation. This thinking employs the intervention of Christina Sharpe's text, *In the Wake: On Blackness and Being*, which is preoccupied with Dionne Brand's elegant *A Map to the Door of No Return*. This book presupposes that a return to that space of liminality is the key to finding a way through and beyond the context of the quotidian Black Death to a true phenomenology of Blackness. It is worth quoting Sharpe here at length to establish this critical point:

> I think this is what Brand describes in *A Map to the Door of No Return* as a kind of blackened knowledge, an unscientific method, that comes from observing that where one stands is relative to the door of no return and that moment of historical and ongoing rupture. With this as the ground, I've been trying to articulate a method of encoun-

> tering a past that is not past. A method along the lines of a sitting with, a gathering, and a tracking of phenomena that disproportionately and devastatingly affect Black peoples any and everywhere we are. I've been thinking of this gathering, this collecting and reading toward a new analytic, as the wake work, and I am interested in plotting, mapping, and collecting the archives of the everyday of Black immanent and imminent death, and in tracking the ways we resist, rupture, and disrupt that immanence and imminence aesthetically and materially.[2]

It is perhaps useful here to situate myself relative to the door of no return in order to synchronize this project with the thinking of Brand and Sharpe.

Notice to Mariners I: The Plantation Notebook

My father celebrated his eighteenth birthday on September 29, 1963. In a functional world, he and his father would have journeyed to the Hale County Courthouse to register to vote. At that time, Hale County, Alabama, the epicenter of what is known as the Black Belt, a county known for the lynching and mysterious deaths of Black people, had virtually no registered Black voters and nothing my father or my grandfather could say or do would change that fact. What the government did provide my father was a personal letter from the Department of Defense inviting him, without the possibility of refusal, to report for induction into the U.S. Army for service in the Republic of Vietnam. He returned from Southeast Asia physically unscathed but with no accounting for the wounds to his spirit that must necessarily attend being both denied citizenship in one sense and required to serve because of citizenship in another. It is the legacy of this wound that concerns me here and that wound's common genealogy to the Door that seems to offer no possible return.

As a child, I spent summers in the home where my father was raised and had journeyed from both to be rejected by the voter's commission and inducted into the army. As the story goes, by the age of six, I became preoccupied with a notebook that lay on a shelf in my father's childhood home, somewhere between the family Bible and the high school annuals of my dad and his siblings. The book, I am reminded, represented the life's work of my many-times-great-grandfather who was born in the 1840s and enslaved on the Samuel Pickens Plantation in what was then known as Sawyer Depot in what was Greene County and is now part of Hale County, a geographic space that is currently known as Sawyerville. "Sawyer" is a notorious name in the annals of enslavement. As fate would have it, the Pickens, who established this forced labor camp in Alabama, had relocated from Cabarrus County,

North Carolina, in the 1820s. North Carolina also happens to be the state of residence of Samuel Tredwell Sawyer, the lawyer, congressman, and rapist of Harriet Jacob's whose *Incidents in the Life of a Slave Girl*[3] chronicles her escape into an attic for seven years while she awaited manumission of the children fathered by Sawyer. Jacobs was literate; my many-times-great-grandfather was not, but his notebooks were composed of dozens of drawings depicting his life as an enslaved person on the Samuel Pickens Plantation. I say "were" because the notebooks are lost. Upon my grandfather's death, family members descended upon the house and the book disappeared and no one has admitted in the half century that has elapsed that they have it.

Despite this apparent loss, the notebook lives on in my imagination, and I allow myself to believe that its loss is only in theory and my preoccupation with the excesses of the plantation is in large measure a ramification of the direct evidence my many-times-great-grandfather left us through his art practice. This binary imaginative effort—my ancestor's art practice and my effort to fill in the blank those images have left—is the basis of a new form of Black Being. This process and its role in this project are intellectually indebted to both Saidiya Hartman's "Critical Fabulation" and Christina Sharpe's "Wake Work." In working with my imagining of the imagination of my grandfather many times over, I believe that I can recall the texture and smell of the book; more parchment than paper and bound together with heavy string across the top that allowed me to flip through the images. If there is color, I'm convinced it is a figment of my imagination. What I wonder about is what my many-times-great-grandfather included and what he left out. Is the home of his enslaver depicted, their animals, his fellow victims, instruments of torture, birds, trees? I've resisted the urge to inquire about its whereabouts because the truth of its complete loss is too great a burden to bear, so instead of that understanding I might offer the corpus, the whole of my work, as restitution, exchanging the meta for the physical.

The reverberations of the Middle Passage and the place of entry that promises the impossibility of return forces one to think about the possibilities that lie within our problems. In this sense, the void that the Middle Passage institutes, which, in a way, can be partially filled by the knowledge of the absence of the Plantation Notebook, presents a space for radical theory. As mentioned earlier, in concert with the important notion of Critical Fabulation from "Venus in Two Acts," which Hartman describes in the following fashion, we find the foundations of an approach to resolving this complexity:

> I have chosen to engage a set of dilemmas about representation, violence, and social death, not by using the form of a metahistorical discourse, but by performing the limits of writing history through the act of narration. I have done so primarily because (1) my own

> narrative does not operate outside the economy of statements that it subjects to critique; and (2) those existences relegated to the nonhistorical or deemed waste exercise a claim on the present and demand us to imagine a future in which the afterlife of slavery has ended. The necessity of trying to represent what we cannot, rather than leading to pessimism or despair must be embraced as the impossibility that conditions our knowledge of the past and animates our desire for a liberated future.[4]

What that tool allows for is the possibility to look backward and forward in order to fill in the blanks that represent subjective futurity to propose a new way of Being-as-Black.

Resistance, Rupture, and Disruption

In returning to Brand and Sharpe, I am preoccupied with the tripartite notions of resistance, rupture, and disruption that Sharpe places before us. I imagine that the place to focus the force of this effort is at the seemingly impenetrable portal itself in order to render inoperative the resistance to return. In fact, to imagine a place of impenetrability that is still understood to be a door or a portal is to allow a faulty description of reality to outstrip reality itself. By walking to the threshold of that obstruction and pushing through it, the fact of the fiction becomes apparent. The first problematic that confronts this effort is grasping hold of the slippery point of transition between Afropessimism and Morrison's "*third, if you will pardon the expression, world*," which I understand as a foundational element of the Black Radical Tradition or Black Critical Thought/Theory that Anthony Bogues describes as:

> A tradition of critical interdisciplinary thought that poses questions about the human condition and the social world that human beings have made. It does so from the perspective of the historical and also of the contemporary human expression of the formerly enslaved Black Body . . . and the colonized native. It is a tradition of thought that critiques forms of human domination and reaches for practices of freedom that cannot be subsumed under conventional conceptions of liberty.[5]

In working with the definition provided by Bogues, it is the notion that this form of critical inquiry is preoccupied with the human construction of the social world that, in the first instance, will confront the subject framed in negatively formed Blackness. This serves as the initial point of inquiry. What this implies is that human thinking has produced a condition for which a form of oppositional human thinking can be employed to unravel or dismantle its logic. Africana Philosophical Thought is just such an oppositional practice. What that means, concretely, is that at least since the encounter of Europeans with the people of Africa, an event that in many ways signaled the beginning of modernity, the existential viability of the Black subject has been under assault, and the foundational preoccupation of Africana Thought has been resisting that cataclysmic threat to Black Being. That opposition often is pursued through the production and maintenance of a competing canon that endeavors to stabilize the subject in question and that effort often appears as the careful dismantling of the logic of white supremacy. The project of destabilization is often pursued through close and careful engagement with the essential threads of the *(il)logic* of Black inferiority that, taken together, create the interlocking modes of subjugation that predate the Middle Passage and appear to stretch beyond our current moment into a future that is certain about the uncertainty of Black Being. The effort to attend to the first goal, elaboration of Blackness under coercive threat, requires that we deconstruct the terms and conditions of the foundation of marginalized Black Being.

Scholarship has revealed that an essential element of the effort to destabilize the subjectivity of people of African descent is the erasure or fracturing of a coherent relationship to historical memory. Orlando Patterson's *Slavery and Social Death*, in an effort to describe the elements of the enslaved condition, proposes that "natal alienation" is one component of that practice:

> Not only was the slave denied all claims on, and obligations to, his parents and living blood relations but, by extension, all such claims and obligations on his more remote ancestors and descendants. He was truly a genealogical isolate. Formally isolated in his social relations with those who lived, he was also culturally isolated from the social heritage of his ancestors. . . . Slaves differed from other human beings in that they were not allowed freely to integrate the experience of their ancestors into their lives, to inform their understanding of social reality with the inherited means of their natural forebears, or to anchor the living present in any conscious community of memory.[6]

It is just this sort of notion, regarding the isolation from the social heritage of people of African descent, generally, and the enslaved, specifically, that is an essential element of the ethos of racists in that Black bodies were not just ideally suited for the peculiar institution but were subjectively formed to be excluded from robust participation in the pantheon of human actors as individuals and collectively. This is the set of ideas that preoccupies the oppositional philosophical practice of Toni Morrison.

Returning to ideas introduced in the Introduction, it is important to note that the thinking Morrison seeks to implode is encumbered with a series of binaries: inside/outside, Negro/American, Enslaved/Human, all of which are explained by the thinking of Georg Wilhelm Friedrich Hegel. Thinking that has found itself prominently a part of the work of, perhaps most obviously, Du Bois and Fanon. Hegel and his thinking are necessarily explored in some detail here as providing a point of entry into the epistemology of white supremacy, which must be thoroughly understood to effectively theorize its demise. The intellectual labor of wrestling with the thinking of Hegel is necessary in that it must be thoroughly probed to identify the point of rupture. The point of weakness in Hegel is situated here as the point of weakness of the Anti-Black World or $World_1$ that must be exploited to reveal the threshold of the door we intend to open. It is worth noting, Hegel is not the only way to locate the place of rupture but rather "a" way.

Blackening Hegel or "This Is What Happens when Black People Read Hegel" (RA Judy)

This book has made it a primary goal of its method to practice the nondialectical nature of Morrison's resistance to Du Bois's double consciousness. However, to exceed boundaries, one might want to be assured, to as great an extent as possible, of exactly what they happen to be. With that in mind, the architecture posing as the World of Anti-Blackness is, in many ways, ably described rather than brought into existence by G.W.F. Hegel. Rei Terada's 2023 text, *Metaracial: Hegel, Antiblackness and Political Identity*, also highlights the omnipresence of Hegel, which, in the progress forward that this project presupposes, must be dealt with. Terada offers the following apology, which I adopt and extend: "While I feel apologetic for returning to the 'seemingly interminable question of the master-slave dialectic' (Scott 2021, 152), there seems to be no way around it."[7] I mention Terada here in the sense that, to get around Hegel, we have to clarify and map the boundaries of his argument that depends upon binaries, which are both geographic, temporal, and material as well as aspatial, atemporal, and immaterial. All of them general and, at the same time, particular. That effort allows us to witness in clear terms the actual fragility of these seemingly impenetrable claims. Ultimately, the goal here is to offer an account of the way Hegel's philosophical musings about the relationship of Blackness to worlding and, further, the manner in which he describes the physical and metaphysical imperative of death, generally, and Black Death, in particular, function to deliver the fun house of the illogic of white supremacy that imposes itself upon us and appears to be unavoidable.

At the outset, I situate our exploration of the limits of Hegel's thinking by proposing that his system in its internal workings is analogous to a billiard table. This provides us with a way to think about the functioning of Hegel's system through its similarity to a game of pool and to pay careful attention to the inner workings of the table itself. The player in this analogy stands in as the Lord, the cue ball as the Bondsman, and the other balls represent the thing between them: that which must be worked on. The white ball, properly employed, is used by the player(s) to clear the table of the other balls. Improperly employed it goes into a pocket but the properties of the ball and the table itself are such that it is returned to the Lord to be used again and again until its utility is completely exhausted. The other balls come to rest and are tallied to determine the victor between two competing Lords/players until another game begins. The cue ball can only be resolved and recognized through constant labor, its color notwithstanding. Here it is, its weight or what Hegel calls "specific gravity," in §288, which is relevant here:

> In the first place, this inner of the shape of the simple individuality of an inorganic thing is *specific gravity.* As a simple being, specific gravity can be observed just as well as can the determinateness of number, the sole determinateness of which specific gravity is capable; or it can be found through the comparison of observations, and in the way it seems to furnish one component of the law.[8]

I will mangle this section because of what the actual functioning of these claims portends for the question of the construction of the natural versus unnatural and what that means for the possession or lack of possession of reason. Hegel understands specific gravity to be the manifestation of a series of identifiers of an inorganic thing (§290). What is important to understand is how the inorganic relates itself to the "organic" and speaks to the ineluctable Otherness of Black subjectivity that this logic imposes without a relationship to objective reality.

This is resonant with §256: "The organic does not engender something; it merely *conserves itself,* that is, what is engendered is, as it is engendered, equally already present."[9] The organic is, therefore, directly related to the thing from which it comes and further, in temporal fashion, represents the midpoint of the existence of a thing: "What corresponds to the organic itself is the inner activity lying midway between what is first and what is last for it insofar as this activity has in it the character of individuality."[10]

For purposes of this argument, this place between first and last must be something like "Life" or "Living," which represents the recurrent midpoint (considered in its totality) between the distinct moments of birth and death.

Further, Hegel understands that the organic thing is mechanically related to an "organic system":

> It turned out that for there to be such a law, the relationship had to be such that the universal organic *property* would have made itself into a thing *in* an organic *system* and would have its own shaped imprint in it, so that both would be the same essence, available at one time as a universal moment and another as a thing.[11]

So, for the organic thing to be fully "organic," it finds itself existing in a system that valorizes its existence through the foundational agreement at the level of "essence" or the thing itself. The inorganic thing functions differentially in that as the outer of the organic is related to the inner, rendering its appearance for an observer coherent as it is synchronized (§284), the "inorganic" does not represent this unity: "The *other* appears at first as its outer inorganic nature."[12]

Hegel situates the concept such that the inorganic being is untrue to itself and, therefore, "out" to the coherent relationship of the organic property to the organic system that functions according to particular laws. What I'm curious about is the object that is true to itself but finds itself "resident" in an organic system that renders the object always already "inorganic" to the organic nature of the environment. Let's return to the Hegelian Billiard Table.

The preoccupation is not so much with what occurs on the top of the table but more so with the system in the interior that has mechanisms to determine the "true nature" of a ball that enters its realm. As a practical matter, the player might elect to add the cue ball to the group of balls in play, rather than use it as dictated by the rules, and select one of the other balls, the eight ball for the sake of argument, to serve as the "cue ball." The game will proceed as expected, in general, if one ignores the color of the cue ball, but, when the "cue/eight ball" finds itself in a pocket, it will *not* be returned through a special path back to the players. Likewise, to the extent the eight ball knocks the white ball into a pocket, the white ball will be returned unlike the other balls in play. In each case, the true nature, with respect to the design of this system, of the balls will be revealed by their interaction with the inner/invisible workings of the table. Only the ball with the proper "specific gravity" will be revealed to be the true tool for the labor at hand. We might call this the "Mechanics of White Supremacy."

The inner workings of the billiard table, which judge the relationship of the outer appearance/function of the ball against its inner truth (specific gravity), are analogous to Hegel's system of dialectical recognition, which is able to valorize a predetermined set of traits. For this effort, it means that an entirely separate type of evaluation or cognition is required to realize a system that facilitates an egalitarian praxis of inclusivity that accommodates an array of figures who are self-determining the way in which they interact with society. Hegel guards against this probability by asserting it is fear that demonstrates the existence of reason on the part of the Bondsman writing in §195:

> However the feeling of absolute power as such in the various particularities of service is merely dissolution *in itself*, and, although the fear of the lord is the beginning of wisdom, in that fear consciousness is the "it" that is "for itself" but it is not fully *being-for-itself*.[13]

I am concerned here with the implication of this passage for the "Negro" existing within this system and that subject's relationship to what Hegel calls "fear consciousness," generally, and "fear of the lord," more specifically, as the path to positive self-consciousness. This presents a problem of sequentiality even within the asynchronous nature of Hegel's System of Science. Recall that Hegel asserts the spatiotemporal place of the organic is at the midpoint between the beginning and the end, which I have proposed is something like "living." It also might be considered, within Hegelian dialectics, as the midpoint between Consciousness and Absolute Knowledge, which seems to be something like his account of Reason. If we take Hegel at his word and accept that fear consciousness is the first step toward wisdom, it would seem that the emotion must arrive outside of experience and remain the constant companion of knowing subjects that desire true self-consciousness. This fear must be the fear of death (embodied as the Lord), which becomes the thing (life) that must be put at risk to achieve self-consciousness. This fear serves as the obstruction of efforts to remove the Lord from the place of absolute authority.

Hegel's gloss on the "trial by death" in §188 is the crux of this matter as we understand that, ultimately, we must turn our attention to the phenomenon of "Black Death" or the Black(ness) of Death.

> However, this trial by death likewise sublates the truth which was supposed to emerge from it and, by doing so, completely sublates the certainty of itself. For just as life is the *natural* location of consciousness, that is, self-sufficiency without absolute negativity, death is the *natural* negation of this same consciousness, negation without self-sufficiency, which thus persists without the significance of the recognition which was demanded. Through death, the certainty has been established that each has risked his life, and that each has cast a disdainful eye towards death both in himself and in the other. But this is not the case for those who pursued this test in this style.[14]

Hegel is adding the risking of metaphoric death to the metaphoric personae of Lord and Bondsman in his system. This is his attempt to analogize the struggles of everyday life—say, for instance, an argument with a dry cleaner over damage to a garment—to the struggle to preserve life, but he leaves aside the actuality, in his parlance, the "immediacy," of enslavement, mastery, and the specter of real death. Black Consciousness, in the World of Anti-Black Racism, must account for these real and omnipresent facts.

It is necessary here to bring Hegel's methodological intervention that describes the way a subject embarks on a journey from sense certainty/consciousness to being for the self in the immediacy of self-consciousness to bear on the relationship between the master and the enslaved Black body as an *actual* rather than a *representational* set of subject positions. The point of reference here are the well-known passages (§§178–196) of the chapter titled "Self-Consciousness," in subsection A, "Self-sufficiency and Non-self-sufficiency of Self-consciousness: Mastery and Servitude," which is the object of Terada's concern through Scott, referenced in the opening moments of this section. My attention is immediately drawn to the closing moments of §184, "They *recognize* themselves as *mutually recognizing each other*."[15] What I take Hegel to mean here is that the two players in this encounter see themselves in the other, which seems to amount to a mutual acceptance of the humanity if not the human(ess) of the other even to the extent that they are engaged in conflict. This does not serve as a condition of the possibility for interaction between beings recognized as fully human, or, in the parlance of the *Lectures on the Philosophy of History*, "Historical," and with those (mis)recognized as (sub)(in)human or nonhistorical. This is a type of imperfect recognition, on the part of the structurally (en)mastered, of not only the fact that recognition is not between them and this Other but also the fact of the impetus of that lack.

Here we have the core of an essential claim that serves as the engine of Hegel's *System of Science, First Part: The Phenomenology of Spirit* (hereafter and in endnotes, the short title used to refer to this book will be the subtitle: *Phenomenology of Spirit*), which is the assertion that the process of mutual recognition renders the particular as universal in its universality and at the same time the universal as particular in its particularity. Section 117 speaks to this argument, "The object that I take up presents itself as *purely One*. I am also cognizant of the property in which it is *universal*, but as a result I go beyond individuality."[16] For Hegel, the individual is universal in that it is the One like all other individuals and in that commonality is universal. One can readily see the way Hegel's wholesale erasure of "Africa Proper," which we unpack shortly, creates a universal and particular understanding of *worthful worthlessness*. The "Negro" in Hegel's account is neither universal nor particular in that they exist in the nonexistence of historical subjectivity as an object of knowledge. This is a devastating condition in Hegel's account, which is laid bare in the text of §93:

> A *knowing* that knows the object only for the reason that the object *is* but which itself can just as well be as not be. However, the object *is*: it is the truth and the essence. The object is indifferent as to whether it is known or not known. The object remains even when it is not known, but if the object does not exist, then there is no knowing.[17]

There is some common sense in this assertion. One cannot have knowledge of eighteen-foot-tall German Shepherds because they do not exist as objects to know anything about except to know about their nonexistence. This is fine for fictional creatures but a completely separate matter for actual beings. What Hegel has done through his wholesale dismissal of an entire factually existing continent full of people is to render them illegible: what Ralph Ellison understands as "invisible." Substantively, what the internal workings of Hegel's recognition machine accomplish is that, to the extent one encounters an eighteen-foot-tall German Shepherd, it would remain nonexistent to this system of knowing because its only point of reference is that of its nonexistence, and, therefore, it is necessarily seen as something other than what it is in order to comport to this engineered erasure. This is shorthand for Hegel's notorious assertion that Africa and Africans lack any relationship to history as he defines the term in his *Lectures on the Philosophy of History*. Hegel situates his analysis of history as traceable through the development of "four historical worlds":[18]

> While theorizing on the conceptual planes of the dichotomy between East and West, Hegel identifies four historical worlds—Oriental, Greek, Roman and German. . . . Africa is not among Hegel's four cultures of civilization.[19]

In the text of the *Lectures on the Philosophy of History*, Hegel proposes that to properly consider Africa, the continent must be divided:

> . . . into three parts: one is that which lies south of the desert of Sahara—*Africa proper* [my italics]—the highland almost entirely unknown to us, with narrow coast tracts along the sea; the second is that to the north of the desert—European Africa (if we may so call it)—a coast land; the third is the river region of the Nile, the only valley-land of Africa, and which connects with Asia.[20]

The careful delineation of Africa into three parts sets the stage for Hegel's effort to separate what he understands as "Negroes" from areas of the continent that would undermine his blanket assertion of the depraved nature of the African continent and its inhabitants. It is critical to note here that this is a description of the way the logic of white supremacy endeavors to develop an architecture of its own imaginary that then poses as world:

> Africa proper, as far as history goes back, has remained—for all purposes of connection with the rest of the world—shut up; it is the gold-land compressed within itself, the land of childhood, which lying beyond the day of self-conscious history, is enveloped in the dark mantle of night.[21]

So, we are to understand that with respect to the exclusion of Africa from the pantheon of historical worlds, Hegel really only means "Africa Proper," which he notes is shut off from positive contact with the world prior to the world of Anti-Black Racism. I say "positive" contact because Hegel is fully aware of the slave trade and states that "the only essential connection that has existed and continued between the Negroes and the Europeans is that of slavery."[22] The geographic distinction of Africa as a discernible and recognized landmass is inconvenient for Hegel's endeavor to separate "Negroes" from consideration as human actors who might *desire* (this is an important Hegelian term) self-consciousness. It is critical to mark the importance of Terry Pinkard's 2018 translation of the *Phenomenology* employed here. With respect to the notion of Self-Consciousness as elaborated by Hegel, the relevant passage of §167 is rendered in part here:

> As self-consciousness, it is movement, but while self-consciousness *only* distinguishes *itself* from itself *as itself*, that difference as an otherness is, to itself, *immediately sublated*. There simply *is* no difference, and *self-consciousness* is only the motionless tautology of "I am I." . . . This unity must become essential to self-consciousness, which is to say, self-consciousness is *desire*, full stop.[23]

What Hegel really means is that "Negroes" are not to be considered as historical actors wherever they happen to find themselves. This seems clear in that the transportation of bodies from the African continent does not, in the thinking of Hegel, lead to any advancement toward the type of recognized humanity that he explores in his philosophical system. He is explicit on this point. "The Negro, as already observed, exhibits the natural man in his completely wild and untamed state."[24] He continues:

> Another characteristic fact in reference to Negroes is *slavery*. Negroes are enslaved by Europeans and sold to America. Bad as this

> may be, their lot in their own land is even worse, since there a slavery quite as absolute exists; for it is the essential principle of slavery, that man has not attained a consciousness of freedom, and consequently sinks down to a mere thing—an object of no value.[25]

There are several problems here, not the least of which is Hegel's reductive and convenient misapprehension of the facts of the matter with respect to the differences in forced labor practices between the Atlantic World and "Africa Proper." For our purposes here, and this is explored in much greater detail in various places in this text, Hegel's preoccupation with slavery or *unfreedom* as a master signifier, and its relationship to its polar opposite, mastery or freedom, is essential to keep in the forefront of our thinking since slavery becomes an essential element of the fulfillment of historical consciousness that must somehow endeavor to exclude the exemplar of that condition: the enslaved Black body. Note the last clause here, "an object of no value," which illustrates the way the corporeal and metaphysical existence of the enslaved has no value unless and until the labor of both body and soul are exploited. This is resonant with the fact that negatively framed Blackness is meant to equate to worthlessness up to some event of extraction of value for the depraved system of valuation relied on by the proponents of this violence: labor, sexual assault, other forms of mental and physical harm. Humiliation. All serve as the events that introduce the possibility of positive valuation of Blackness for white supremacy.

With respect to the way Hegel's system of science operates, generally, and with respect to the Black subject, specifically, it must be asserted that it is not separable from white supremacy as a system of knowing. To the extent this epistemological predisposition has always already dismissed the possibility of the historical "Negro," in that the possibility is immediately recognized as nonexistent, it, therefore, represents an object for which there can be no knowledge. We need to hold onto this understanding.

Returning to the passages that form the central preoccupation of the discussion of Mastery and Servitude, we find that the two self-consciousnesses encounter one another and place a "thing" (*das Ding*) between them that serves as the medium by which the Lord and the Bondsman are identified/revealed. Section 189 reads:

> It is through that experience that a pure self-consciousness is posited, and a consciousness is posited which is not purely for itself but for an other, which is to say, is posited as an *existing* consciousness or consciousness in the shape of *thinghood*.[26]

This subjective progress proceeds with the following lines in §190:

> The master relates himself *to the servant mediately through self-sufficient being*, for it is on this very point that the servant is held fast. It is his chain, the one he could not ignore in the struggle, and for that reason he proved himself to be non-self-sufficient and to have his self-sufficiency in the shape of thinghood. However, the master is the power over this being, this being, however, is the power over the other, so that the master thus has within this syllogism the other as subordinate to him. The servant, as self-consciousness itself, relates himself negatively to the thing and sublates the thing. However, at the same time the thing is for him self-sufficient, and, for that reason, he cannot through his negating be over and done with it, cannot have eliminated it; or, the servant only *possesses* it.[27]

We must tread carefully here because, in this instance, in the critical movement of consciousness to self-consciousness and then forward to the ultimate place of resolution, Absolute Knowing, Hegel has rendered the servant able to move forward through labor that apparently can be rendered here as "self-consciousness itself" or "desire." Care must be taken because the possibility of the enslaved-in-fact recognizing themselves as this figure with a system of possibility before it within the superstructure of the System of Science is intoxicating but doomed to fail for at least two reasons.

First, the figures that Hegel situates here have *thinghood* as distinct from their subjectivity and, in that labor, can be exerted *upon* the thing. For the "Enslaved Proper," there is no possibility of separating the labor from the subject. The enslaved is recognized as "alive" and to have "World" in this system only through labor, and, when labor is alienated from the body, the body is no longer recognizable within this system and ceases to exist.

The "Negroes" as enslaved and inseparable from labor and, in Hegel's proposition, don't matter. Labor becomes the critical middle term here. Not because one party (the Lord) is in anticipation of being rewarded by being able to "consume" the fruits of the labor of the Bondsman, but, in the case of the enslaved Black Body, the labor *is* the body and subject to being consumed at the whim of the master. This requires a return to the question of the differentiation of the universal from the particular to the extent it is possible. Recall that for the normative functioning of Hegelian dialectics the subject is both universal and particular. For white supremacy, the "Negro Proper" is neither universal nor particular. The "Negro" just *is*, and, in the fractured relationship to being recognized as particularly universal, they are rendered *No Thing* as opposed to *the Thing*. It is not the case that the Black body becomes the Thing between a metaphoric Bondsman and the actuality of a Lord/Master: that is, the Bondsman represents the market; the Lord, the plantation owner; and the Thing, the cotton produced by the labor of the enslaved. That facilitates the alienation of the enslaved body from the object produced by the labor of the enslaved and creates a duality that facilitates an escape route to personhood: Hegel and white supremacy are interested in no such trap door. The Black body is bound to labor in this paradigm as the limit condition of corporeal and recognizable existence in that the subject is already dead in its social existence.

What I am characterizing as a "trap door" here is Hegel's preoccupation with death (again, for him, generally, meant metaphorically in the same manner that the notion of Lord and Bondsman are metaphors for other relationships) as the thing that must be risked to facilitate forward progress. Patterson demonstrates that, for slavery proper, this is a moot proposition in that death as an agential proposition has already been rendered impossible for the enslaved, writing:

> Perhaps the most distinctive attribute of the slave's powerlessness was that it always originated (or was conceived of as having originated) as a substitute for death, usually violent death. . . . Archetypically, slavery was a substitute for death in war. But almost as frequently, the death commuted was for some capital offense, or death from exposure or starvation.[28]

What Patterson describes as a "substitute," in my reading of this passage and its relationship to Hegel's dialectic in chief, is that, at the moment of that substitution, the future prospect of self-referentially risking life to expand the horizon of human possibility has been foreclosed. The point, here, is that death is omnipresent for the enslaved; however, it does not serve as the vehicle for progress within the Hegelian System of Science. Patterson critically proposes that:

> The condition of slavery did not absolve or erase the prospect of death. Slavery was not a pardon; it was, peculiarly, a conditional commutation. The execution was suspended only as long as the slave acquiesced in his powerlessness. The master was essentially a ransomer. . . . Because the slave had no socially recognized existence outside of his master, he becomes a social non person.[29]

Patterson's formulation is important for the thinking here, but I want to pay close attention to this notion of becoming a "non person." A subject cannot and need not "become" something that it already happens to be, and also it does mean that the becoming functions as a terminal subject position.

To be clear: Black people were persons before being framed as nonpersons by slavery, and the fact of the artificial nature of that positionality indicates that they were never actually nonpersons but only framed as such.

A principal methodological argument of this project is that it is presupposed that Hegel has accurately described the machinations and ambition of white supremacy. Further, that in doing so, he extracts the "Negro" from the fullness of participation by inserting the same figure in the fullness of explicit exclusion. This being said, it is necessary to account for the manner in which the enslaved is included through exclusion here. One aspect of this is the imperative to ensure that the "Negro" remain excluded from the fullness of resolved Being. The second reason might have to do with Hegel's topsy-turvy world, which exists as a necessary counterpoint to the world in which he lives and is described essentially by what it is *not* and, by extension, who is *not*. The essential question driving this thinking is how inverted is the inverted world in Hegel's account, and, more to the point, which elements remain static between the opposed worlds and facilitate awareness that his inverted world is categorically not Morrison's "*third, if you will pardon the expression, world*"?

Lewis Carroll's *Through the Looking-Glass* is instructive here. Alice's observations serve as the representatives of the sensibility of the reader to allow for awareness of the "inverted" nature of Wonderland. If a subject were totally immersed in Wonderland it would cease to be wonderful and would just be "land." Recall what Hegel establishes (in §158) as the condition in the topsy-turvy world: "where what is despised in the former is honored, and what is in the former honored meets with contempt."[30]

Perhaps ironically and, at the same time, predictably, what Hegel holds in place in order to witness the alteration of existence is the imperative of contempt for some subject and exaltation of others. It is not that the world becomes one in which *no one* is despised but rather that the formerly valorized becomes despised. Avoiding this wholesale, perhaps revolutionary, disorientation of the valuation of subjects serves an important function for the maintenance of white supremacy as explicated by Hegel. That function is the absolute imperative that "Negroes" never become the arbiters of Right, because, to the extent that the world is inverted in this fashion, white people become the "Negroes" and Europe (broadly considered) becomes a land of no historical existence. Fanon marks this potentiality in *The Wretched of the Earth*, proposing "for if the last shall be first, this will only come to pass after a murderous and decisive struggle between the two protagonists."[31] This, for Fanon, is a stage in the progress toward what he calls the "New Humanism" that is implicated in Hegelian categories and the imperative of a struggle to the death. To articulate a way of Being-as-Black, not just as an oppositional System of Science to Hegel's white supremacist superstructure but also to oppose the conditions of the topsy-turvy world, we must first deal with the experience of death within the current system of existence for the Black subject.

The question for me can be effectively pursued by interrogating the notion that fear of the master is the threshold condition for wisdom. What this seems to portend for the Black subject is that fear of death (corporeal), in that the subject is always already rendered metaphysically dead as marked by the erasure and separation from their historical Being, is realized as fear of death at the hands of the master for endeavoring to be human. Zakiyyah Iman Jackson's essential *Becoming Human: Matter and Meaning in an Antiblack World* places stress on the status of the human, writing:

> I argue that the recognition of humanity and its suspension act as alibis for each other's terror, such that the pursuit of human recognition or a compact with "the human" would only plunge one headlong into further terror and domination. Is the black a human being? The answer is hegemonically yes. However, this, in actuality, may be the wrong question as an affirmative offers no assurances. A better question may be: If being recognized as human offers no reprieve from ontologizing dominance and violence, then what might we gain from the rupture of the "human"?[32]

Stated differently, to the extent that the socially dead subject moves to ameliorate that condition, white supremacy/Hegel has *weaponized* self-consciousness by making death the means by which one advances toward it. This leaves the figure mired in Hegelian categories of thinking with two bad choices: the first is to do nothing for fear of death and the second, to do something and die. In the latter, the actual versus the metaphoric death of the subject terminates progress toward Absolute Knowing and solidifies the fact that the Black subject is mired in the condition of servitude. This is not an abstraction. Black life is policed, and that activity is designed to hang the specter of death over the life of the "Negro," which destabilizes the coherence of organic being by bringing the final term "Death" to the midpoint "Life." Lynching (broadly defined) is the mechanism for this understanding.

The fear and phenomenon that bears critical inquiry is the policing of Black bodies as different from, though obviously inextricably related to, the institution of the police. I mean that the violence against Black bodies that is memorialized or covered in the same manner that lynchings were archived on postcards in the twentieth century lumps together those murdered by the police (Breonna Taylor) with those murder by civilians (Trayvon Martin). The purpose of this policing is to reinforce Hegel's condition of wisdom: *Fear*. And there is always Death. The death that Hegel must believe I was meant to fear and grow up understanding that Black people ought not to ever feel safe in the presence of white people.

Hegel situates the Bondsman as the figure that travels through the dialectic. This presents at least a linguistic problem or paradox if not an existential threat to the notion of white supremacy in that, and here we adopt Hegel's employment of "proper" to demarcate the spatiality of the "Negro," *Slavery Proper* must be somehow different from the slavery or servitude that he allegorizes in the dialectic of Lord and Bondsman because "Negroes" as nonhistorical beings cannot be understood to have the potential to achieve Absolute Knowledge. Stated differently, one should be careful not to understand the "slave" of Hegel's dialectic as the slave of the plantation without careful qualification of the relationship between the two figures. Further, we must be careful not to allow the term "slave" to retain its power over the ontological nature of Blackness. Hegel, by bounding the "Negro" as outside the limits of reason, has disallowed that figure from participation as an active member of the dialectic and its progressive resolution. This is primarily a product of the notion that as far as Hegel's Negro is concerned, there is no distinction between enslaved as status and enslaved as ineluctable subjectivity. This is categorically false.

It is this lack of separation between the subject and the status of the subject as enslaved and the dehumanizing nature of the practical exclusion of "Negroes" from mattering historically that rings the alarm bell and the necessity for Frantz Fanon's engagement with Hegel in *Black Skin, White Masks.* We turn briefly to Fanon here in that I read his text as being directly engaged with Hegel's *Phenomenology* from the third sentence of the Introduction, which reads "I'm not the bearer of absolute truths."[33] Since the second sentence declares the untimeliness of the encounter, "It's too early . . . or too late,"[34] it is clear that the subject concerning Fanon is out of time (positively nonhistorical), fully and only present, and, therefore, incapable of Absolute Knowledge and, at the same time, potentially resident in a generative node like that conjured by Bob Marley or, as we see soon, exploited by Ralph Ellison. The subject in being both too early and too late is simply *Now.* When Fanon directly engages Hegel by name in the subsection, titled "The Black Man and Hegel," of chapter 7 ("The Black Man and Recognition"), he lays bare the insufficiency of the dialectic in that it fails in its structural bias, writing:

> But the former slave wants to *have himself recognized.*
>
> There is at the basis of Hegelian dialectic an absolute reciprocity that must be highlighted.
>
> It is when I go beyond my immediate existential being that I apprehend the being of the other as natural reality, and more than that. If I shut off the circuit, if I make the two way movement unachiev-

able, I keep the other within himself. In an extreme degree, I deprive him even of this being-for-self.[35]

It is a fairly well accepted fact that there is plasticity in the narrative voice in *Black Skin, White Masks*: the "I" that becomes "we," as one example, and the appearance of Fanon himself as both analyzer and analyzed in the narrative. Here, I would perhaps propose a more dramatic form of shape-shifting in the passages under consideration. For much of the section "The Black Man and Hegel," there is an argument to be made that the text accommodates a reading whereby there is the presence of Hegel himself talking *at* rather than *to* or *with* the *Black (hu)Man* about the manner in which the exclusion and erasure we have been referencing functions. Ultimately, the Black subject appears to respond and, in so doing, proposes a way forward with Hegel's system as the point of departure through rupture:

> I ask that I be taken into consideration on the basis of my desire. I am not only here—now, locked in thinghood. I desire somewhere else and something else. I demand that an account be taken of my contradictory activity insofar as I pursue something other than life, insofar as I am fighting for the birth of a human world, in other words, a world of reciprocal recognitions.[36]

This "ask," on the part of Fanon, is deepened by reading it alongside Morrison's tracing of a "*third, if you will pardon the expression, world*," which, in concert with these lines, requires a new form of reciprocity that the novelist asserts is framed with relation to the contradiction of double consciousness. Further, as noted earlier in this section, by reading self-consciousness as literally desire, Fanon's notion, through and in discourse with Hegel, is perhaps more provocative when reimagined to read something like:

> *I ask that I be taken into consideration on the basis of my self-consciousness. I am self-conscious somewhere else and something else.*

To be clear, this somewhere and something (or being some other) is found in Morrison's "*third, if you will pardon the expression, world.*" Fanon is deeply immersed in a struggle with Hegel because of his racism and its implications for the futurity of Black Being. Fanon is only one such example. Hegel is never far from an explicit and/or implicit point of reference within the intellectual tradition dedicated to the recovery or, perhaps more carefully, recognition of what W.E.B. Du Bois marks as "true self-consciousness" in *The Souls of Black Folk*. Du Bois, like Fanon, is part of a pantheon of thinkers within the Black Radical Tradition for whom Hegel is an interlocutor as well as opponent: C.L.R. James's *Notes on Dialectics* engages Hegel's *Science of Logic* in its totality through a Marxist reading of the text proposing that a philosopher might assert, "We are not Kantians. We are dialecticians of the school of Hegel developed by Marx."[37]

Situating "Death," for Hegel and, therefore, white supremacy, as the way forward is meant to drive the Black body to the place of its destruction. That is, in the effort to employ this paradigm for purposes of liberation, we will have caught up to the Hegel we want to leave far behind. The reference now is §451, having already arrived at Spirt and still concerned about Death.

> Death is the consummation and the highest work that the individual as such undertakes for the polity. However, insofar as he is essentially *singularly individual*, it is contingent as to whether his death was both immediately connected with and was the result of his work for the universal.[38]

The German's description of the world, where Black subjectivity goes to die, simultaneously refutes and reinstates Hegel's "Negro," in the same manner that the "Negro" is removed and at the same time required in the *Phenomenology* through slavery and its place in the *Philosophy of Right* is substantively a trap for the Black subject. The engine of Hegel's machine that produces his knowing subjects is fueled by death. Here, at §187, the self-consciousness of the Bondsman encounters the self-consciousness of the Lord, and the thing that is between them, serving at once both to differentiate them and to unite them, is their relationship to death:

> To the extent that it is what is done *by the other*, each thus aims at the death of the other. . . . The relation of both self-consciousnesses is thus determined in such a way that it is through a life and death struggle that each *proves its worth* to itself, and that both *prove their worth* to each other. . . . And it is solely by staking one's life that freedom is proven to be the essence.[39]

But, in the phenomenology of Blackness within the system of Hegel, this metaphoric death that Hegel allegorizes here is all too real, and, therefore, as we know from Du Bois, there is no possibility of finding this "essence." Those versed in the canon of Africana thought are thoroughly immersed in the Du Bois of *The Souls of Black Folk*, generally, and his formulation, in particular, which I have called in other work "Tripartite Subaltern Self-Consciousness" as the label for the interlocking concepts of *second sight, double consciousness, and twoness.*[40] Proposing that Hegel's "Negroes" are not able to locate the essence of being necessary for the proper encountering of the essence of an opposed subject is to follow the Du Boisian articulation of existence in "a world which leaves him no true self-consciousness."[41] This is what Hegel describes in §235 as the insufficiency of the "*in-itself*" for recognition, writing:

> Self-consciousness and being are *the same* essence, or *the same* not in comparison with each other, but rather the same in and for itself. It is only a one-sided, bad idealism which lets this unity again come on the scene as consciousness on one side and an *in-itself* on the other side.[42]

The resonance of Hegel's (mis)understanding of the subjective value and humanity of the "Negro" is present here in Du Bois's characterization of this "world," which I propose is his description of the same "world" that is the object of analysis for Hegel and is mapped here and named the Anti-Black World, or World_1:

> After the Egyptian and Indian, the Greek and Roman, the Teuton and Mongolian, the Negro is a sort of seventh son, born with a veil, and gifted with second-sight in this American world—a world which yields him no true self-consciousness, but only lets him see himself through the revelation of the other world. It is a peculiar sensation, this double-consciousness, this sense of always looking at one's self through the eyes of others, of measuring one's soul by the tape of a world that looks on in amused contempt and pity. One ever feels his twoness—an American, a Negro; two souls, two thoughts, two unreconciled strivings; two warring ideals in one dark body, whose dogged strength alone keeps it from being torn asunder.[43]

There is explicitly one world here and, by implication, two others that have already been mapped in Figures 1, 2, and 3 in the Introduction. The "American world," which we have indexed as the Anti-Black World or World_1, delivers this result. Here Du Bois, rather than endeavor to establish an alternative system of cognition, is careful to establish the invalidity of Hegel's arguments from the *Lectures on the Philosophy of History* by asserting a historical narrative for the Negro, writing:

> The history of the American Negro is the history of strife—the longing to attain self-consciousness, to merge his double self into a better and truer self. In this merging he wishes neither of the older selves to be lost. He would not Africanize America, for America has too much to teach the world and Africa. He would not bleach his Negro soul

> in a flood of white Americanism, for he knows that Negro blood has a message for the world. He simply wishes to make it possible for a man to be both a Negro and an American, without being cursed and spit upon by his fellows, without having the doors of Opportunity closed roughly in his face.[44]

There is much to unpack here, but what is critical for evaluating this element of Du Bois's thinking, which I wish to put into conversation with Hegel at the outset and then with Morrison, is the manner in which he recognizes that the "world" structurally denies "Opportunity" to the Negro. This is most obviously understood to be related to the primary elements of civic existence—the economy, education, social status, and so on—but the capitalization of the term seems instructive. Accepting this, pushing beyond these surface manifestations of citizenship, I am proposing that there is a way in which Du Bois is bearing witness to the foreclosure of the dialectic as a vehicle of progress toward Absolute Knowing for the Negro. Because of the inability marked here of the Negro to locate "essence" for material recognition, Hegel's structure is *designed* to fail the ambition of the "Other." As a practical matter, for Du Bois and others, the term self-consciousness must be resituated when it comes to Black subjectivity.

Hegel asserts the historical significance of what he calls the "Negro" by asserting the historical insignificance of what he calls the "Negro." What this then means for the subject so included through exclusion for this system of cognition is that the subject Hegel understood as the "Negro" represents "Conditional" being as the oppositional authorizing necessity of what he calls "Unconditional" being in §26:

> For its part, science requires that self-consciousness shall have elevated itself into this ether in order to be able to live with science and to live in science, and, for that matter, to be able to live at all. Conversely, the individual has the right to demand that science provide him at least with the ladder to reach this standpoint. The individual's right is based on his absolute self-sufficiency, which he knows he possesses in every shape, whether recognized by science or not, and no matter what the context might be, the individual is at the same time the absolute form, or he has *immediate self-certainty*; and, if one were to prefer this expression, he thereby has unconditional *being*.[45]

This paragraph suggests robust agency with regard to subject formation, "an unconditional being" that has the right to demand access to the system whose terminus is Absolute Knowledge. That agency is the "ladder" required to move both upward and forward. This seems to allow for, within the circularity of Hegel's thinking, where the beginning is in many ways indistinguishable from the end and even the most marginalized sentient subject is "able to live with science and to live science, and, for that matter, to be able to live at all."[46]

Another critical aspect of this relates to what this seeming universality of agency means for Hegel's "Negroes," who are historically excluded and "non-living" in that they are always already "socially dead" in the manner that Patterson proposes. The argument is that this exclusion creates a form of coercively imposed conditional being without access to the ladder internal to Hegel's system of science, which situates the "Negro" as unable to live with science, unable to live science, and, therefore, unable to live at all. Achille Mbembe reveals this as the "Necropolitical" core of Western thought, which creates the living/dead subject.[47]

It is important to deal with the nature of dialectical relations both inter and intra Worlds or systems of cognition. It is well tread territory and establishes the nature of dialectical subject formation within Hegel's system of science or white supremacy. Hegel also establishes, through the articulation of the "inverted world," that the "verted" world exists in contradistinction to the "inverted" form of existence. My reading of Du Bois and Fanon, and here I'm thinking of the color line and the boundary between colonized and colonizer, is that both these formulations are encumbered with their dialectical relationship to Hegel's dialectics. Morrison is not interested in subjectivity formed against walls of resistance to positive existence. Recall her description that reads:

> Beyond the outside/inside double consciousness, this new space postulates the inwardness of the outside, imagines safety without walls.[48]

What this appears to propose is that there is a technology of being that is not subject to the necessity of particularity through contact against arbitrarily formed points of comparison. In that way, this third way is significantly different from the commonly employed theories of the subject that are indecipherable and indiscernible without contrast. This theory of the Black Subject, to be specific, requires knowledge of white supremacy but does not resolve itself through subject forming opposition to it.

The imperative to positively locate the Black subject spatially is the corrective response to the efforts by Hegel et al. to dislocate the Black Body by rendering it spatially negated through its relationship to "Africa Proper." The typology of spatiality referenced here is both physical and metaphysical but can never be fully one or the other and relates itself to the corporeal nature of the (re)claim(ation) of Black subjectivity. The Black Body becomes the vehicle for progress through the *counterphenomenology* here, the vessel for being-toward-resolution, and the final resting place of the relevant subject. RAJudy's essential and demanding *Sentient Flesh: Thinking in Disorder, Poiēsis in Black*, deeply interrogates this thinking:

> Windham's "us is human flesh" troubles this orientation in a way that cannot be easily dismissed. Rather than giving temporal primacy to flesh as stolen sign, his statement presumes that meaning and form are expressed spontaneously: the flesh is *with* and not *before* the body and person, and the body and person are *with* and not *before* or even *after* the flesh.[49]

The body here serves as the boundary of the corporeal political space, with its flesh functioning as a border that can be violated as well as protected. The embodied nature of positive Black subjectivity, particularly with reference to the diasporic subject, disallows the negating resonance of the (Long) Middle Passage while at the same time affirms the agency of the body in question to be valorized where and when it finds itself.

As mentioned earlier, Hegel's schizophrenic relationship to the presence, or lack thereof, of Black being(s) in his system of thinking is deepened in some sense by his 1821 text *Elements of the Philosophy of Right*. In that text's opening moments, §2 of the introduction to be precise, he notes, "In Roman law, for example, no definition of a *human being* would be possible, for the slave could not be subsumed under it; indeed the status of the slave does violence to the concept."[50] The problematic for definition that Hegel ascribes to the Romans also haunts his own system of thinking. The "slave" and slavery, and the manner in which Hegel's historical argument witnesses that institution as the manner in which the Negro encounters Europe, literally pierces the hermetically sealed nature of his account of consciousness.

In order to elide it, we must develop and effectively employ new modes of cognition in service of new modes of consciousness. This requires that we first understand the way in which cognition functions in the Anti-Black World and then the way in which it can be short circuited to deliver the technology required here. Early in the text of the *Phenomenology*, specifically in the opening paragraph of the introduction (§73), Hegel situates cognition as an *instrument* for seizing hold of the truth or "absolute essence":

> For if cognition is the instrument for seizing hold of the absolute essence, then it becomes immediately clear that the application of an instrument to a thing no longer leaves the thing as it is for itself, but rather goes about forming and changing it.[51]

For this book, this means that, to the extent we accept the "rules" of Hegel's world regarding the (dys)forming effects of cognition, the system under examination will, in fact, be altered by examination. Hegel pushes on this as §73 proceeds:

> What is absurd is that we are making use of a means at all. It does indeed seem that this defect can be remedied through cognition of the way in which the *instrument* works, for such cognition makes it possible to subtract from within the result that part which, in the representation we obtain of the absolute through the instrument, belongs to the instrument; and so such cognition makes it possible to obtain the truth purely, however, this improvement would in fact only bring us back to where we were before. If we again subtract from a formed thing what the instrument has added to it, then the thing—here, the absolute—is again for us exactly as it was prior to this consequently superfluous effort.[52]

Hegel's account of the net zero effect of cognition is bounded within his system, which assumes the participants in this form of thinking are necessarily *within the boundaries* of that system. Understanding that the "Negro" is outside the system, we see the first element of the instrumentality of a system of Black Phenomenology, in that we need to develop an account for the integrity of systems examined by those outside of the system. It is important to consider that thinking carefully about a system designed to erase a particular subject, as the erased subject, must necessarily destabilize and disfigure the system itself. I emphasize that what we are witnessing is that the system of cognition explicated by Hegel is designed to necessarily exclude Black Being from registering as worthwhile in the most basic sense of the term. The primacy of cognition, here an improvisation of Maurice Merleau-Ponty's *Phenomenology of Perception*, is the reason that cognition as such is the first technology that must be explicated in service of the destabilization and replacement of the system that erases Black subjectivity.

The Play of Cognition(s)

The primacy of cognition in this project is due to the fact that it serves as the point of entry into a bounded system of Being and functions as the limiting condition of subjective potentiality. To the extent that a cognitive system is designed to prevent "seeing" certain subjects and/or their attributes, then consciousness and Being are necessarily bracketed within that limitation. Further, a subject who is overdetermined by a cognitive system is at least assumed to be if not, in fact, bound within that system of knowing. This is the gist of the notion of second sight that Du Bois asserts can never deliver a subject a true understanding of the self. It is one level of "security" that the Anti-Black World has designed, built, and maintained; in that this cognitive realm, in its seeming totality, refuses the aggrieved subject the benefit of seeing themselves differently or through a different cognitive lens.

What Hegel understands about that system is the manner in which various typologies of Death serve as the final layer of security for the cognitive system that denies Black subjects' knowledge of themselves. The border wall of the Anti-Black World or World$_1$, architecture posing as world, is a cognitive feedback loop, feeding on its on misinformation. The way out, the Door of ~~No~~ Return, is thus effectively barred by the omnipresence of Death, posing as the way forward.

The following section reveals a series of diagrams, "cognitive maps," that illustrate what I am calling the "Play of Cognition(s)," the last of which unlocks the door to Morrison's "*third, if you will pardon the expression, world*." Four questions serve as the driving force behind this thinking:

1. What happens when a maligned subject finds itself within a system of cognition that is dedicated to maintaining the conditions of marginalization?
2. What happens when a negatively framed subject attempts to introduce an alternative mode of cognition to disrupt the prevailing system?
3. What happens when an opposing system takes hold within a negating system of cognition?
4. What happens when two opposing systems confront a similar object?

The stage is set for this work, as mentioned earlier, by a close reading of Merleau-Ponty's *Phenomenology of Perception*, where he proposes the following:

> Because we are through and through related to the world, the only way for us to catch sight of ourselves is by suspending this moment, by refusing to be complicit with it or as Husserl often says, to see it *ohne mitzumachen* [without taking part], or again, to put it out of play.[53]

To put the self out of play, with respect to the back-and-forth of negatively framing modes of cognition, requires examination of the state of play expressed by the cognitive map that delivers the negatively framed Black subject to the world and to the Black Self. The first step is to deal with question one in the list, which lays out the base case of cognitive play in the anti-Black World.

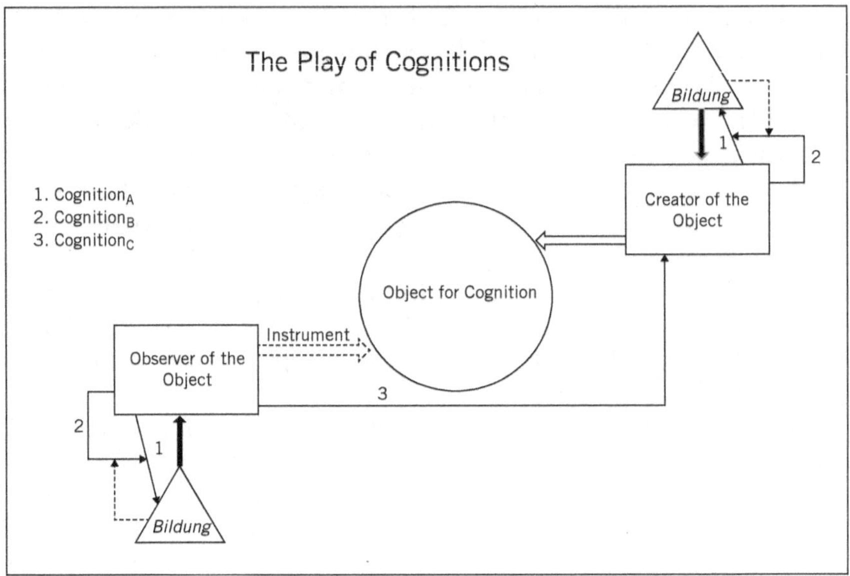

Figure 4 The Play of Cognitions under the conditions of white supremacy.

Figure 4 depicts the way an object is created and delivered for cognition to observers from the imagination of those who have established themselves as the hegemon. Here, the Creator of the Object for Cognition, in order to create the object, has cognition of the culture that informs the creation of the object: Cognition$_{A.}$ The next level of cognition for the creator subject is cognition of Cognition$_A$: labeled here as Cognition$_B$, which amounts to an understanding of why this is all happening in the first place and is understood to be driven, if not necessarily accounted for, by the *Bildung* of the creator.

The Observer of the Object for Cognition has a similar series of interlocking moments of cognition or cognitive events. First, there is the Instrument of observation that is itself cognition, as outlined in §73. That instrument is informed by the first moment of cognition, which is the examination of the *Bildung* of the observer that causes the employment of the instrument in the first place: Cognition$_A$. The second moment of cognition is Cognition$_B$, which is, as in the system of the Creator, cognition of the manner in which *Bildung* informs the functioning of Cognition$_A$. The third moment of cognition is the examination of the Creator of the object under consideration: Cognition$_C$. What should be clear here is that, in the case the Object for Cognition is the description of the Observer of the Object, there is no clear way for the Observer to see themselves differently from what is established by the *Bildung* of the Creator. The case that concerns us here is when the cultural education of the creator of the object for cognition includes the description of the Black subject as irretrievably negative. The Instrument for cognition, here depicted as a dotted arrow, is the product of this negatively framed system and is designed to deliver a description of the object by the object that is infected with this harmful logic. This is another description of the mechanism of Du Boisian second sight and also a way to clarify what Merleau-Ponty means by what must be "put . . . out of play."

The second permutation of this cognitive map follows the same logic as the first, except that the *Bildung* of the Observer of the Object has a different idea about the character of the Object for Cognition but, at this stage, is still employing the negatively framed and, therefore, faulty instrument for cognition. This delivers what Du Bois understands as double consciousness, which resolves itself as twoness. The subject is aware of the competing ways to understand (consciousness) the self but is unable to do more than resolve to hold the contradictions in place. This is the dialectical relationship that Morrison implores us to resist and to understand as the product of choices and not the result of unavoidable logic. This scenario also does not, following Merleau-Ponty, take the problem out of play.

The third way to consider this paradigm is one in which the *Bildung* of the Observer of the Object develops an instrument for cognition that is not related to the *Bildung* of the Creator of the Object. What this achieves is a description of the object that, in its totality, creates a new object, which, in its thorough description, resides at a remove from the dialectical system here.

This creates a new subjective form that exists on its own without reference to a negatively framed version of the self. What happens here is that the *Bildung* employed to create the alternative system of cognition must necessarily deal effectively with the memory of the former mode of understanding and the way in which it delivers defective results. Again, the Merleau-Ponty of *Phenomenology of Perception* is critical here. As Merleau-Ponty grapples with "the role of memory in perception,"[54] he proposes the following:

> Prior to any contribution by memory, that which is seen must currently be organized in such a way as to offer me a scene in which I can recognize my previous experiences. Thus, the appeal to memory presupposes what is meant to explain, namely the articulation of the givens, the imposing of a sense onto the sensible chaos. The evocation of memory becomes superfluous the moment that it is made possible, since the work that we expect from it has already been accomplished.[55]

See Figure 5, "The Play of Cognitions," which is rendered here to demonstrate the manner in which Hegel's brand of cognition renders the neces-

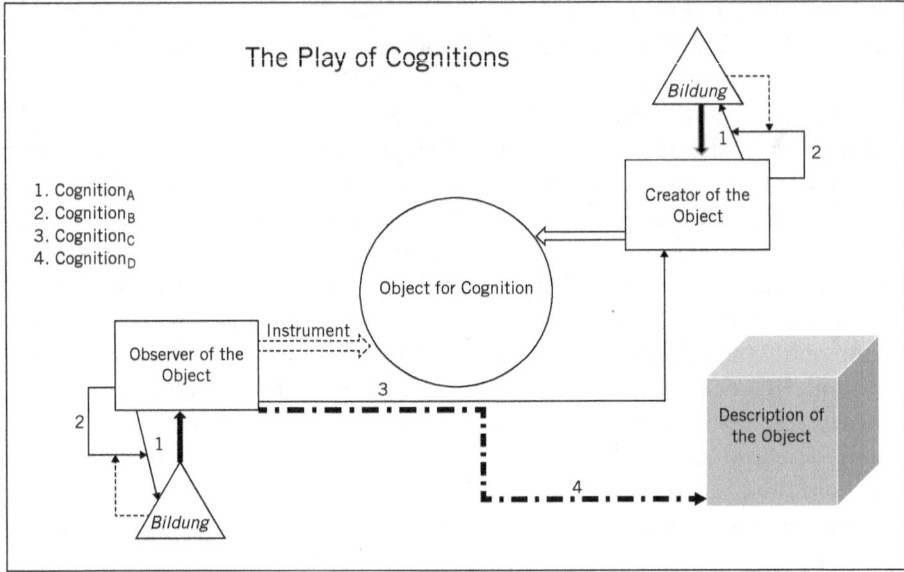

Figure 5 The Play of Cognitions destabilizing white supremacy.

sity of Morrison's exposition of a "*third, if you will pardon the expression, world*" for eliding Du Bois's telos.

For Morrison's "*third, if you will pardon the expression, world*," there must necessarily be an alternative system of cognition that is the unique providence of those whom this system is designed to exclude. To deal effectively, and by that I mean to dismiss the preconceptions that memory delivers, Toni Morrison explicates the process of Rememory, which serves as the Instrument for altered cognition. Morrison's relationship to nonlinear time is, in fact, the foundation of a form of cognition we label both "Rememory" and "Thirdsight," which allows access to the terms and conditions of a "*third, if you will pardon the expression, world*." Additionally, it is important to note that Morrison employs fractured temporality and genealogy, or, more specifically, the notion of "Rememory" as the cognitive tool/reality for navigating this system of harm and perceiving a space of positive resolution. In the text of *Beloved*, Morrison's character Sethe offers this explanation of the to-be-resolved confusion caused by these interlocking events of ramification that are the awareness of both Transsubjective and Transgenerational trauma.

It may be useful to ensure that we are properly oriented by revisiting briefly the plot of Morrison's *Beloved*. The story is set in Ohio in the years following the Civil War and Emancipation. Sethe, the protagonist if we need to name one, escaped from slavery while pregnant to join her grandmother in Ohio, where her other daughter had already found some modicum of safety. Sethe becomes a victim of the Fugitive Slave Act when slave catchers from her former plantation have successfully tracked her down. Rather than have her children and herself returned to slavery, she attempts to kill them and is only successful in murdering the daughter who had preceded her to Ohio. The ghost of the child returns to haunt Sethe and her family to understand why her mother killed her. This "return" obviously disorients the progress of linear time, a concept that had troubled Sethe before the apparition:

> "I was talking about time. It's so hard for me to believe in it. Some things go. Pass on. Some things just stay. I used to think it was my rememory. You know. Some things you forget. Other things you never do. But it's not. Places, places are still there. If a house burns down, it's gone, but the place—the picture of it—stays, and not just in my rememory, but out there in the world. What I remember is a picture floating around out there outside my head . . ."
>
> "Can other people see it?" asked Denver.
>
> "Oh, yes. Oh, yes, yes, yes. Someday you be walking down the road and you hear something or see something going on. So clear. And you think it's you thinking it up. A thought picture. But no. It's when you bump into a rememory that belongs to somebody else."[56]

I reference this confusion as a "to-be-resolved" state of affairs in that the true nature of this Transsubjective and Transgenerational cognitive state, in spite of Sethe's ability to explain and note its existence, must necessarily elude the awareness of the mother who elects to kill her child. It is not clear to me, and this is perhaps the key to unraveling this problematic, that our prevailing system of cognition, which is rendered coherent by the telos of birth to death, is sufficient for the task of reckoning with Transsubjective and Transgenerational cognition. This is clear, though unstably so, from thinking through the important and devastating (mis)understanding that informs Sethe's decision to kill her children and successfully only murdering the child known, prior to her "resurrection," as "crawling already?"

What I mean here is that the tragic reality of the existence of the binary proposition of transsubjective and transgenerational cognition, fueled by Morrison's notion of trauma-induced "Rememory," at the level of the cognition of phenomenological reality, doesn't matter if "crawling already?" is freed from the experience of slavery by death because she has and is already transsubjectively and transgenerationally suffered(ing) and will continue to suffer its excesses. This, at some level, must be what causes the confusion for Beloved who returns to find out why Sethe murdered "crawling already?"

The fact of this lies in the inability of Beloved to resolve the sweep of "her" cognitive awareness, which is also the dominant system of confusion for the other inhabitants of 124 as well.

This "confusion" is, perhaps, usefully explored through the following thought experiment that has as its objective an "understanding" of the cognitive map Morrison establishes as the phenomenological reality for marginalized Blackness that must be resolved to exceed the bonds of anti-Blackness. Imagine that *Subject A* finds themselves a passenger on a train that feels as if it is headed down a track. I say "feels as if" because there are no windows on the side of the train and, therefore, movement is conveyed via two screens at the front of the car that are labeled "Left" and "Right" and show a landscape on each that is rapidly moving by. This gives our passenger, *Subject A*, the notion that they are proceeding forward at a rapid pace. At the same time, *Subjects B* and *C*, are aboard trains that are hundreds of miles away from one another as well as hundreds of miles from the location of *Subject A*. Both *B* and *C* are filming out of the left and right side of their respective train cars and broadcasting to the left and right screens in the view of *Subject A*. This means that the sense-certainty of *Subject A* is based on spatial, positional, and subjective disorientation because what they believe represents their cognitive experience is that of another. To further complicate this, *Subject B* has their camera aimed at a forty-five-degree angle in the direction of travel and *Subject C*'s camera is focused at a forty-five-degree angle away from the direction of travel. Additionally, *Subject B*'s footage is from one hundred years ago and *Subject C*'s is from fifty years ago. Nothing about *Subject A*'s perception of the world, including that of the car being in motion, is synchronized with what is best understood as physical reality.

This is sufficiently complex and destabilizing to linear systems of cognition, and Morrison introduces an additional layer of complexity that enriches the cognitive tool she is developing. *Subject B* and *C* are also out of synch with what we may erroneously understand as the normative cognition of reality, in that the images they encounter may or may not be first-person cognitive events, and, again, what enriches these encounters is that they (1) cannot tell whether they are a result of primary cognition and (2) it, in fact, doesn't matter.

To say it doesn't matter is to substantively miss that, as far as Morrison is concerned, whether events are "real" or not misunderstands the expansive nature of "the real" in this system of thought. However, it deeply matters in grappling with the author's extension through improvisation on the thinking of both Du Bois and Fanon.

Recall that in the essay mentioned earlier here from *The Source of Self-Regard*, Morrison, perhaps, admonishes us to understand both that "W.E.B. Du Bois's observation is a strategy, not a prophecy or cure" and, further, that "beyond the outside/inside double consciousness, this new space postulates the inwardness of the outside." Morrison's decision to focus her attention on the middle term of what I have termed "Du Bois's Tripartite Subaltern Consciousness"[57] is important. By centering her attention on the "sensation" of Double Consciousness that Du Bois exposes as "a peculiar sensation . . . this sense of always looking at one's self through the eyes of others, of measuring one's soul by the tape of a world that looks on in amused contempt and pity,"[58] Morrison understands the rigidity of Du Bois's system of consciousness, which lands on twoness, "An American, a Negro, two souls, two thoughts, two unreconciled strivings; two warring ideals in one dark body, whose dogged strength alone keeps it from being torn asunder,"[59] to be relatively pessimistic and the product of the cognitive trap of constructing awareness of the self through the vision of those dedicated to purposive destructive (mis)understanding and (mis)recognition of the other. Substantively, Du Bois's cognitive map is encumbered by its continued relationship to the play of cognitions that circles around itself and even in its awareness that the "object" formed and maintained by the *Bildung* of white supremacy/Anti-Blackness is not real, the foundational information is present in the attempt at revolutionary self-re-definition by this Other/Object that results in an irreconcilable binary being: Twoness. Tracing Morrison's intervention, proposing that this form of consciousness represents "a strategy, not a prophecy or cure,"[60] it must then be the case that even a cognitive system marred by its relationship to the logic of white supremacy is one of only several ways to disable this attempt at establishing inescapable abjection for Black people, her project being structured around what she calls the "inwardness of the outside."[61] The phenomenology of Blackness, proposed by Du Bois, which struggles to find its way out of the result of the absorption of negatively framed Blackness into the system of cognition of the self of the Black subject, is recalibrated and, therefore, extended by Morrison through the obliteration of a worldview that presupposes the good as existing only in counterpoint to the bad: the inside as oppositional and structured against the outside.

Morrison, here, is employing the thinking of both Du Bois and Fanon to inform the necessary existence of the "*third, if you will pardon the expression, world*" described as "already made for me, both snug and wide open with a doorway never needing to be closed."[62] The bridge from Morrison to Fanon, which has as its point of departure Du Bois, is designed to address the two foundational thinkers' preoccupation with the white gaze and the implications thereof. I'm thinking specifically of the Fanon of *Black Skin, White Masks*, whose encounter with the white gaze at the opening of chapter 5, titled "The Lived Experience of the Black Man," reads "'Dirty, nigger!' or simply, 'Look! A Negro!'"[63] It asserts that the white gaze alters the subjective potentiality of the Black subject, in that the regard of the Black Self by the

Black Self is calibrated by a relationship to whiteness. The relevant quotation reads:

> Ontology does not allow us to understand the being of the black man, since it ignores the lived experience. For not only must the black man be black; he must be black in relation to the white man.[64]

The concern with ontology and its relationship to phenomenology, and what that portends for the stability of the Black self, maps alongside what we have established as the telos of the Du Boisian theory of the Black subject, whose system of cognition leads to a barely sustainable existence in conflict with an internalized whiteness disguised as the "American." Morrison proposes a different view of this problematic that resides in the relational interstices between ontology, phenomenology, and radical subject formation.

In *Beloved*, Sethe encounters the white gaze during the critical moments of her escape from Sweet Home, the forced labor camp, when Amy Denver, also in flight of a different sort, sees her and reacts by exclaiming, "Look there. A nigger. If that don't beat all."[65] Here, this encounter leads down a path different from that explicated by the Fanon of *Black Skin, White Masks*, and, importantly, the Du Bois of *Souls*, where he writes, "I remember well when the shadow swept across me."[66] The story is a familiar one. The young Du Bois has his calling card refused by a girl in his class:

> Then it dawned upon me with a certain suddenness that I was different from the others; or like, mayhap, in heart and life longing but shut out from their world by a vast veil. I had thereafter no desire to tear down that veil, to creep through; I held all beyond it in common contempt and lived above it in a region of blue sky and great wandering shadows.[67]

Morrison takes a different tack, employing what might be productively called an utilitarian approach to the reality of white supremacy. Amy Denver and her unavoidable (at least for white people) "look a nigger" moment is confounded by the ability of Sethe here to do what the subjects in the ruminations of Du Bois and Fanon cannot: enjoy sufficient subjective plasticity to, at the same time, both be in the way to receive some form of "help" from white people while, at the same time, erecting a barrier of personal safety and subjective sovereignty by giving her a fake name.

> "What they call you?" she asked.
>
> However far she was from Sweet Home, there was no point in giving out her real name to the first person she saw.
>
> "Lu," said Sethe. "They call me Lu."[68]

Like Ishmael in the opening of Melville's *Moby-Dick*, Sethe (here "Lu") announces herself by prefacing her name with a "call me" as a disguise but with an important caveat. While Ishmael has the agency to order himself to be addressed in a certain manner ("Call me Ishmael"), Sethe possesses neither the authority to name herself to white people nor, perhaps more importantly, the ability to do so safely, so she makes up a name as a claim of subjective sovereignty and defense mechanism ("They call me").

This thinking must be indexed against the point of entry here, specifically the emphasis Morrison places on interrogating Du Bois's understanding of subaltern self-consciousness. Sethe, upon encountering the white gaze, even in her state of physical and mental disability, accesses two states of being that are not accounted for or, perhaps, not part of the awareness of both Du Bois and Fanon but are products of "Third-sight/Rememory." First, the possibility of the animal:

> Down in the grass, like the snake she believed she was, Sethe opened her mouth, and instead of fangs and a split tongue, out shot the truth.[69]

Du Bois's formulation has the telos of "twoness" within the Black Body: two incompatible ways of being, Negro and American. For Morrison, neither one of these unresolvable subject positions is compatible with her reading of the self-authorizing Black subjectivity that resists what she understands as an avoidable result of the system of cognition, double consciousness, which drives Du Bois's rigid system and is illustrated here in the play of cognitions as awareness of the cultural content of object making. What is essential to understand is that it is the relationship between Morrison's Transsubjective and Transgenerational system of cognition that allows the Negro/American binary to be displaced, within the same "dark body," by the Human and the Animal. The journey to that space of subjective possibility is solely dependent on an abandonment of double consciousness as the cognitive tool of the Black subject to be replaced by Morrison's Transsubjective and Transgenerational way of knowing. This means that, in opposition to Du Bois's assertion of the Black subjective awareness that comes to be(ing) through the eyes of another bent on the destruction of the subject in question, Morrison's subject knows about themself through the eyes of those who are similarly subject to the white gaze and its destructive effects.

Morrison demonstrates here in these passages that there is a new way of Being-as-Black: Subjectivity that accommodates Self-defining Humanity and its positive relationship to the Animal. This concept is not without complication beyond that of the question of the possibility and then the practice of accommodating multiple and potentially competing subject positions. I'm thinking here with and through Jackson's interrogation in *Becoming Human* of these elements of Morrison's work. Jackson requires that we account for the legacy of questioning the humanity of Black people through the assertion of animality:

> The bestialization of blackness has been central, even essential, to reanimations of antiblack discourse from the early days of the American republic until today. Often when this occurs, the evocation of black animality is either unquestioningly reified or criticized for reinforcing antiblack racism and quickly dismissed. Toni Morrison avoids both approaches; instead, she problematizes these strategies by critically engaging the assumptive logic of racialized animality and redirecting antiblack animal imagery.[70]

The relevant scene is set when Denver "easily slipped into the told story that lay before her eyes,"[71] which is the account by Sethe of the moments before she encountered Amy Denver. Denver, yet to be born, is experienced physically by Sethe as a "little antelope . . . [that] rammed her with horns and pawed the ground of her womb with impatient hooves."[72]

The fact of the matter here is that Sethe has no frame of coherent reference to be aware of the existence of the animal known as an antelope, having lived in the southeastern United States her entire life. She resolves the cognitive confusion by accepting the fact that her memory is out of time as well as out of place:

> She guessed it must have been an invention held on to from before Sweet Home, when she was very young. Of that place where she was born (Carolina maybe? or was it Louisiana?) she remembered only song and dance.[73]

What we learn as this passage unravels itself is that the text accommodates the understanding that this "memory" is a "Rememory" that belongs to Sethe's unnamed mother from her time (or a Rememory of a Rememory of some other subject in Africa) *before* the Middle Passage:

> Oh but when they sang. And oh but when they danced and sometimes they danced the antelope. The men as well as the ma'am's, one of whom was certainly her own. They shifted shapes and became something other.[74]

This means that the choice to represent herself to the white gaze at the cognitive threshold of this "*third, if you will pardon the expression, world*" allows for the two internally coherent possibilities of Black Being that comprise this subject: Human and Animal as opposed to the impossible to resolve Negro and American. The Human and the Animal contain within them a complex series of identities. With respect to the Animal, Morrison reveals several like the snake, the hawk, the calf, to name a few. With respect to the

Human, one of the most interesting notions exposed by Morrison here is that Sethe often refers to the "ma'am" as a separate identity from herself. These passages reveal Sethe's understanding; the first, "concerned as she was for the life of her children's mother"[75] and later, "I believe this baby's ma'am is gonna die in wild onions on the bloody side of the Ohio River"[76] where the "she" the "mother" and the "ma'am" are all Sethe discussing herself as another. This ability to observe, from a separate space, the manifold internalized ways of being as if they are outside is the performance of the notion of the place of safety elaborated by Morrison as the result of altered cognition.

The circular and interlocking nature of cognition in the Hegelian understanding of World, which roughly maps on top of what we have identified here as the Anti-Black World or $World_1$, is the framework that Morrison's system destabilizes, if we allow that distinction, from the World, which is important to mark. Morrison's Rememory, in its transsubjective transmission of experience, renders the subject permeable and in excess of itself through this transmission and receipt. This is an especially fraught process for a subject who is in the process of bearing witness to their own erasure. The analogy would be being present to observe your own birth and death as coincident events by the observer/actor who's pre- and afterlife are somehow bracketed by *Birth/Death* and *Death/Birth* rather than the normative nature of "living" being bracketed by being born and dying. With this in mind, we can turn to a careful examination of the lurid discourse of Black Death, which we have identified as the structural obstruction to positive Black subjectivity within the Anti-Black World that itself is the constant reminder of the prudence of the fear we have highlighted here.

The hangman's noose, be it real or metaphoric, is a continuous presence because it is lynching that serves the purpose of establishing a regime of rational fear of the irrational violence against Black bodies. The predictable unpredictability of Black people encountering white people is the irrational nature, the unreasonable reason, that Hegel marks as fear of the master.

The insertion of Death and the fear of the master at so critical a moment in subjective development by Hegel accurately depicts the state of play for the epistemic maintenance of white supremacy. The modern institution of policing and its relationship to the slave patrols cannot be overemphasized. Slave patrols were responsible for returning runaway slaves to their masters, enforcing laws that prevented Black people from traveling without passes or permits, and preventing revolt. It is the notion of motion (traveling) that serves as the point of dialectical tension between master and slave. Recall that Hegel proposes the proper functioning of the dialectic situates a "thing" between Lord and Bondsman that reveals the status of the antagonists. The party that is compelled to work on the thing is the Bondsman, the party that enjoys the fruits of that labor is the Lord. The question that must be dealt with to resolve this aspect of Hegel's phenomenology, in order to leave it behind, is What might be the "thing" to be worked on between the Black subject and the anti-Black racists? Morrison, Du Bois, and Fanon have different ideas about this.

In Hegel's metaphoric meeting between subjects that arrive at the point of dialectical tension, unaware of their status as Lord or Bondsman in this particular instance for this particular encounter, things can go either way. For purposes of Hegel's engagement with the manifold condition of the "Negroes" proper that occupy his imaginary, the Black subject, historically unimportant and enslaved in order to be free, must necessarily always already be and remain the Bondsman. By having the status of Bondsman *presupposed* by the structure of the Hegelian System of Science for the "Negroes," it establishes the presumption of fear, which the figure in question can never be without, within the ever-defended walls of this worldview. The fear of the master is what I understand as fear of death in a much different sense than the fact that mortality is just that: we all must die.

The fear memorialized here by Hegel is meant to substantively be the fear of death that arrives as a reaction to endeavoring to unlock the dialectic in order to render it determinative rather than reifying. For the part of the culture that establishes the manner of seeing the world that informs Hegel's Anti-Black Racism, it is the coercive power of the state that serves to render "real" the fear that he understands to be the threshold indicator of wisdom and, for that matter, reason: in that it is unreasonable not to be in fear of that which intends to kill you, and the fact of Black inferiority maintained through fear is the condition of a reasoned existence for the white supremacist. Recall in §451 Hegel reminds us that "death is the consummation and the highest work that the individual as such undertakes for the polity."[77]

Notice to Mariners II: Niggers Beware

I was first pursued by a mob of white racists who were intent on policing my body when I was ten years old in 1977. I am able to triangulate the event based on three navigational aids: Stevie Wonder's *Songs in the Key of Life*, the bicentennial celebration, and my birthday.

Songs in the Key of Life was released in the fall of 1976, and I remember going to Sears with my parents, my father buying the record, and, as we were leaving the store, seeing the red, white, and blue ABA Rawlings basketball I asked for as a gift for either the fast approaching Christmas holiday or my March birthday. It arrived for my birthday, but, as is typical of Chicago, there was really no springtime so using the ball had to wait until it was warm enough to go to the outdoor courts near my home. This is where the story becomes complicated.

I lived with my parents and my little brother on the far south side of Chicago where the street numbers were into the hundreds and the city proper threatened to run out: what is known today as the "Wild 100s." I grew up within blocks of the home my mother had grown up in, which had been torn down in order to make room for the expressway. Honestly, it wasn't until I attended a Jesuit high school in downtown Chicago and had to travel through the entire city to get there that it became clear to me that white people actually lived in Chicago. To our west was the white neighborhood known as Beverly, and, somehow, when we had driven through that area, I had seen and marked in my memory the well-kept basketball courts in one of their (white people's) parks. I extracted a promise from my father that we would drive over there for me to break in my new basketball on those hoops rather than the run-down rims in our neighborhood.

I believe it was May or June because it was the kind of hot that only Chicago can deliver. The kind of heat that makes the asphalt molten and the air above it come to life, looking like what we called "monkeys dancing." I had finished helping my father mow the lawn, and I was lying on my back in the front yard. The clouds were moving so rapidly that I imagined I could feel the rotation of the Earth. Finally, my dad said the word and my brother and I jumped into the back seat of the car and his youngest brother, my uncle, rode in the front seat for us all to go try out the ball.

We drove to the park and headed through the gate onto the courts I had been dreaming about and found them to be empty. What we also found was that one of the backboards that faced the interior of the park had a skull and crossbones with the admonition "Niggers Beware!" affixed to it. I don't remember much of what immediately transpired, but I do recall not feeling comfortable shooting the ball toward the basket and rather just dribbled it around a bit, really wanting to go home. I'm not sure that it registered the "Niggers" who needed to beware included me and my family, but I knew for sure that it wasn't a place I wanted to be any longer. My memory of the events becomes vivid again when the once empty court was suddenly filled with white people who began yelling at the four of us.

My father and his youngest brother were survivors of the killing fields of Hale County, Alabama, and had migrated (fled?) to Chicago to get away from just this type of chaos. I imagine that they must, at some point, have thought that this type of mob violence would give way to less kinetic forms of attack in a place like Chicago, at least by 1977. The white kids who encircled us hurled insults and racial epithets, while the boldest of them lunged within inches of my dad and uncle, who, upon reflection, seemed to be involved in a rite of passage that was meant to render any assumption of progress demonstrably false. The Chicago summer that had pushed aside the winter to allow me to go out and play had been replaced with the thick acrid and poisonous humidity of Alabama, and it must have felt all too familiar to my dad and uncle. It would, from that moment forward, be a part of the lives of my brother and me as it had been for our ancestors back to the encounter with white people in Africa: the one line of genealogical and historical relation that white supremacy had no intention of interrupting.

I had never seen children, and here, looking back, they were clearly teenagers, attack or even scream at adults. It makes me wonder two things: first, what had they seen their parents do to Black people to assure them that no Black person, no matter any characteristic one might name about them, need be respected, and, second, what would have happened if my five-year-old brother and I had been there alone. There is something important about the fact that these children were formed into this mob.

My father worked for the City of Chicago as a building inspector, and he had a badge that I imagine he had to show to gain access to properties. He pulled it from his back pocket and held it toward one particularly aggressive kid who was getting really close to us, and, somehow, they retreated to a corner of the court to decide what they were going to do and how they were going to do it. Thinking about this now, this was probably a particularly dangerous moment in that they may have been encouraged to go find an adult, and, worse yet, the adults may have involved the actual police.

I still had the ball in my hands, and my father pulled me to the free throw line and told me to shoot it, then, he said, we could go home. I half-heartedly threw it toward the hoop, missing all construction, and my uncle caught it and bounce passed it back to me. Take your time and shoot it like you know how, my dad said. I cast a wary eye at the gathering and re-forming mob and this time got the form right enough for it to make it through the hoop. My uncle rebounded the ball, and we made a beeline for the car and headed directly back home. None of us, to my knowledge, ever spoke again about this, and I wonder if my dad and uncle ever talked together or with anyone else about it. It was, in reality, not necessary, in one very tragic sense, and really necessary, in another important way. It registered with them just like any other rite of passage I imagine. My brother and I finally became a particular kind of Black by way of being called Niggers, and there has never been as much time as I would like to have elapsed between the instances when I felt like I was ten years old again, standing at a free throw line while a mob of anti-Black racists conspire to harm me.

Six Hundred Pounds

On Friday, December 22, 2023, the two paramedics who administered a lethal dose of ketamine to Elijah McClain were convicted for their actions.

Predictably, in the aftermath of this guilty verdict, *The Sentinel* published an article with the headline: "Experts Say Convictions of 2 Aurora Paramedics in the Death of Elijah McClain Could Have Chilling Effect on Rescuers."[78] It is probably worth substituting the term "chilling effect" with something that approximates "fear" since that is the realm we are operating within when it comes to the complexity of Black Death as a corrective to notions of self-consciousness. It is also important to be aware that this verdict is one of several that have been rendered in this case, some being acquittals and others being convictions, but we must never lose sight of the fact that, at the end of the day, Elijah McClain is dead for no reason.

So, "first responders," whose job it is, putatively, to save people from harm, in this instance decided to kill the person in danger. Or, more correctly, the first responders were, in fact, representative of real danger to Black people. The guilty verdict, designed to, in fact, make the responsible parties "fearful" of taking actions that are detrimental to the well-being of the people they are supposed to serve and protect, has instead inspired them to busily work to reverse the vector of fear back to the public. They need you to know that the next time they show up to find the police abusing someone they may choose to do nothing (also a crime, by the way, but perhaps "better") rather than do something that may, in fact, be lethal.

But, of course, they, the first responders: charged, some convicted and some acquitted, all describe that they were, in fact, afraid for their lives while dealing with Elijah McClain. The recording of the incident is examined here in some detail, but there is one moment that requires us to conclude that the cognitive realm of white supremacy and Anti-Blackness is, in fact, dissonant with respect to reality to the detriment of the safety of Black people. Claudia Rankine's formulation is operative here "because white men can't / police their imagination / black men are dying."[79]

To be clear, the coroner reported that Elijah McClain was five feet, six inches tall and weighed 140 pounds.[80] The sound recorded that night—notably, all of the responding officers' body cameras had mysteriously "fallen off"—includes the recording of the assertion that McClain had "incredible, crazy strength."[81] This strength was displayed when one of the officers claimed that Elijah McClain, five feet, six inches tall and 140 pounds, "almost did a push-up with all three of us on top of him." They had reason to be afraid, obviously, because the superhuman strength that would allow a person of any size to do a push-up, even "almost," with more than six hundred pounds of police on his back fighting to restrain him would necessarily require a lethal dose of ketamine to calm him down.

This pain comes to us on waves of fear. Fear of the sudden predictable unpredictability of encounters with institutions of white supremacist coercive force.

Let's further memorialize, through examination, the existence and death at the hands of police of Elijah McClain. Death, embodied as the Aurora Colorado Police Department, met Elijah on August 24, 2019. Seven months before the murder of George Floyd and Breonna Taylor at the hands of police, and six months before a mob of white people pursued and murdered Ahmaud Arbery while he jogged.

Elijah is heard on a recording saying the following while the police murdered him:

My name is Elijah McClain.
I was going home.
I'm an introvert.
I'm just different.
That's all.
I'm so sorry.
I have no gun.
I don't do any fighting.
Why are you attacking me?
I don't even kill flies.
I don't eat meat.
But I don't judge people who do eat meat.
Forgive me.
All I was trying to do was become better.
I will do it.
I will do anything.

We know that this is Elijah McClain because he says so. We know what he is/was doing because he tells the police. The next four phrases bear examination as a combined declaration in service of unearthing their relationship, and, in fact, this event's relationship, to Hegelian categories of thinking, which we have found here, that seem to mire the Black subject in "Negro-ness Proper."

I'm an introvert.
I'm just different.
That's all.
I'm so sorry.

I am interested in first making some gesture at the Cartesian elements here that, following Du Bois, create the assertion for Elijah that he can be nothing but sorry for his self-confessed "difference." We explore the necessity of positive self-reflection in due course, but it is also proper here, while we interrogate the imperative of fear for wisdom and consider what this must mean for the corporeality of Elijah McClain while he finds himself caught in the maelstrom of the System of Science . . . in it but not of it.

Descartes requires that the normative Western subject turn inward and regard the self to come to achieve an awareness of the actuality of their Being. Further, one must imagine that this form of self-reflection elicits, in the normative case, awareness of the situatedness of the subject, which we can index here to include, but not be limited to, historical awareness and recognition, spatial stability, coherent temporal existence, and membership in a polity. What this means for the moment of self-reflection for the normative subject is that they find themselves members of a coherent historical continuum, aware of their place in the world and the stability of it, existing at and in the midpoint between birth and death, what I have called living, and fully as a citizen.

Elijah McClain who admits (?) to being an introvert reflects on himself, finds that he feels himself to be "different," and, in his perception, that is "all": in the place that he has found himself "all," in that it is an overabundance and not enough to keep him safe, it is also too much to be the just enough just enough for continued existence in Aurora, Colorado.

Elijah is afraid, but, in this instance, his fear only serves for these police as chum serves great white sharks. It is his motion, "I was going home," that has ceased, and he is well aware of being frozen in this moment where the end point, Death, has been folded over to encounter what should be his long midpoint, Life. Note that he reveals his awareness of the danger in that he is no longer going home having replaced that assertion of being in motion: "I am going," with the awareness of his demise: "I was going home."

Here, Death, arriving out of sequence coincident with Life, is the locus of Elijah's temporal disorientation that is a product of the arrest of his momentum toward home, which can't be the Home proposed by Morrison, and the awareness that the cessation of the linear progress from here to there is the threshold condition for Death.

It is the arrival of what, in one sense, appears to be an irrational coercive threat by the state but, in another sense, is predictable. "Why are you attacking me?" affirms that Elijah is not a citizen, in that he has no expectation of being treated with respect by the state. He is to fear the state. The fact that his fear of the master, which we have framed here as fear of death, must exist prior to the actual experience of the thing makes his assertion, "I'm just different," the trace of the foundation of Hegel's Anti-Blackness and the forces arrayed to prevent confrontation that may trend toward the dismantling of the mechanisms of white supremacy.

I'm just different.
That's all.
I'm sorry.

For any other subject this would have been enough to prevent escalation, but we know now as Elijah knew then that his luck had run out. He *was* going home. He would never get there.

We can take the last four phrases as a coherent whole.

Forgive me.
All I was trying to do was become better.
I will do it.
I will do anything.

The threshold has been crossed. Elijah McClain is no longer mortal per se and is hurtling toward his event of (im)mortality. Empty of the self. Turned inside out.

He has time now because he no longer belongs to himself but is both in the possession of the polity who has taken his death to serve it and in the possession of us who now memorialize him. Immortal in his mortality. Turned inside out. Hegel anticipates this: §784 is instructive.

> The *death* of the divine man, as *death*, is *abstract* negativity, the immediate result of the movement which only comes to an end within *natural* universality. In spiritual self-consciousness, death loses this natural significance, that is, it becomes its already stated concept. Death is transfigured from what it immediately means, i.e. from the *non-being of the individual*, into the *universality* of spirit which lives in its own religious community, dies there daily, and is daily resurrected.[82]

Giorgio Agamben is, perhaps, helpful here, and I am thinking with and through his understanding of the *Sacer* expressed in his 1998 book *Homo Sacer: Sovereign Power and Bare Life*. Therein, Agamben proposes the following, quoting Festus:

> The sacred man is the one whom the people have judged on account of a crime. It is not permitted to sacrifice this man, yet he who kills him will not be condemned for homicide. . . . This is why it is customary for a bad or impure man to be called sacred.[83]

For Agamben's part, through his preoccupation with the Camp, he locates the reemergence of the Sacred Man from Roman Law. For our purposes here, it serves to locate the possibility of a body beyond the boundary of the human. A juridical figure for whom humanity, if we accept humanity having as a component of its existence the right to security in the body and the notion that violation of that security will elicit punishment, is *not* the normative condition. Sacrifice, both here and in Agamben's employment of Festus, becomes the way backward and forward to Hegel in that he situates death in §451 as the ultimate sacrifice for the polity and, in so doing, requires there to be a structural "work around" to take proper (dis)account of Black deaths, which serve the collective only in being different from other forms of death. Hegel consciously renders the Black Body outside of the possibility of serving the polity as a sacrifice *for* but rather establishes the subject as sacrificed *to*, which is coincident with the separation between being for the self as opposed to being for the other. Recall the notion explicit in Agamben's *Homo Sacer* marshaling Festus that asserts the *sacer* could not be framed as a sacrifice and the companion notion by Hegel that death is the ultimate service to the body politic. Both of these conditions are coherent in the Anti-Black World of Hegel's *Phenomenology.* Elijah's death, following Festus, is not a sacrifice within the four corners of that world and, for Hegel, serves to buttress the state in its spectacular murder that reifies the fear of the master/death that occupies a primary point of inflection for his system.

However, Elijah, Breonna, George, Trayvon, Sandra, Michael, the names are endless, "will do it" and "will do anything," and this final assertion is the bridge through Death to the formation of a new system of science to disrupt the world of Hegel. These deaths are meant by the state to be worth something only in that they, these people, were worthless until the moment of death and the payment of settlements or even the rare juridical punishment is meant to seal the system from destabilization.

Being-as-Black, in its robust manifestation, will not countenance this. These deaths open the breach to new ways of knowing and framing the self, which will arrive through the next "step" in the process: examining the valuing of the formerly devalued as a product of their death.

"Just Enough Just Enough" or "You're Nobody (Till Somebody Kills You)"

> . . . but . . .
>
> —Stevie Wonder, "Living for the City"

> I spit phrases that will thrill you / You're nobody till somebody kills you.
>
> —Notorious B.I.G., "You're Nobody (Til Somebody Kills You)"

The Sublime Paradox of Black Life/Death

The opening epigraph of this section, the single word "but" preceded by ellipses, is extracted from one of the many fraught and generative moments of Stevie Wonder's 1973 masterpiece *Innervisions*. Here the song quoted is "Living for the City." The lyrics read:

> His sister's black, *but* she is sho'nuff pretty
> Her skirt is short, *but* Lord her legs are sturdy
> To walk to school, she's got to get up early
> Her clothes are old, *but* never are they dirty
> Living just enough, just enough for the city

We will deal with the "just enough(s)," but first we must account for the series of problematic binaries that lead inexorably to being just enough, barely enough, for the city. These binaries exemplify the ubiquity of the harm done and maintained by the cognitive realm of white supremacy and Anti-Blackness in the Anti-Black World. Stevie Wonder, despite his consciousness and expressions of the beauty of Blackness here, at this moment, is unable to derive subjectivity in the self-referential fashion necessary to realize Morrison's "*third, if you will pardon the expression, world*." Stevie, at this moment, buoyed by the lush electronic bridge of the Fender Rhodes, which hides the ominous bass line from the opening of the song, reveals the telos of the coercive environment of white supremacist ways of knowing. *But.*

His sister is Black . . . *but* . . . she is pretty. In spite of, not as a predictable and inevitable aspect of the aesthetic of Blackness. She is pretty in spite of being Black. Lest one be accused of making too much of this line, one need pay careful attention to the series of "buts" that appear here as the predictable result of the descriptive opening verses.

She, we have witnessed, is Black *but* pretty. Her skirt, short as it is, finds itself oppositional to the sturdiness of her legs. Her clothes are old "*but*" not dirty, and all of that is just enough just enough for some time and someplace like the city that appears as a place of flight from "hard time Mississippi."

I'm thinking about Stevie Wonder's "just enough" as exhaustion, technical and subjective in the sense of just barely, as opposed to the possibility of having something in reserve and using only what is necessary, and these "*buts*" as a last-ditch effort to extract some good that leads, however, to the doubling that Morrison tells us to avoid. There is nothing that remains here. Stevie signals this by the title that excises the just enoughs in the song that lands on Black consciousness. One just enough is not enough just enough. The double just enoughs are absorbed by the living (barely) and the city (barely) to render their presence in the title superfluous and redundant.

"Living for the City" in this perception is always already understood to be just enough just enough.

And now I'm thinking about two very distinct figures who predictably express abjectly different understandings about the method by which one becomes "somebody," or, more carefully, how one ceases to be "nobody" and at the same time whether any of this is enough or just enough of just enough. For Dean Martin, from his position of always-already-drunken white privilege, it is love that will sustain his "somebody-hood" through the inevitability of his old age in the tune "You're Nobody until Somebody Loves You." For the Notorious B.I.G., it is upon the untimely and violent arrival of death that the body that will never grow older vacates itself of no-body-ness and becomes somebody. The closing moments of the song tell the tale of a legendary figure who, in spite of everything known about him can only be truly recalled upon recollection of his murder with apologies for the language in advance:

A fuckin' shame, dude's a lame, what's his name?
Darkskin Jermaine (see what I mean?)

Note here the Blackness in excess of the Black that is Jermaine that jogs the memory. It is reminiscent of the Notorious B.I.G. of "One More Chance/ Stay with Me," where he substitutes Stevie's "but" with his own "however":

Heartthrob never
Black and ugly as ever
However
I stay Gucci down to the socks
Rings and watch filled with rocks

Dealing with his ever Black ugliness with a veneer of diamond jewelry and designer accessories. And, at the same time, in excess of the depraved self-reference, there is always the Death that preoccupies, occupies, and obstructs.

I am drawn to think with and through the manner in which Black Death establishes the notion of relation that did not preexist the event.

Reminisce on dead friends too
You're nobody 'til somebody kills you

Now I'm thinking of Breonna Taylor who I wish I had never heard of. What I really mean is that I wish Breonna Taylor only ceased being *nobody* in the same way we are all nobody to those who don't know us until they get to know us rather than becoming somebody upon the moment of her death. Through the lurid cooperation between murder and the technology to document and distribute it, Breonna became our "dead friend too." To be more precise, I wish I had never heard of the Breonna Taylor who showed up on the cover of *Vanity Fair* magazine, who I call here *Breonna Taylor II* as distinct from the person formerly known as Breonna Taylor who I understand as *The Real Breonna Taylor.* I wish I never knew about *Breonna Taylor II,* who was, in some way, eulogized by Ta-Nehisi Coates and depicted by artist Amy Sherald, which is to say that I wish that *The Real Breonna Taylor* had never been murdered and become somebody when somebody killed her and had just grown old in obscurity with those who loved and knew her rather than becoming my "dead friend too." I don't mean that *The Real Breonna Taylor* was "nobody," but I do mean that she was nobody who would be depicted as a hipper version of Michelle Obama by Amy Sherald whose portrait of the First Lady dressed like *Breonna Taylor II* hangs in the National Picture Gallery. *The Real Breonna Taylor* is also nobody who would show up in an essay about her actual life that ended in a barrage of gunfire from the police, while her boyfriend called the same police to tell them what they already know: that they had "kicked in the door and shot [his] girlfriend." Only *Breonna Taylor II, partially resurrected* from the tragedy could have an essay written in its Wake, titled "A Beautiful Life," in the (non)sense that *it,* her actual life, would attract any of the attention she has achieved because of her tragic end, which, somehow, is folded over onto the quotidian nature of the life of *The Real Breonna Taylor,* who then is rendered in its hideous end as "Beautiful."

We are back to Hegel by way of Bed-Stuy and Biggie Smalls: some where—and when—we must label The Sublime Paradox of Black Life/Death.

The Black(ened) Bodies that concern Biggie, exemplified by *The Real Breonna Taylor,* are subjectively inert, existing as nonsubjects. No Bodies, excluded from the possibility of citizenship as a corporeal being mired in Embodied-No-Body-Ness, at the point of impact with the kinetic power of white supremacy, are transformed into figures like the *Dis-Embodied-Some-Bodied Breonna Taylor II.* The Beautiful Life that only arrives with Death.

The possibilities here confound forward progress. If we take Hegel's reading of white supremacy for its word the life of *The Real Breonna Taylor* only becomes abstractly valuable with the corporeal death of *The Real Breonna Taylor* who is resurrected as *Breonna Taylor II,* unrecognizable even to herself.

What I am compelled to wonder is what *The Real Breonna Taylor,* in some surreal encounter with the future and nonexistent *Breonna Taylor II,* who stands in for her, would think of herself postmortem. The proposal is that to accept Coates's characterization and Sherald's transubstantiation, one must reckon with what that acceptance portends. Basically, Black Subjects achieve disproportionate *worth* against and through disproportionate *worthlessness* (in the reckoning of white supremacy) through an encounter with untimely death. With this in mind, we cannot, therefore, allow these deaths to be a terminus in the sense of having no value postmortem nor can we allow the value of Black Life to appear only as a result of coercive threat. Properly Being-as-Black disallows death as a terminus for subjects who have lived a life in constant engagement with catastrophe; a state of affairs that I am reading as different from a catastrophic life. Trying to stay alive gets in the way of living. When death arrives implicated, or perhaps cloaked, in white supremacy, cutting against Hegel's self-serving (the self being whiteness) admonition to the included-through-exclusion to be afraid, it serves as a clearing or point of transition that is heavy with the weight of what I understand to be three different ways in which to describe the three-dimensional box that arrives through the Black Subject's engagement with the Play of Cognitions: Du Bois's V(v)eil, Fanon's zone of nonbeing/hachures, and Christina Sharpe's Retinal Attachment. All three of these ways of thinking would most productively be revealed simultaneously rather than as palimpsest, but, in lieu of that possibility, they are approached one at a time in the chronological order of their articulation and established as essential points along the way to Morrison's "*third, if you will pardon the expression, world*," in addition to being heavy with Rememory.

We encounter the power of simultaneity in addressing the events that concern us here by witnessing the interlocking modes of Black Death across a horizontal reckoning of events that stretches backward and forward and must be corrected to realize other ways of Being-as-Black. There is a cognitive realm that can be witnessed and brought to Consciousness only by the tool of Morrison's Rememory, which is obscured by the tidal flows of the eternal recurrence of Black Death in the horizontal reckoning of then, now, and when that makes them into an already and always Now.

Recall here Chandler's important gloss on the horizontal within the white world, which is replicated in the Black World. That replication is rendered invisible to those outside the Black World by the veil, and the most important division for our thinking here is also generally invisible to those inside the Black World because of the Veil. The distinction here requires attention.

The Big "V" Veil

The work of W.E.B. Du Bois continues to push scholars in the Black Radical Tradition to grapple with the complexity and durability of his system of thinking. One particularly important element of that project is to ensure that a central element of his argument from the canonical text, *The Souls of Black Folk*, the concept of the V(v)eil, be awarded its proper weight as a result of a careful reading of the text. Stated succinctly, Du Bois describes two distinct "veils" in his system and to confuse them as a single thing is to miss an essential element of his system and, further, to misapprehend the manner in which the existence of an alternative space of knowing, a unique and self-referential place of Black Being, is represented in that text. I mentioned this earlier and the distinction is depicted in Figures 1–3 from the Introduction, but the complexity still bears careful consideration.

In *An Africana Philosophy of Temporality: Homo Liminalis*, I explored this by first making reference to a provocative line in Du Bois's *Black Reconstruction in America: 1860—1880*, where he writes, "Beneath the Veil lay right and wrong, vengeance and love, and sometimes throwing aside the veil, a soul of sweet Beauty and Truth, stood revealed."[84] My text glosses this line with the following: "[the term 'veil'] is rendered as a proper and improper noun: upper and lower-case, which implies that Du Bois is writing about two different ideas."[85] He is, in fact, doing so, and that differentiation is in the details of the referenced diagrams.

What Figure 2 is meant to assert is that the division between the Black and white worlds is rendered by Du Bois as both the "color line" and the small-v-veil, which is often conflated with the big-V-Veil. The latter being the locus, or perhaps the line of demarcation between common Black existence and the space of radical self-awareness. The ubiquity of this confusion is made apparent in the important introduction to the 1999 Norton Critical Edition of *The Souls of Black Folk*, edited by Henry Louis Gates Jr. and Terri Hume Oliver. In the subsection labeled, "Double Consciousness and Tripartite Yearnings," they write:

> In the Forethought of *Souls* Du Bois provides a metaphoric explanation for the division between the white and black world. He speaks of black life as within a veil, and he promises to step "within the Veil, raising it that you may view faintly its deeper recesses—the meaning of religion, the passion of human sorrow, and the struggle of its greater souls." Du Bois's veil metaphor—"and he saw himself—darkly as through a veil"—is an allusion to St. Paul's famous phrase ("For now we see through a glass darkly") in his first letter to the Corinthians, and Du Bois's use of it suggests, among other things, that the African American attempt to gain self-consciousness in a racist society will always be impaired because any reflected image coming from the gaze of white Americans is necessarily a distorted one, and quite possibly a harmful one as well.[86]

The first quoted sentence, the one in which Du Bois proposes he will step "within the Veil" should signal the reader that something is going on. As a practical matter, if the veil separates the white and Black worlds, then Du Bois, unless he somehow has found himself resident on the white side of things, doesn't need to journey into a place where he already resides. Second, regarding his control over access to the Veil—"raising it that you may view, faintly its deeper recesses"—if we allow ourselves to conflate the two veils, it would mean that Du Bois has control over the durability and fixity of the separation between Black and white people: he does not.

A careful hermeneutics of the text in question reveals that it is clear Du Bois wishes to hide in plain sight the thing that is a central preoccupation of the book: mapping the gateway to, if not the clear articulation of, the existence of a world that *does* offer the Black Subject true self-consciousness in a space both impervious to and unaffected by the white gaze. This is critically important because it points to the possibility of destabilizing the system of marginalized self-consciousness, which confounds the subject formation of Du Bois's Negroes. I say "destabilizes" here because Du Bois's canonical formulation of the interlocking modes of cognition articulated in *Souls*—second sight, double consciousness, and twoness—which he describes as sequentially, *only*, *always*, and *ever*,[87] must find a space in which these imperatives fall away. I believe that the solution provided by Du Bois ultimately proves insufficient, in that it continues to be dialectically opposed and existing in opposition to the world of white supremacy as illustrated by Figures 2 and 3, which show that the Veil remains inside of the Anti-Black World. Fanon takes a somewhat different approach. Recall that we are tracing three ways of viewing this possibility from different though related thinkers: Du Bois, Fanon, and Sharpe.

The Fanon Zone(s)

"Falling away" is the term I am interested in pursuing through examination of the next element of this thinking: Fanon's *zone of nonbeing* and *zone of hachures*, which I am separating here to mark the fact that the two "zones" function in markedly different ways. The passages in question appear in the introduction and in chapter 3, titled "The Man of Color and the White Woman," of *Black Skin, White Masks*. The passage in the introduction reads:

> There is a zone of nonbeing, an extraordinarily sterile and arid region, an incline stripped bare of every essence from which a genuine new departure can emerge. In most cases, the black man cannot take advantage of this descent into a veritable hell.[88]

The concept that attracts my attention here, spaces of subject reformation, also appears in chapter 3 of the text and reads, "out of the blackest part of my soul, through the zone of hachures, surges up this desire to be suddenly *white*."[89]

It is imperative to note that what Fanon proposes "happens" to subjects who are able to enter a space of subject de-re-construction is that the form of radical self-reflection he proposes serves as an *Event*. To be clear, what is being proposed here is that this "Event" be analogous to the event of Death, which Hegel situates as the way forward for marginalized subjects. What both Du Bois and Fanon have proposed is the notion that an *Event* of subjective destabilization can, for properly situated subjects, propel the subject in question to a space Hegel is desirous of hiding. This is also indicative of the cognitive incapacity of the white supremacist epistemologies, as they can see themselves only positively against the negatively framed "Other," in this case the rational disability of Hegel's nonhistorical Negroes. Further, Du Bois and Fanon propose that common Black folks are only incidentally aware of the existence of the world behind Du Bois's Veil and Fanon's dual zones of differential possibility.

On the part of Du Bois, there is his articulation of the exemplary presence of the Talented Tenth, which can, through a process of higher education and cultural fluency, access the realm of the True Black Being. But what of the Black Commons? Here I am using the term "Commons" modified by Black as an honorific rather than a way to index cultural naivete. First, it is important to note that Du Bois also came to want to be done with the notion of the Talented Tenth. I quote here from Rodney J. Reed's *A Grand Journey: The History of Sigma Pi Phi Fraternity 1904–2010*:

> Archon W.E.B. Du Bois delivered the memorial address [at the Nineteenth Grand Boulé in 1948 in Wilberforce, Ohio] entitled "The Talented Tenth." On this day Archon Du Bois began his speech by explaining that his original use of the phrase, the "Talented Tenth" had been intended to emphasize the need for higher education to develop leadership among the brightest and the most able black Americans, who would then be capable of leading the black community forward. Over the years, however, he felt that this description had been misconstrued as an intent to build an aristocracy, neglecting the masses, and thus he wished to reexamine the concept. He argued that, in addition to building leadership, it was important to focus on the masses of black people and to provide them with the skills and knowledge they needed to acquire . . .
>
> . . . He further posited that leadership committed to self-sacrifice and a willingness to plan for the redistribution of wealth was a requisite to fulfilling the agenda he advocated. He proposed that the "Talented Tenth" be replaced with the concept of the "Guiding Hundredth."[90]

This important rethinking of this canonical concept on the part of Du Bois did not receive the attention it deserved, both predictably and paradoxically, because the address was during the closed and generally secret proceedings of his fraternity, Sigma Pi Phi.

Fanon makes a similar argument in his exposition of the zone of nonbeing in the introduction, where he warns, "In most cases, the black man cannot take advantage of this descent into a veritable hell."[91] It is important here to mark that Fanon seems to articulate a fork in the metaphysical road to Black Being in the following fashion. The zone of nonbeing leads to the type of existence Fanon unveils in the next paragraph of the text:

> Man is not only the potential for self-consciousness or negation. If it be true that consciousness is transcendental, we must realize that transcendence is obsessed with the issue of love and understanding. Man is a "yes" resonating from the cosmic harmonies.[92]

In contrast, to the extent the subject is traversing through the zone of hachures, they find themselves wanting to be "suddenly white."[93] There is little doubt here that Fanon is dealing with Hegelian categories of subject creation, generally, and the reality of the inverted world, specifically. Fanon writes:

> I want to be recognized not as *Black*, but as *White*.
>
> But—and this is the form of recognition that Hegel never describes—who better than the white woman to bring this about? By loving me, she proves to me that I am worthy of white love. I am loved like a white man.
>
> I am a white man.[94]

Recall the description of the world in §158 of Hegel's *Phenomenology* that reads, "What is black in the former world is white in the latter."[95] The notion of revenge populates the emerged subjectivity from the zone of hachures, where Fanon notes that his access to a white woman's love:

> opens the illustrious path that leads to total fulfillment. . . .
>
> I espouse white culture, white beauty, white whiteness.
>
> Between these white breasts that my wandering hands fondle, white civilization and worthiness become mine.[96]

Earlier in this text, I proposed that the functional error in Hegel's understanding of the world that may very well allow his "Negroes" to assume a place of historical significance is that, for him, this altered state of being must necessarily be in dialectical relation to the diminution of white subjectivity to an abased status. Here, Fanon demonstrates the flawed nature of Hegel's world, in that it is *not* the place of love and understanding he situates as the telos of traversing the zone of hachures that I am reading as leading to Hegel's inverted world as opposed to the telos of the zone of nonbeing, which leads to a state of Being-as-Black.

Retinal Attachment

Morrison's variation, the third leg of this effort, triangulates the "doorway" to self-referentially validated Black Subjectivity and is usefully examined through the thinking of Christina Sharpe in the essential text *In the Wake: On Blackness and Being*. The preoccupation here is with what Sharpe refers to as "Retinal Attachment," a subsection of the chapter, "The Hold." Here, Sharpe analyzes the visual artist Kara Walker's description of the creative space she (Walker) periodically finds herself inhabiting that is presented in Arthur Jafa's film *Dreams Are Colder Than Death*:

> When I find myself in this schism, in this kind of mercurial space that's sort of nongendered and nonraced and constantly being sort of encroached upon . . . my skin keeps trying to stick itself back on. . . . I'm working and then I become aware of the skin and everything that comes with it and I kind of like detach, just slightly, not all the way, it's not into that space. I'm getting this image of retinal detachment or something. The skin is literally kind of pulled away and it's kind of gory and grotesque and that's where I feel at home. It's not a safe space to be, but it's one where you can kind of look at the underside of race a little bit.[97]

Sharpe reads this notion of retinal detachment as a technology (my term) that "allows for powerful forces and images to emerge from and move through her [Walker] but . . . only within a particular range."[98] I agree with this reading that proposes a narrowing, if not bracketing, of "vision" here but endeavor to read it against and through Fanon back to Du Bois and then forward to the potential of a new opening that promises new possibilities.

Working, as I have proposed, in some sense, "backwards" from the description provided by Walker that this is "not a safe space to be, but . . . one where you can kind of look at the underside of race" seems resonant with Fanon's admonition regarding access to the zone of nonbeing that reads "in most cases, the black man cannot take advantage of this descent into a veritable hell."[99] The French term employed by Fanon to describe the goings-on within the zone of nonbeing, *dépouillée*, is translated in this version as "bare," but it is more accurately rendered as describing something akin to plucking the feathers from a chicken or a depilatory. Obviously, this echoes the description by Kara Walker of the creative space where her skin "is literally kind of pulled away."[100]

Additionally, Walker points us to the possibility of a new type of "seeing," which I understand to be different from the Du Boisian "seeing" of second sight. Walker notes that, in this "schism," she can "kind of look at the underside of race."[101] This is at odds with the manner in which I am reading the first movement of Du Bois's system of Tripartite Subaltern Self-Consciousness: second sight, which is a gift that "only lets him see himself through the revelation of the other world."[102] In Walker's space of "schism," we witness altered states of cognition that map onto Rememory/Third-sight, which serves as at least the entrepôt to the "*third, if you will pardon the expression, world*," in that she is able to see the underside of race (as I read it here, the truth of the matter), which is necessarily different from seeing oneself through the cognitive regime of racists. Pace Du Bois, Walker reveals the next step along the way, which is resonant, in the sense of contrapuntal, to Du Bois's description of double consciousness. For Du Bois, this stage of consciousness is a "peculiar sensation . . . [a] sense of always looking at one's self through the eyes of others, of measuring one's soul by the tape of a world that looks on in amused contempt and pity."[103] This is not what Kara Walker describes, which, as a product of what Sharpe describes as "retinal detachment," is where "the skin is literally kind of pulled away . . . and that's where [she] feel[s] at home."[104] The final step or movement in this advance beyond Du Bois's trapped subject, what he describes as twoness, is where Walker is again out of phase with the unresolvable tension between "Negro" and "American" that threatens to destroy the "dark body."[105] Instead, Walker describes a "mercurial space that's sort of nongendered and nonraced"[106] but still unstable because it is "constantly being [. . .] encroached upon . . . my skin keeps trying to stick itself back on."[107]

It is this instability, the impermanence, or, perhaps more carefully, the unreliability of the schism that indicates that the space being described here is one of liminality or transition rather than the "*third, if you will pardon the expression, world*," a new space of Being-as-Black that we are seeking. It appears, and here the palimpsest has been established through the sequential reckoning with the Veil, Fanon's two zones, and Sharpe's preoccupation with Walker's schism, to become a collage of these images that approach our cognition as they may rather than in order. Here, in this space, at this threshold, Du Bois's Veil has been lifted to allow for descent into Fanon's dual zones of subjective reconstruction, where Walker feels the negatively framed Black(ness) being stripped away from her body as her body that is Black in its otherness from the Black of the white gaze, which throws us back to the competing images of Breonna Taylor and what I understand as a resurrection or raising of the body. Recall I marked the *partial resurrection* of Breonna Taylor as *Breonna Taylor II*, a riff on the reality of the murder of Breonna Taylor, who lives again as a poor simulacrum of herself and suddenly my "dead friend too."

Raising of the Body

Here I'm thinking of Jean-Luc Nancy's short text *Noli me tangere: On the Raising of the Body* that takes careful stock of the scene of the risen Christ who, upon encountering the Magdalene, warns her:

> Touch me not; for I am not yet ascended to my Father: but go to my brethren, and say unto them, I ascend unto my Father, and your Father; and to my God, and your God.[108]

Here, behind the Veil, in the depths of the Fanon's Zones, as the skin is pulled from the body, in the Wake, the Cut, the Break, as before the vacant tomb, the no-longer-dead-body is subject to an altered regime of cognition that Nancy recognizes as parable. Parable, again in the sense of the biblical notion, that Nancy productively glosses in the following fashion tracing the contours of the definition of parable by Jesus to the disciples in service of explaining his use of the rhetorical vehicle. They are meant, Christ says:

> for those to whom it is not "given . . . to know the mysteries of the kingdom of heaven." Meant for those who "seeing, see not; and hearing they hear not, neither do they understand," the parable might be expected to open their eyes, informing them of a proper meaning through this figurative system. But Jesus says nothing of the sort . . . mak[ing] one of his most well-known and paradoxical statements: "For whosever hath, to him shall be given, and he shall have more abundance; but whosoever hath not, from him shall be taken away even that which he hath." Thus the objective of the parable is first to sustain the blindness of those who do not see. It does not proceed out of a pedagogy of figuration (of allegory or illustration) but, to the contrary, out of a refusal or a denial of pedagogy.[109]

With this understanding, I am preoccupied with sorting through the manner in which the actual life of *The Real Breonna Taylor*, at the point of death, is recast as *The Parable of the Beautiful Life of Breonna Taylor II*, the iconography or visual documentation of which, similar to the resurrection of Christ, is unrecognizable to those who knew *The Real Breonna Taylor*.

Nancy continues to be relevant here in his careful analysis of the "event" of Mary Magdalene's encounter with the newly risen Christ and artistic representation of the same. To return to the site in front of the now empty tomb, Mary Magdalene encounters a figure who she believes is the gardener:

> Another aspect of the intrigue of vision involves the mistake Mary Magdalene initially makes when she thinks she is seeing the gardener. For this mistake to be possible, Jesus must not be recognizable, or at least not immediately so. . . .
>
> The difficulties involved in recognizing Christ have a two-fold significance. On the one hand, it is as if his resemblance to himself were a suspended and floating moment. He is the same, altered within himself. . . . He has already left; he is no longer where he is; he is no longer as he is. He *is dead*, which is to say that he *is not* what or who he, at the same time, is or presents. He is his own alteration and his own absence: He is properly only his impropriety.
>
> On the other hand, the difficult and uncertain recognition bears the stakes of faith. It does not consist in recognizing the known but in entrusting oneself to the unknown.[110]

It is truly what goes on "within" the tomb, behind the Veil, in the zones and the schism, that will ultimately be the point of focus, but it is here on the other side that we "see" Christ as unrecognizable in the same manner that *The Real Breonna Taylor* bears no resemblance to *Breonna Taylor II*. The question, substantively, is whether the death of *The Real Breonna Taylor* has resulted in a "positively" altered being that appears as *Breonna Taylor II* in the same manner as the resurrected Christ. Mapping this on top of the fork in the reconstruction of the subject road we have been tracing in this book, the way through the zone of nonbeing and/or the zone of hachures, *Breonna Taylor II* must, necessarily, be the result of one or the other of these typologies of subject de-re-construction. In the case of the examinations we have of the resurrected Christ and the inability of his intimates to recognize him without further context, it is clear that the "process" has resolved itself positively. Stated differently, the unrecognizable nature of the risen Christ is indicative of a transformation to a higher state of Being that is no longer subject to the problematics of marginalized human existence. "Do not hold on to me, because I have not yet ascended to the Father" (John 20:17). As Nancy asserts, "The scene is organized around vision."[111] It is the result of the resurrection that has altered Christ, which Nancy describes in this fashion:

> The resurrection is not a resuscitation: it is the infinite extension of death that displaces and dismantles all the value of presence and

> absence, of animate and inanimate, of body and soul. The resurrection is the extension of a body to the measure of the world and the space in which all bodies meet [*côtoiement*].[112]

In this case, the discourse around what I am framing as the resurrected figure that appears as *Breonna Taylor II* is, likewise, organized around the vision or, more directly, the creation and/or manipulation of the corporeality of *The Real Breonna Taylor.* As with what transpires before the now empty tomb, we likewise are standing in the aftermath of the burial space and time of Breonna Taylor (who we will never know and is distinct from both *The Real Breonna Taylor* and *Breonna Taylor II*), now murdered, now buried, and now appearing in diaphanous robes of seemingly impossible to realize seafoam green that belie the life darker than blue that ended tragically. Here, unlike the sanctified and resurrected corporeal appearance of the risen Christ, the Breonna that our eyes have before us, *Breonna Taylor II*, is not a vision of positively resolved subjectivity. At least the context of visuality that we possess on this side of the Veil, zones, Break, and Wake does not afford us eyes with which to see what has truly become of the Breonna Taylor who has passed from this world and is ideally bounded and stable in a resolved space of Phenomenal Black(ness), a space that we must first locate and understand, which is perhaps distinct from the space from whence Morrison's Beloved arrives.

This argument improvises on Christina Sharpe's concern that Kara Walker's Retinal Detachment "hinders one's vision"[113] and is preoccupied with Retinal *Attachment*, providing a different manner of seeing, which I am positing is the mechanism by which the body that we cannot see and/or recognize stands revealed. Sharpe's thinking here is instructive:

> We are positioned in the knowledge that we are living in the afterlives of slavery, sitting in the room with history, in a lived and undeclared state of emergency. The ground of compromise, the firmament, the access to freedom and democracy, littered with Black bodies. With the optic of the door of no return on our retina, we might envision, imagine, something else—something like what Joy James (2013) calls a "liberated zone" even though under siege.[114]

It is possible that two things are happening at once to a subject like Breonna Taylor who encounters this form of subject-(dys)forming death. At the same time, we, the observers of the phenomenon, like Mary Magdalene, have not ourselves journeyed through the "tomb" and are not able to witness anything but the garbled cognition that appears as a gardener until the proper context for seeing is granted and consciousness arrives. The point here is that, because of the unaltered system of seeing of those who observe the "Transformation/Transubstantiation" of the subject (second sight, *Retinal Detachment* or *Attachment*), they are not able to see anything but the misrendered subject. This then requires an account of the manner in which the true nature of the subject who has journeyed through the *zones of nonbeing* and *hachures* can be witnessed/recognized/rendered by outsiders who themselves have not completed the journey. The body, chastised through this discourse with death, is effectively doubled. The discernible subject is implicated in the continued malformation of Black Being that renders Breonna Taylor recognizable by being unrecognizable. The second body has moved on to the second form of phenomenological apparition, which will only be recognizable when the observer has been properly resituated to see differently. Until we have articulated that practice, we must first deal with the reality of the deformed experience of Black subjectivity that is still tethered to this world.

Fanon explored this in his essay, "The Algerian Family," where he exposes the impossibility of the proper memorial of death under conditions of colonial occupation:

> The classic mourning tears are hardly any longer to be found in Algeria. . . . These collective deaths, without warning, without a previous illness that had been treated and fought, abandoned in the ditch on the side of the road, cannot set into motion emotional mechanisms that are homogenous to a society. Lamentations and grief-stricken faces are part of a patterned stable world. One does not weep, one does not do as before when one is faced with multiple murders. One grits one's teeth and prays in silence. . . . It must not be believed, however, that the traditional ceremonies are repeated in the case of natural deaths, resulting from illnesses or accidents. Even then, it seems virtually impossible to revive the habitual techniques of despair. The war has dislocated Algerian society to such a point that any death is conceived as a direct or indirect consequence of colonialist repression. . . . The Algerian people have thus decided that, until independence, French colonialism will be innocent of none of the wounds inflicted upon its body and its consciousness.[115]

We deal with this formulation again in this project.

Fanon, Melville, and Sharpe are all concerned with the totalizing effect of this form of death that renders the body absent and incapable of being properly memorialized. What this means for this argument is the form of faith that allows us to recognize the unrecognizable, which is marred by Anti-Black Racism, is the result of a form of cognition that will not allow us to witness

Morrison's "*third, if you will pardon the expression, world*." The Faith that allows what should be the incomprehensibility of the juxtaposition of Breonna Taylor, *The Real Breonna Taylor*, and *Breonna Taylor II* is belief in the crushing weight of impending doom. What Christina Sharpe calls "the everyday of Black immanent and imminent death."[116] This represents the awareness that all Black people are subject to the discourse of (dys)formation through improper memorial of death as a result of (un)lawful death at the hands of the state; acts that are done in service of reinstating, on a constant basis, the Fear of white supremacy: Hegel's fear of the master.

Melville writes "but Faith, like a jackal, feeds among the tombs, and even from these dead doubts she gathers her most vital hope."[117] This Faith is not the good news that the Magdalene leaves the garden with but Faith in the savagery of white supremacy. This atmospheric pressure is what I am proposing represents the engine of Afropessimism that sees no way in which the condition of Anti-Black Racism can be ameliorated much less eradicated. This thinking is, in many ways, encapsulated in a formulation in Frank Wilderson's recent text, usefully titled *Afropessimism*, where he reflects on the durable nature of Anti-Black Racism in this political perception:

> The U.S. government *could* become a democracy for people of color who are not Black (it's not likely, but it is certainly possible); but if it ever rid itself of the central ingredient that overdetermines its conditions of possibility—that is to say, if the United States of America were to somehow not be anti-Black—then we would no longer have a country; the United States of America would cease to exist. Just as tomatoes overdetermine gazpacho soup! No tomatoes, no gazpacho. No anti-Blackness no nation.[118]

In thinking with, about, and through Wilderson's admonition, it is first necessary to understand that, here, the United States of America stands in as the exemplar for a worldwide system that has Anti-Blackness as its foundational ethos. Understanding this, we then can propose that the worldwide system of white supremacy, which is driven by Anti-Black Racism, is the operating system for the "world," which has appeared in this project up to this point. What this means for the progress of this text is that the world in question functions, mechanically, through Anti-Black Racism that expresses itself in various physical ways: the police violence we have explored here in some depth being one such manifestation of this phenomenon. Following Wilderson, it seems important both to identify the ingredients of the recipe and to propose the "Laws of Motion" that dictate the ways things work in this perception. This is in aid of an attempt to locate the elements of the world that Wilderson proposes overdetermine the manner in which it works and propose the manner in which the effective "removal" of certain ones of them would lead to the collapse of the system. That effort will effectively lead us to the threshold of the seemingly impenetrable, or perhaps hidden, Door of No Return in order to effectuate its penetration in the progress toward a way of Being-as-Black.

Laws of Motion

The title of this section of this project, "Laws of Motion," is meant to capture the proposition that the metaphysical ideology of white supremacy, fueled by Anti-Black Racism, manifests itself in physical forces that act upon bodies. These bodies then react in predictable ways that can be productively described in the same manner as the laws of motion that govern our physical world. Ta-Nehisi Coates makes a similar argument, in his book *Between the World and Me*, that I want to mark and carefully demonstrate where this project expands on his thinking. Coates writes:

> Americans believe in the reality of "race" as a defined, indubitable feature of the natural world. Racism—the need to ascribe bone-deep features to people and then humiliate, reduce, and destroy them—inevitably follows from this inalterable condition. In this way, racism is rendered as the innocent daughter of Mother Nature, and one is left to deplore the Middle Passage or the Trail of Tears the way one deplores an earthquake, a tornado, or any other phenomenon that can be cast as beyond the handiwork of men.[119]

A recurring trope for this narrative has been the notion of "World," which has appeared explicitly in the work of Du Bois, Fanon, and Hegel and implicitly in Sharpe, by juxtaposition through Wilderson's employment of the United States as exemplar of the irreducibly white supremacist nature of the world, and, finally, in the ambition of Morrison's "*third, if you will pardon the expression, world.*" Coates here wants us to think about the complicated way in which the notion of a natural world, a place with rules that are unaffected by humans and must be obeyed, is used to solidify and authorize racism as the result of the careful study of the natural differences between the races. I want to slightly modify the provocative notion presented here that race and racism are the progeny of Mother Nature and the results like natural disasters and instead propose that the totalizing fiction that is white supremacy and its companion, Anti-Black Racism, are made to appear the fundamental force of all of the universe, gravity. What this means is the result of a racist event, like the killing of Elijah McClain, is only the physical manifestation of the unavoidable power of gravity that acts outside of the limitations of space and time and can only be managed but never dispensed with.

This is consciously related to the kind of cosmogony that is employed to define the physical manifestation of this world. This is usually related to theories of the origin of the universe that have generally found themselves gesturing at, if not fully embracing, the notion of the Big Bang as the event that set the cosmos in motion. The central complication here is that the Big Bang is often understood to have originated out of "nothing," which stresses, to the point of collapse, the cause-and-effect relationship that dictates the way the World operates. Put simply, Newton's Third Law of Motion asserts that for every action there is an equal and opposite reaction. This is obvious in the physical world and is, arguably, the principle upon which dialectical reasoning derives its coherence. It is the nature of the universe arriving ex nihilo that calls into question the Third Law of Motion. This complication finds itself exposed in the metaphysics of Aristotle, in his text predictably titled *The Metaphysics.* Aristotle arrives at the existence of a deity, which is outside of the logic of action/reaction in "Book Lambda 7" of *The Metaphysics*. There, he offers the following:

> The account that we have offered is a coherent one. If it is incorrect, then there is no alternative to the world's generation being from night and from everything being together and from that which is not. I take it that this confirms our solution: there is something which is always moved through an uninterrupted motion, and this motion is circular (as is evident not merely by argument but as a matter of fact), and consequently the primary heaven will be eternal.
>
> But there will then be something that moves them. And since that which is moved and which also moves is intermediate, it follows that there must be something that moves without being moved. This will be eternal, it will be a substance and it will be activation.[120]

The unmoved mover, pure substance that is always/already in motion, is implicated here in the effort to define the forces at play in the creation of marginalized Blackness and the possibility of transformation of that status to something altogether different though related. It is reasonable to consider that, in the "space" (here the term "time" is irrelevant) "prior" to the Big Bang, there were forces in and at play that are not within the range of our perception but were translated into a form that is cognizable by humans, or, more precisely, cognizable by various modes of human perception and description, through some event. Here, the Big Bang represents either just such an event or the physical manifestation of the crossing.

The relevance for this bracketing of the point of transition/transmission from one complex system of knowing (world) to another is severalfold. First, to draw into conversation the point of transition/transmission from ideas to action; here, to explore the manifestation of the metaphysics of white supremacy into the physics of white supremacy. Second, to pay close and careful attention to the manner in which the first preoccupation is related to the transubstantiation of ideas of Black inferiority into the physical manifestation of the "Negro." Third, to probe the point of transition/transmission from the world of Anti-Black Racism to a World without it that, like the Big Bang, appears to be without a cognizable accelerant and enjoys a stable existence with laws of motion that appear to be unrelated to the elements that require their existence in the first place.

I am interested here in thinking about the notion of a retreat behind some barrier that serves to obstruct the functioning of forces from the World, which is resonant with the material covered that proposes Du Bois, Fanon, Sharpe, and Walker are all describing, in substantive fashion, just such a space of subject re-creation. This thinking presupposes a full, complete, and irreversible departure from the old world to a new one. The challenge here is one that has replicated itself over and over again in and around the Black Radical Tradition: what to make of the necessity of accounting for the fact of Anti-Black Racism in all of its forms while seeking to imagine a way of being without it?

In order to properly deal with what must be left behind in one world in favor of new modes of being in another, the details of the operation of the world to be abandoned must be delineated. As I have mentioned before, it is my contention that the ideological forces of white supremacy exert themselves in the same manner as forces of nature. In pursuit of that understanding, the first step here is to examine the primary force in this world's existence, gravity, as a corollary force to the way I am seeking to characterize white supremacy and its force in the same system of existence.

Gravity

To argue that white supremacy and Anti-Black Racism manifest themselves in the world in a fashion that appears to function with the same unavoidable force as the laws of nature requires some detailed examination perhaps best done via an exemplar of the case.

For instance, Ronald McNair, on January 28, 1986, must have been briefly relieved to be slipping the confinement of gravity aboard what proved to be the ill-fated launch of the space shuttle *Challenger.* McNair, who, in the summer of 1959 at the age of nine, had been refused the right to check books out of the Lake City Public Library (a facility that now bears his name), had earned a Ph.D. in physics from MIT, and his constant need to challenge gravity, both physical and metaphysical, had earned him a seat on a spacecraft for the second time.

The physical manifestation of gravity is, at least on the surface, a seemingly more obvious phenomenon. Since the work of Sir Isaac Newton, humankind has been in a position to learn more about this force, but this has brought our collective understanding to the point of concluding that we really know very little about it. Some progress toward understanding has been made, principally the fact that quantum mechanics has concluded that gravity is actually a warp in the space-time continuum. The physicist Brian Greene endeavors to render this complex notion accessible in his text, *The Elegant Universe*, writing the following:

> In Newtonian gravity the sun keeps the earth in orbit with an unidentified gravitational "tether" that somehow instantaneously reaches out across vast distances of space and grabs hold of the earth (and, similarly, the earth reaches out and grabs hold of the sun). Einstein provided a new conception of what actually happens . . . [principally] that the presence of mass, such as the sun causes the fabric of space around it to *warp* . . . the difference . . . is that unlike Newton, Einstein has specified the *mechanism* by which gravity is transmitted: the warping of space. The agent of gravity, according to Einstein, is the fabric of the cosmos.[121]

So, returning to the physical and metaphysical forces of gravitation that acted upon the body of McNair, the first is the complex relationship between space, time, and mass that accounts for the "rightness" of Newton's explanatory observations and the theoretic layer of complexity opened by Einstein. The metaphysical force that I wish to analogize in some sense to the force of gravity is the omnipresence of white supremacy that serves to *warp* the life force of whatever "objects" find themselves subject to its pull. I am proposing that white supremacy, like gravity, is an omnipresent force in the "world" as we understand it. The term "world" here continues to be employed to adopt its value in marking the space that Du Bois carves out early in *Souls*, is apparent in the opening chapter of Fanon's *The Wretched of the Earth*, and has served as the telos of this project, which is preoccupied with Morrison's "*third, if you will pardon the expression, world*" while also acknowledging that it is truly "only" architecture. Here Fanon, like Du Bois, articulates a specific form of World in this case, the "colonial world," which is the international corollary to the uniquity of the American experience, writing in successive paragraphs the following opening sentences: first, "the colonial world is a world divided into compartments"[122] and, second, "the colonial world is a world cut in two."[123]

By rendering this notion of World formal, there follows the need to articulate the laws of nature that govern existence in these realms, and, like the cosmos that concerns Newton and Einstein, there is a force that sets this world in motion, and, in this case, it is white supremacy. In service of fully situating this claim against the cut of Einstein's understanding that the mechanism for the transmission of gravity to do its work on the objects within its apparently infinite reach is through the warping of space, it is necessary to examine the two phenomenon for analysis. With the understanding that gravity and white supremacy are the binary forces under consideration here, we must then make an argument for the manner in which the latter force is transmitted to bodies. At the risk of oversimplifying the complex simplicity of the transmission of gravity by the warping of space, I propose that it is violence that serves as the vehicle for the transmission of white supremacy. This requires some further development of the analogy operating here. If we accept that white supremacy and gravity operate in the same manner, we understand that we have engineered various structures to make it appear that gravity/white supremacy is not a concern.

For instance, to the extent that I am sitting on the second floor of a building as I write this, a complex understanding of the manner in which gravity functions informed the construction of the structure that resolves all of the forces in play and renders it stable. To the extent that there is no unresolvable force—earthquake, tornado, and so on—the structure remains stable, and all of the forces summed together net to zero. Likewise, to the extent that I remain within the structure of the building, my relationship to gravity is also stable. However, to the extent that I need to go to the second floor of a building on the other side of the street and elect to walk out of the window rather than go down to the ground floor, cross the street, and go up to the appropriate office, I will become familiar with the force of gravity very quickly. The same goes for white supremacy.

Over the span of the existence of the Anti-Black World or $World_1$, we have erected structures in the form of laws and evolved customs that are designed to make it *appear* that the force of white supremacy has disappeared or become inert. One important caveat is that these laws and customs, the "structures" designed to resolve the force of white supremacy, are necessarily ontologically compromised by their inextricable relationship to the thing itself. This means that the "structures" I am referencing here, things like the Voting Rights Act, *Brown v. Board*, Title IX, and so on, are mechanisms that give the *appearance* that white supremacy has been suspended, when in reality the force is dispersed in the same manner that the load-bearing wall of a building nets all of the forces to zero. This also means that these "structures," like the load-bearing wall, are only functional because of the continued relevance of white supremacy, and, to the extent that it disappears, the structures themselves become immediately incoherent.

Pushing further along this line of reasoning, in similar fashion to the meditation on the reality of gravity and the trip to the second floor, as one gets to the edge of the structures designed to obscure the existence of white supremacy, the reality of its existence can have catastrophic consequences. Here, I am reminded of the opening of Toni Morrison's essential *Song of Solomon*, which is dedicated to a long meditation on the ability of Black people to defeat gravity and fly. Morrison opens the novel with these lines:

> The North Carolina Mutual Life Insurance Agent promised to fly from Mercy to the other side of Lake Superior at three o'clock.[124]

The insurance man, Mr. Smith, is only the first example of the defiance of gravity and, at the same time, defiance of white supremacy in the text. I'm thinking with, through re-dis-orienting the axis of the argument to the vertical rather than the horizontal, in the story of flight that RAJudy describes in his essay "Restless Flying, A Black Study of Revolutionary Humanism." Judy draws two geographically and necessarily temporally separated events of flight. The first Aimé Césaire's 1956 poem, *Le verbe marroner*,[125] from which Judy renders the relevant lines as "Shall we fly away Depestre, shall we fly away?" The second is a verse from the seventeenth-century Abbasid poet, al-Mutanabbi, which Judy renders as "Restless as if riding the wind Steering me South or North."[126] The point here by Judy is that "each is invoked with regard to mid-twentieth century projects of national liberation." The ability of Morrison's characters and the poetics of Césaire and al-Mutanabbi to elide oppression through flight, either vertical or horizontal, cause some Black people in the Morrison, like Astronaut McNair, to meet with the tragic mathematics of the force of gravity. But recall it is violence that I named as the vehicle for the transmission of white supremacy, and here I am first led to think of Emmett Till, just as Morrison does, writing, also in *Song of Solomon*:

> A young Negro boy had been found stomped to death in Sunflower County, Mississippi. There were no questions about who stomped him—his murderers had boasted freely—and there were no questions about motive. The boy had whistled at some white woman, refusing to deny he had slept with others, and was a Northerner visiting the South. His name was Till.[127]

Mamie Till, the child's mother, gave us access to his body in order to discipline our cavalier awareness of the force of white supremacy, and, based on that legacy, I will take the liberty of revising his name to further explore the concern here and render it *(un)Till*, meaning that the death of Emmett *(un)Till* is a moment that has not quite arrived, in that, in its recurrence across time and space, it represents just the type of warp in the fabric of the stuff of perceptual existence that preoccupied Einstein. The unadorned nature of our encounter with the broken body of Emmet *(un)Till* is necessarily different from that which we have explored regarding the altered visual tableaux of Breonna Taylor, *The Real Breonna Taylor*, and *Breonna Taylor II*. By leaving his body unadorned from its coercion, Mamie Till, like Mary Magdalene, allows the subject to travel in uninterrupted fashion. A fashion that presents the provocative potentiality of the existence of the warp in the coherence of the world we are searching for, where the laws of motion that are dictated by white supremacy fail and allow access to the realm of substantive subject re-creation. I'm thinking of what I had forgotten and was reminded by Morrison's prose that it was stomping that killed *(un)Till* and that requires gravity and that is why we call it a Lynching. The gravity-exploiting murder of Emmett *(un)Till* is bracketed by the opening moment of gravity-defiance and the closing passages where the protagonist of Morrison's narrative discovers that he is part of a tribe of Black people who can fly. The text is instructive here:

> "Yeah. That tribe. That flyin' motherfucking tribe. Oh, man! He didn't need no airplanes. He just took off; got fed up. *All the way up!* No more cotton! No more bales! No more orders! No more shit! He flew, baby. Lifted his beautiful black ass up in the sky and flew home. Can you dig it? Jesus, God, that must have been something to see. And you know what else? He tried to take his baby boy with him. My grandfather. Wow! Wooee! Guitar! You hear that? Guitar my great-granddaddy could flyyyyy and the whole damn town is named after him. Tell him, Sweet. Tell him my great-granddaddy could fly."
>
> "Where'd he go Macon?"
>
> "Back to Africa. Tell Guitar he went back to Africa."
>
> "Who'd he leave behind?"
>
> "Everybody! He left everybody down on the ground and he sailed off like a bald eagle."[128]

Morrison's prose allows us to witness the relationship I am leaning on here that proposes the earthly and measurable toll of white supremacy; here cotton, bale, orders, and broadly defined "shit" are only substantively overcome by slipping the bonds of gravity. Here, where the law of gravity is interrupted, Macon Dead posits the possibility of a space that allows a return "to Africa" that necessarily leaves stranded those still subject to its logic. This is resonant with Du Bois's first attempt to elide the logic of white supremacy by elevating himself above the fray. This fails in that the structures that require the flight remain intact.

And now I'm thinking about George Floyd.

There are periods of time to consider here that have been warped by the mass of the objects, these Black bodies, that we are considering. There is first the "until" between August 28, 1955, and May 25, 2020, and the *(un)till* between the beginning of the encounter we can bear witness to, if you so choose, of the eight minutes and forty-six seconds or the more precisely documented nine minutes and twenty-nine seconds revealed at the trial, which could just as easily have been four hundred years give or take. Both long in their own ways and breathtakingly short in others, when it comes to the disregard for Black bodies that allowed four officers, in broad daylight, on a city street populated by people with a camera phone in every hand, to stretch a body out where the black top ends and the gray of the concrete begins and smash his still-Black face against the white lines by the weight of the blue line *(un) till* . . . and all of this requires gravity. And now I'm thinking about Laura and L. D. Nelson on March 25, 1911, and their lynching at the hands of a mob.

And naturally I'm thinking about gravity and its corollary force, white supremacy, that are all brought together here in a photo that Rememories this diabolical resolution of forces. The architecture of the bridge become gallows over the North Canadian River south of Okemah, Oklahoma, has been demolished. The event lives on because of a photograph of the catastrophe taken by George Henry Farnum that became a popular postcard. One can imagine a glibly scribbled "Wish you were here!" above the signature of the mailer, while the image on the other side of the card continues to haunt us. It is here that all of the strands of this argument cruelly intersect with the employment of this tragic geometry to convert gravity into a tool of white supremacy; white supremacy as the medium for the transubstantiation of gravity itself into a tool of political terror that resolves this malevolent mathematics with a noose.

The accounting here is revelatory. It must not be lost on this argument that the bridge had been erected to span a cut in the stolen land of Indigenous people. The applied science of civil engineering, refined over the ages, allows the mass of the metal bridge to be effectively distributed back to the earth on either side of the chasm that needs crossing. The white mob of murderers have the weight of their bodies overflowing with the venom of their hatred added to the mass of the bridge that is likewise distributed to the surrounding earth and netted to zero by the equal and opposite forces that respond. The mathematics becomes more complex because the bodies of Laura and L. D. Nelson must be put into motion, accelerated, with sufficient force to shatter their lives but with insufficient force to part the ropes that must also leave undisturbed the barbaric stasis of the bridge. Newton's equation, Force being equal to mass multiplied by acceleration, his elegantly simple algebraic representation of the force of gravity, at the point of putting the Nelsons into flight, totals the weight of these Black people times the sum of the unchangeable constant that is the acceleration of gravity and the additive of the push from the hands of their murderers. For this complex misuse of the force of gravity to serve a political purpose, the bodies of Laura and L. D. Nelson must be rendered substantively weightless, zero acceleration, which gives the appearance that there is zero force, in order to serve as the spectacle of the potentiality for political terror that gravity possesses.

In the spirit of this accounting, this is the time to do so for the transubstantiation, if I can be allowed that term, of the force of gravity and the ideology of white supremacy into political violence. Hegel, in his *Phenomenology of Spirit*, proposes in §135 the following:

> The universal is in its own self in undivided unity with this multiplicity, which means, however, that these matters are each where the other is; they reciprocally permeate each other—without, however, touching each other because, on the other side of the coin the many distinct matters are likewise self-sufficient . . . This moment is, however, what is called *force*.[129]

This thinking facilitates a moment of clarity for me via the Fanon of *Black Skin, White Masks*, who posits, "Society, unlike biochemical processes, does not escape human influence. Man is what brings society into being."[130] Here, I render these lines useful for this argument and improvise the theme as "white supremacy, unlike the laws of physics, does not escape human influence. Man is what brings white supremacy into being," and, then, to resolve the tension here, we must remind ourselves that the ultimate goal of that oppressive force is to make you believe that it is as unavoidable as a force of nature and without the possibility, once set in motion, of human influence.

Now I'm thinking about two things at once. The architecture of the National Memorial for Peace and Justice in Montgomery, Alabama, and John Edgar Wideman's novel *The Lynchers*.

In Montgomery, visitors to the museum walk beneath massive steel plinths, suspended by cables in the ceiling to memorialize the employment of gravity as a tool of white supremacist political terror. Visiting this space is at one and the same time an act of rebellion and a profound awareness of the sheer weight and the "gravitational pull" of white supremacy.

Visitors to this memorial have the collective weight of these sculpture hanging over their heads in the same way that the collective weight of white supremacy exists in Damoclean fashion over all of our bodies. In point of fact, the very same deployment of gravity as a means of political coercion here is the silent partner in this art piece that makes all too apparent the danger this logic portends. But, in that space, where the bodies of the lynched become impossibly heavy, the sheer mass renders them quantum and a glimpse, if not a breach, into a world where Newton's system that depends on a classical notion of gravity fails and introduces what physicists Hall, Deckert, and Wiseman elaborated in their 2014 paper titled "Quantum Phenomenon Modeled by Interactions between Many Classical Worlds." Here, and I will be brief to the point of banality, objects can be implicated in what is known as superposition that allows an object to interact with multiple systems of existence or Many Interacting Worlds. In the essay, "'Theorizing in a Void': Sublimity, Matter, and Physics in Black Feminist Poetics," Zakiyyah Iman Jackson asks:

> Why have black feminists turned to physics metaphors, in particular, to articulate a paradoxical space of visibility/invisibility in the grammar of the Human?[131]

Jackson's work and this poignant query, in particular, is generative for this project that goes to the point of positing that the turn to various elements of what can most accurately be described as "physics" perhaps is not metaphoric. To focus in on what I mean, here, is to say that we have explored several manifestations of Black bodies reacting in a manner that indicates an existence that is, at least in the liminal space, between worlds, if not actually appearing in both. Here the point of interaction is between the world where white supremacy is the established order and another where Black bodies can fly or alter the vector of the violence of which I am preoccupied. As we see later, the Morrison of *Beloved* explores the space of observation between worlds that serve as the place and time of the confusion of Sethe's "returned" daughter.

I'm thinking now about Wideman's 1973 novel *The Lynchers*, which I believe seeks to reverse the vector of the force of gravity and the logic operating here. It follows the efforts of four African American men who hatch a plot to lynch a white police officer in retribution for hundreds of years of Black people being terrorized by white supremacy, writing:

> - Now I'm not talking about grabbing just any old body and stringing him up to the nearest lamp post. That's not it at all. . . . I mean a formal lynching. With all the trimmings. . . . I would eschew that western model, go to the South where tradition means something.
>
> - Mr. Neegro swinging in the breeze. You recall now, charred blacker than you ever were in life. . . . Forked log swinging in the heavy air, black pendulum, tolling power, power, power. White power.[132]

Here, Wideman makes a clear reference to the morbid poetry of the lamentation, "Strange Fruit" that alerts us to "Black Bodies swingin' in the Southern breeze / Strange Fruit hangin' in the poplar trees."[133] This poetry leads me to consider another gesture toward the political consequences of gravity and its corollary force, white supremacy, in Gil Scott Heron's poem "Whitey on the Moon":

> A rat done bit my sister Nell.
> (with Whitey on the moon)[134]

It is clear that in the wake of the Apollo landing, Heron wants to question the prioritization of space exploration over decent housing and medical care or, more concretely and completely, over the positive existence of Black people. In concert with the argument here, I read this as much about the gravitational force of white supremacy, which tethers Nell to the Earth, and the dangers of rabid vermin, while the equal and opposite reaction to the force of white supremacy over Black bodies is the gravity defiance of the Moonwalking Neil Armstrong.

In this vein, on September 2, 2020, in the wake of the plague of police violence and COVID-19, the former NASA astronaut Leland Melvin told a panel assembled to consider Black lives in the space industry the following:

> I've been on this rocket with millions of pounds of thrust and not once was I afraid of space. . . . It's when I've been stopped by police officers that I didn't even know. . . . I was starting to sweat and just holding the steering wheel really hard.[135]

On the part of Black bodies, to slip the bounds of white supremacy, according to Astronaut Leland, one must leave the Earth. Jason R. Young's piece in the *Journal of Africana Religions*, titled "All God's Children Had Wings: The Flying African in History, Literature, and Lore," speaks to the mythology, some say, of Black people who are not limited to existence under the threat of gravity and, ultimately, by analogy or in point of fact, white supremacy. Young, in responding to a critique of the first published draft of this paper is forced to respond to the criticism, no doubt deemed devastating to the argument by the critic, that "the laws of physics apply to everyone . . . including Africans."[136] The author clarifies his claim in the second edition of the paper, proposing:

> And so they do. [they being the laws of physics] The idea that the interminable laws of physics apply always to everyone, everywhere rooted is a practical, commonsense view of the world. . . . As it relates

> to the study of the past, the commonsense view of the world has served to delimit what sorts of human experiences and activities can legitimately be included in the canon of history.[137]

The revolutionary act I am tracing here reveals itself in two parts: first, recognizing the force-driven transubstantiation of the human designed idea of white supremacy into a demiforce of nature for what it is, and, second, beginning to accept that there are bodies black enough for whom the laws of this form of physics are inoperative. This is the space of transition that requires our attention because it is arguably the threshold of the Door that for one world offers no return and for another affords just that in the form of passing forward to a previous futurity where Blackness is self-referentially so. As we draw closer to the threshold of the point of transition, it is imperative that we assert the architecture of this perception by thinking carefully about space and place.

Mapping the Territory

A guiding principle of this project that is inextricably related to space is best expressed by Sylvia Wynter's essay "On How We Mistook the Map for the Territory, and Reimprisoned Ourselves in Our Unbearable Wrongness of Being, of Désêtre: Black Studies toward the Human Project." Here, Wynter situates as her point of departure the provocative assertion by Amiri Baraka that "the idea that Western thought might be exotic if viewed from another landscape never presents itself to most Westerners."[138] What is critically important in this quotation for this effort is the manner in which Baraka renders cognition as markedly different as a function of the space ("landscape") from which the object for cognition is encountered. Wynter elaborates on this theme and exhorts us to be certain that the effort to distance oneself from the metaphysical and physical territory of white supremacy is not confounded by mistaking the representation of the space for the space itself, whether physical or metaphysical. Wynter believes that it is just this sort of debilitating exercise in mistaken identity, confusion of cause and effect, and categorical error that encumbers the efficacy of Black Studies, writing:

> In effect, because the systematically induced nature of Black self-alienation is itself (like that correlatively of homosexual alienation) only a function (a map), if an indispensable one, of the enacted institutionalization of our present genre of human, *Man* and its governing sociogenic code (the *territory*), as defined in the ethnoclass or Western bourgeois biocentric descriptive statement of the human on the model of a natural organism (a model which enables it to over-

> represent its ethnic and class-specific descriptive statement of the human *as if* it were that of the human itself), then in order to contest one's function in the enacting of this specific genre of the human, one is confronted with a dilemma. As a dilemma, therefore, that is not so much a question of the essentializing or non-essentializing of one's racial blackness as Gates argues, but rather that of the fact that one *cannot* revalorize oneself in the terms of one's racial blackness, and therefore of one's biological characteristics, however inversely so, given that it is precisely the biocentric nature of the sociogenic code of our present genre of being human, which imperatively calls for the devalorization of the characteristics of blackness as well as of the Bantu-type physiognomy, in the same way it calls, dialectically, for the over-valorization of the characteristics of whiteness and of the Indo-European physiognomy.[139]

Wynter's several concerns here are essential for this work. The prevailing "sociogenic code," what I am calling the "Laws of Motion," render it impossible to develop, much less sustain, self-authorizing Blackness. Further, it is clear that the dialectical nature of the relation of Black to white must be abandoned in that it serves to "impose upon us 'an unbearable wrongness of being.'"[140] In order to destabilize this condition, Wynter calls for a new form of cognition:

> This, therefore, as a hitherto unknown territory, the territory of human consciousness and of the hybrid nature-culture laws by which it is structured, that was only to be identified, in the context of both of the global anti-colonial struggles, as well as of the social movements internal to the West itself, by the political activist and psychiatrist Frantz Fanon in his book *Black Skin, White Masks*, doing so from the ground of the particularity of black experience.[141]

It is this "particularity" that has been the preoccupation to this point of this text, which is endeavoring to locate the *territory* and then accurately *map* it in service of describing the phenomenology of Blackness under these conditions and then locate and map the territory of a nondialectical phenomenological experience. It requires that we read across Wynter's work in order to properly triangulate the nature of her understanding of the concept of new forms of cognition. In the essay "The Ceremony Must Be Found: After Humanism," Wynter is clear about what is at stake here:

> By marking the mode of Desire—the desire of Life and of Aversion to Death—these structural oppositional codes function to orient the parameters of motivations/behaviors through which each human

> system realizes itself as such a system. The basic law of their functioning must therefore be the interdiction of any ceremony which might yoke the antithetical signifiers and breach the dynamics of order/Chaos through which the order brings itself into living being; a dynamics which functions like the code of the presence/absence of butyric acid for the tick, for example, to prescribe the seeking/avoiding behavior through which one realizes oneself as one or the other form of self-troping rhetorical human.[142]

Wynter here is attending to the concerns covered in this text that allege Hegel situates Death as the way forward in his system that maps white supremacy in order to render "the ceremony that might yoke antithetical signifiers" impossible. Substantively, "active[ly] creat[ing] . . . the type of Chaos which the dominant model needs for the replication of its system."[143] Following Wynter here, and now moving to her essay titled "Towards the Sociogenic Principle: Fanon, the Puzzle of Conscious Experience, of 'Identity' and What It's Like to Be 'Black,'" where her argument reifies the assertion made here that a completely *new* system of cognition is required to extract Blackness from this system of harm; we find it is necessary to be specific about what it is to be Black in this space and that requires what Wynter, following Thomas Nagel, understands as a "'new theoretical' form":

> It's basic feature would have to be the fact that conscious experience is inseparably linked to *what it is like to be* a specific organism, to the way in which the organism subjectively experiences its mode of being in the world.[144]

What this portends for the argument being made here is that the World that is implicated in white supremacy may be exhausted of its possibilities for the creativity (here this term is meant to be taken expansively) of the putatively marginalized Black subject. Additionally, it is also possible, as an "and/or" circumstance, that what it is to be Black in this World context, which Wynter calls the "sociogenic code" and what I am framing as the "Laws of Motion," is technically exhausted. Or there is the possibility that the tool of cognition available to us is technically exhausted of its potentiality to witness the depth and breadth of Blackness under this sociogenic code. This means that what Miles Davis, for example, has expressed as technically exhausted is asserting that there is a mismatch between what is produced by a subject and what other subjects existing in that mode of being are capable of processing. Therefore, the shift to electronic instrumentation in this example is being framed as more about what our situatedness allows us to perceive than what an acoustic instrument's limitations might seem to be. In service of dealing with this complexity, effectively "mapping" the "territory," and then presenting some argument as to the potentiality of those subject to its logic is essential. That means the borders of the worlds in question here must be defined as well as the gateways between them, which speak to the reason that "Space" as a concept is in play here.

Spaces$_{1-3}$

We can return to the Du Bois of *The Souls of Black Folk* here in aid of this mapping. In chapter 1, "Of Our Spiritual Striving," Du Bois is focused on geolocating the subject in aid of defining the terms and conditions of the world and its functioning. This passage is quoted at length for its clarity in defining its significance for the thinking in this project that includes the previous reference to his elevation.

> And yet being a problem is a strange experience,— peculiar even for one who has never been anything else, save perhaps in babyhood and in Europe. It is in the early days of rollicking boyhood that the revelation first burst upon one, all in a day, as it were. I remember well when the shadow swept across me. . . . The exchange was merry, till one girl, a tall newcomer, refused my card,— refused it peremptorily, with a glance. Then it dawned upon me with a certain suddenness that I was different from the others; or like, mayhap, in heart and life longing but shut out from their world by a vast veil. I had thereafter no desire to tear down that veil, to creep through; I held all beyond it in common contempt and lived above it in a region of blue sky and great wandering shadows. Why did god make me an outcast and a stranger in mine own house? The shades of the prison-house closed round about us all: walls strait and stubborn to the whitest, but relentlessly narrow, tall, and unscalable to sons of night who must plod darkly on in resignation, or beat unavailing palms against the stone, or steadily, half hopelessly, watch the streak of blue above.[145]

For Du Bois, as we have seen, the world in which white supremacy serves as the guiding set of principles is divided in two by what he calls the veil or the color line. Du Bois points to a space of some relief from this condition "above it in a region of blue sky and great wandering shadows." The problem here is that the space above the fray, so to speak, is unsatisfying and leaves the system of separation intact, where Du Bois can find only brief solace in defeating his white counterparts, and results in Black subjects continually marginalized and denied access to the "dazzling opportunities" that he craves. The cause of all of this misery remains unperturbed and the frustration of the marginalized appears in what Du Bois ascribes to the Black masses as a series of useless methods of dealing with the circumstances: "tasteless sycophancy or silent hatred of the pale world about them, and mocking distrust of everything white."[146] It is important, when mapping the space Du Bois describes, to be assured that the world as currently constituted and framed in its separation is a totalizing condition and does not have within its borders a place to be relieved of its logic. This means the space behind the Veil, which I argue represents a place of repose and truth, that Du Bois describes as a place where one can witness, by leaving the "world of the white man,"[147] "the meaning of its religion, the passion of its human sorrow, and the struggle of its greater souls,"[148] is also insufficient or more properly not capable of resolving the central problematic. It is tempting to wonder at the possibility that, behind the Veil, there might be a place of permanence and stable existence at a remove from the "white world," but Du Bois is careful to describe it as a place where one "may *view* [my italics] faintly its deeper recesses."[149] I take this description as that of a place of observation, where one can view either, as if in a museum, artifacts from the other world or perhaps a portal to look into that other place. In order to properly map this territory, the space of observation, within the white World, on the Black side of the color line and behind the Veil, we call it *Space*$_1$ in cataloging the spaces that, linked together, will allow access to the other side of the Door of ~~No~~ Return.

The next space that I am proposing appears is the "room" connected to Du Bois's Veil-space or *Space*$_1$, the doubled space of Fanon's Zones: one of nonbeing and the other of *hachures*. The latter, as we have seen, leads its travelers *back* to a return to the sociogenic laws of the white World and the former is where the body is broken in service of the possibility of it being reordered. Returning to Fanon by way of the Sylvia Wynter of "Towards the Sociogenic Principle," we find the following description of this phenomenon:

> Fanon begins chapter 5 "The Lived Experience of the black" with an account of his subjectively experienced response to the hurled epithet i.e. "Dirty nigger" or simply "Look, a Negro"! At this moment, his idea of himself is one who had come into the world infused "with the will to find a meaning in things," one whose spirit had been "filled with the desire to attain to the source of the world" is shattered. With that hurled epithet, that exclamation, "I found that I was an object in the midst of other objects." [BS: 10] All attempts to escape that "crushing objecthood," eventually, fail. The glances of the other fixed me there, in the sense in which a chemical solution is fixed by a dye. [BS: 109]
>
> "I was indignant; I demanded an explanation. Nothing happened. I burst apart. Now the fragments have been put together again by another self."

> This "put together" other self then analyzes his experience, seeing it as one common to all black men. The quality of this experience, he recognizes, was new in kind. They had not known it when they had been among themselves, still at home in the French island colony of Martinique. Then, "he would have had no occasion, . . . to experience his being through others." Here he must directly confront a reality that had not revealed itself in all its starkness, before his arrival—the reality of the "being of the black man."[150]

This space, the way forward through *nonbeing* rather than *hachures*, we designate as *Space*$_2$. The next step, *Space*$_3$, is another doubled space but synergistically rather than oppositionally related and is described by Ralph Ellison in *Invisible Man* as the hole where Jack-the-Bear resides and by Toni Morrison in *Beloved* within the spite-filled walls of 124. To mark the synergistic relationship of these two accounts of the space I am exploring here, we address them simultaneously, by pulling down the barrier between the texts and considering the Hole and 124 as, ultimately, a single place, through an act of Imagination that is the center of the work in Part II.

Threshold

The Play of Cognitions operative here, in multiple ways, particularly here in the Break between Coercion and Imagination or Cognition and Consciousness, is best understood as a slippery slope, in that it can prove to push subjects forward or backward. Envision it as a peak that arises out of the physical, mental, and spiritual journey we have endured to this point that has an equally steep way opposite the path we have traveled, recall both an ascent and a descent at the same time. The gravity from the World of Anti-Black Racism or World$_1$ is particularly strong here and threatens to pull the traveler *back* to where they have journeyed from: a simulacrum of Sisyphus, engaged in an infinite return to the violence of Anti-Blackness. Here, the force of the Gravity we have described is multiplied, in that the threshold of Consciousness provides for the potentiality of envisioning a way forward (again, simultaneously, up and down) that will leave Anti-Blackness as the dominant force of subject (dys)formation behind and, at the same moment, abandon the possibility of the inability to imagine any other way of Black Being. This inability to imagine other forms of Blackness has been documented by others and retraces its central concerns, always and already asserting and reasserting the impossibility of Return. The latter has been ably handled by others and substantively revolves around its logic, always and already asserting the impossibility of Return. Here we are pursuing the former and have the need to linger at the threshold of the portal that is the doubled chamber I have labeled *Space*$_3$.

Recall that the Black Body that concerns us here is bivouacked on this peak carrying more than the system of cognition we are interested in shattering can bear. It must be wrecked, shipwrecked as the threshold condition for philosophizing. I am thinking here of Hans Blumenberg's short text *Shipwreck with Spectator: Paradigm of a Metaphor for Existence*, where he proposes that the metaphor of the shipwreck is foundational for philosophical thought, stating, "Shipwreck, as seen by a survivor, is the figure of an initial philosophical experience."[151] By way of thinking with a new form of self-consciousness and philosophical paradigm, what I am proposing is that the creation of Blackness as a complex way of being, which was inaugurated by the experience of the Middle Passage and its echoes, is just such an experience of catastrophe that opens the breach for new forms of thinking. Blumenberg writes:

> What can be salvaged from the shipwreck of existence proves to be not a possession withdrawn, in whatever way, into interiority but rather the self-possession achievable through the process of self-discovery and self-appropriation. Long before it divests itself of the security of its relationship to the world, skeptical anthropology defines as its property what it can allow as a substance that is not endangered and cannot be lost. To the outside that cannot be reached from the inside corresponds—and in this Montaigne already moves close to Descartes—the inside that cannot be reached from the outside.[152]

Witness here, again, the echo of Morrison's "new space [that] postulates the inwardness of the outside," which, in Blumenberg's thinking, misses the innovation that renders it impossible to reach the outside from the inside because there is no separation between the two: the subject is already there. The idea of the shipwreck is generative here for characterizing the practice that will yield Being-as-Black. All of this shattering, the Black body assaulted by these negative forces of nature that are bloated with metaphysics-cum-physics, renders the body, in the Anti-Black World or World$_1$, disabled.

PART II

Consciousness

Time was as I was, but neither that time nor that "I" are anymore.

—Ralph Ellison, *Invisible Man*

Imagination

Recall the opacity and separation of the box that appears as a result of the careful consideration of the system of cognition that renders the radical Other inside by being outside. Improvising around Jacques Ranciere's system of thinking leads to an awareness of a phenomenon beyond the French theorist's reckoning; *no part of the part of no part*.[1] The box is the necessary resolution of the destabilization of the system of white supremacy by the scrutiny of the oppressed. The place we find ourselves now requires the leap into what only appears to be the unknown or, more precisely, the unrealized. Following the Ellison of this section's epigraph, the motion across the fractured and recursive nature of the temporal framework renders the subject both fluid and static in that fluidity.

The challenge is laid bare by Fanon, again in *Black Skin, White Masks*, where he asserts: "At the risk of arousing the resentment of my colored brothers, I will say that the black is not a man."[2] What Fanon reveals is that within the system of cognition that dominates modernity, the proper situatedness of the Black Body is to understand it as existing at some discernible distance from consideration as human. The problematic that confronted Fanon is (1) that à la Du Bois, the marginalized subject is aware that the condition of abjection is a contrivance of white supremacy; (2) that, in spite of the coercive force of Anti-Black Racism and its subject-dys-forming pressure, the Black subject is aware of their humanity; (3) that these "Souls" have survived and thrived in spite of the force of Anti-Black Racism and have created, through the survival praxis, a state of Being that is to be respected and cherished; (4) that to imagine the end of white supremacy threatens to end the context and stable-instability of that way of being; and (5) that, therefore, there has, to date, been no system of Being or theory of the (Black) Subject that delivers the Black Body to a way of Being-as-Black that brings to ruin the world of white supremacy and the realization of Morrison's "*third, if you will pardon the expression, world*," intact and unburdened.

I have titled this section of the book "Imagination" rather than surrendering to the temptation to call it "Racial Imaginary." This is in large measure influenced by the introduction to the volume *The Racial Imaginary: Writers on Race in the Life of the Mind*, where the editors Claudia Rankine, Beth Loffreda, and Max King Cap effectively map the limitations of the term for this project. The final paragraph of the introduction is rendered here in its entirety for its clarity:

> What we mean by racial imaginary is something we all recognize quite easily: the way our culture has imagined over and over again the narrative opportunities, the feelings and the attributes and situations, the subjects and metaphors and forms and voices, available both to characters of different races and their authors. The racial imaginary changes over time, in part because artists get into tension with it, challenge it, alter its availabilities. Sometimes it changes very rapidly, as in our lifetimes. But it has yet to disappear. Pretending it is not there—not there in an imagined time and space, in lived time and space, in legislative time and space—will not hurry it out of existence. Instead our imaginings might test our inheritances, to make way for a time when such inheritances no longer ensnare us. But we are creatures of this moment not that one.[3]

This intervention is generative for many reasons, but the one that bears serious consideration within the four corners of this effort is the manner in which the volume edited by Rankine, Loffreda, and Cap has established the artistic as the focus of its inquiry. What this means for Rankine, Loffreda, and Cap is that they are concerned with art and, therefore, the Black Aesthetic in a manner that does not completely account for the way in which "art" is generally understood. In this text, alongside the artistic production of novelists, poets, filmmakers, visual artists, and musicians, I include athletes, philosophers, and theorists. This means the admonition the editors of *The Racial Imaginary* present to writers is to be taken seriously for those who "write" within the field of sports or the academic disciplines of philosophy and theory. Max, Loffreda and Rankine posit that "it seems a lot of us here when asked to talk about race are most comfortable, or least uncomfortable, talking about it in the language of scandal."[4] In addition to scandal, the authors also wish to avoid the "common language" of the "sentimental . . . [and] the past tense"[5] in writing artistically about race. I would argue that the limiting language of scandal, the sentimental, and the past tense also encumber the theory, philosophy, and critique that dominate our current discourse around matters of race, which, following Loffreda, Max, and Rankine, is understood as a species of the genus of Racial Imaginary. Additionally, and this is perhaps the crux of the need to take advantage of the opening this assertion provides, this project is, ultimately, concerned with the next moment, not this one.

The shift here to "Imagination" serves several purposes, all of which lead to and are, in fact, dependent on employing new or, perhaps, more appropriately, "newly recognized" systems of cognition, that will allow us to be conscious of Morrison's "*third, if you will pardon the expression, world,*" which has as the necessary condition for its existence a system of thinking that "*imagines* [my italics] safety without walls where we can conceive of"[6] Being-as-Black.

What that passage means for this analysis is that Imagination here is employed to signal thinking *beyond* the limitations of the Racial Imaginary as defined by Max, Loffreda, and Rankine. By doing so, race becomes an element of the type of imaginary constructed and employed here, not the telos. Also, Imagination, as employed here, serves to extricate our thinking about race from the circularity of the Play of Cognitions outlined earlier that will establish and stabilize the safe space exposed by Morrison.

After thinking carefully about the way forward to new forms and levels of cognition, what I am proposing is that it requires a radical act of imagination to disrupt the play of cognitions and establish the distance required to be aware of Anti-Blackness yet free from its logic. The term "logic" here is presupposed to represent a thorough relationship to what we have termed, here, the "laws of motion" of the worlds under consideration. As has been mentioned and reemphasized, but bears marking again, in the world that we find ourselves in, the logic of white supremacy takes on the characteristics of a law of motion, in this case gravity. To fulfill the aspirations of Morrison's "*third, if you will pardon the expression, world,*" two important elements must coexist. One must have both an awareness, in this case through an act of imagination, of what the laws of motion happen to be in Morrison's "*third, if you will pardon the expression, world*" and some understanding of the liminal space: the hinge, the break, the cut between the two, or, what I am calling, here, "the threshold of the door of return" or $Space_3$. It is for this reason, this need for a coherent definition of here and there as well as, critically, the space between, that Black thought has turned to the quantum in order to make sense of this complexity.

Quantum Blackness

I'm thinking here of the work of Michelle M. Wright and her important text *Physics of Blackness: Beyond Middle Passage Epistemologies*[7] and Chanda Prescod-Weinstein's canonical *The Disordered Cosmos: A Journey into Dark Matter, Spacetime, and Dreams Deferred.*[8] This framework requires that we revisit the notion of "World," recalling Figure 1 from the Introduction that depicted an "Anti-Black World" that is entered via the physical and metaphysical existence of the Middle Passage. The Anti-Black World is divided, internal to its logic and geography, into the Black World and the white world. It is important to note that the Anti-Black World is *not* the world upon which all other worlds "hang." There is, as depicted, a world prior to the Anti-Black World, or Black World$_{\text{Prime}}$, temporally before the physics and metaphysics of the Middle Passage and a world temporally after the Anti-Black World's physics and metaphysics. However, the notion of a world or a perception upon which all of these worlds depend is beyond the scope of this project but also keep in mind that a "simpler" resolution to this problematic could be to recognize to the point of understanding the ploy of architecture posing as world. What we do know is that the Middle Passage and, therefore, the "Door of No Return" served as the pathway from the Ante–Anti-Black World to the Anti-Black World.

This point is critical and an examination of Max Born's text *Einstein's Theory of Relativity* sets the stage for dealing with the necessary dynamic for employing the tool of cognition that allows consciousness of the "*third, if you will pardon the expression, world.*" Born elucidates that the first step toward having comprehensive awareness is to establish the coordinate system for locating points or what Hermann Minkowski called "events" or "world points."[9]

> Our graphical method of representation fails for motions in space, for in this case we have three space coordinates x,y,z, and time has been added as a fourth coordinate. But unfortunately, our visual powers are confined to the three-dimensional space. The symbolic language of mathematics must now lend us a helping hand. . . . If physics is to return to its maxim of recognizing as real only what is physically observable, it must combine the concepts space and time into a hidden unity, namely, a four-dimensional expanse. Minkowski called this the "world" (1908) by which he wished to express that the element of all order of real things is not place or point of time, but the "event" or "world point," that is, a place at a definite time.[10]

As a practical matter, all of this depends upon the innovation of Newton and essential assumptions he made that facilitated the possibility of ever more accurate definitions of Minkowski's "events" and "world points." Born describes the problematic in the following manner:

> Newton was therefore confronted with the task of finding the system of reference in which the law of inertia and all other laws of mechanics were to hold. . . . [He] came to the conclusion that there is an absolute space and an absolute time. . . . The definite statement, both in the definition of absolute time and in that of absolute space, that these two quantities exist "without reference to any external objects whatsoever" seems strange from one like Newton [because] what exists "without reference to any external object whatsoever" is not ascertainable and is not a fact. Here we have clearly a case in which the ideas of unanalyzed consciousness are applied without reflection to the objective world.[11]

Incorporating this information into our thinking, we are able to determine that the Anti-Black World or World$_1$ has, "without reference to any external object whatsoever," situated the idea of white supremacy and Anti-Blackness as the system of reference. As subjects who exist within that worldview, and having been acculturated to view events through that system of reference, it is no wonder that it is difficult to see or, more precisely, place "events" or "world points" without reference to white supremacy as the system of reference. Additionally, therefore, it is clear why it is difficult to "see" into the Ante–Anti-Black World or Morrison's "*third, if you will pardon the expression, world*" because the system of reference is dedicated to the maintenance and deepening of that obscurity. That system of reference is primarily designed to render Black Thought (broadly understood) as illegible, meritless, illogical, and fetishized as exotic: anything but a point of discernible intellectual reference.

The challenge, as mentioned before, therefore, is twofold and, in some sense, each of these elements must come into fruition simultaneously. A new system of referentiality must accompany the identification of the condition for crossing into the "*third, if you will pardon the expression, world.*" As a practical matter, the existence of the Black subject is presupposed in all three of the worlds in play here. The question that has been addressed by physics is how to account for the body in motion across these perceptions, which presents itself as the enduring barrier to resolving the eternal return of the same that is the point of resistance. Again, Max Born addresses this complexity:

> Although the laws of mechanics are the same in all inertial systems . . . the so-called transformation equations . . . allow us to pass from one to the other by calculation.[12]

The complex and interlocking World architecture developed here requires the existence and then identification/cognition of three spaces of subject re-de-formation: the *anteliminal*, the *liminal*, and the *postliminal*. It is important here to reestablish an understanding of this architecture before further detailing it, which, again, is the World of Anti-Black Racism or $World_1$. The world prior to the Middle Passage is the anteliminal. The Long Middle Passage serves as the liminal space, where forces (of nature) are constantly working to (dys)form Black subjectivity while at the same time preventing progress forward or backward that would tend to alter to the point of collapse the terms and conditions (forces at work) in this space. The postliminal, the space "after" the Long Middle Passage, includes the space that points to the "*third, if you will pardon the expression, world*" as well as that space itself. It is the preoccupation of this project and the presupposition of the existence of this other world that serves as the prime mover of this thinking.

The complication here is that the *thresholds* of the spaces between anteliminal, liminal, and postliminal are queered, in that all these spaces of subject re/de/formation exist at the same time in the space-time of passage or transference. Understanding and accepting as axiomatic that two objects cannot occupy the same space-time without being the same object is the premise that requires that some discernible space between the spaces, however small or fleeting, exists. The possibilities seem to roughly be the following:

1. Two distinct objects cannot occupy the same distinct space-time.
2. Two distinct spaces cannot occupy the same distinct space-time.
3. The spaces of object de/re/formation are objects in and of themselves.
4. Therefore, these space/objects cannot be in the same place at the same time as another distinct space object.
5. As subjects pass through or linger in these spaces of subject de/re/formation, they exist at some discernible distance from the typologies of the altered self that exist both in these transitional spaces and in other Worlds.

The space between the spaces of recognizable subject re-creation and/or existence are fleeting and difficult to perceive. In *An Africana Philosophy of Temporality: Homo Liminalis*, I addressed this phenomenon from a perspective of its relationship to time with the point of departure being the 1977–1978 Michel Foucault lectures at the College de France, where he wonders at the complexity of perception much less the analysis of transitional phenomena.[13] Here, the analysis necessarily includes thinking with and through temporality but is focused on the spatial nature of transition, which is itself malleable as an event in time. The complexity of dealing with this space is compounded by the fact that three points of possibility are occurring simultaneously: *entry, remaining,* and *departing.* At this point, they combine their collective forces to destabilize the Laws of Motion in this space. Here, the ways of being from the space of entry and the "destination" find themselves mechanically related to one another. A resolution of these manifold forces at play here must occur. Some forces will be static, netting to zero, others will be dynamic, and there will also be forces that do not exist in this world, coming from the other worlds, that find themselves measurable and at play here. It is the latter two that will be the forces that return the subject from whence it came or propel it forward.

The space under scrutiny here, the threshold that deeply matters, is that between the liminal space of the Long Middle Passage and the postliminal, which I am designating as the Door of ~~No~~ Return; the anteliminal space serves as the place of transition to Morrison's "*third, if you will pardon the expression, world.*"

As has been mentioned, this chapter blurs the relationship between 124 Bluestone Road in Toni Morrison's *Beloved* and Jack the Bear's Hole outside of Harlem in Ralph Ellison's *Invisible Man* and find its point of common reference with Melville's Ishmael and his brief visit to a Black church in *Moby-Dick.* These are the three literary exemplars of the space between the spaces that are the focus of the thinking here and as such present themselves as the Threshold(s) of the Door of ~~No~~ Return that contain the required transfer equations. Before engaging that thought experiment, it is important to note that both Morrison and Ellison understand these spaces as *home.* This is problematic quite simply because the subjects who enter this space of subject re-creation must be prepared to leave, not situate the space for a stable-unstable existence.

Further, the simulation of the sonic presentation of information, basically "song," has appeared early here and requires clarity to establish its theoretical importance. It is Lyricism that sets the flow in motion and archives its truth, serving as the vehicle for forward progress. The moral correction to the ~~Slave~~ Ship is the Soul Ship that sails along and through the Ocean that becomes a river for our purposes.

Lyricism

> Therefore pass these Sirens by, and stop your men's ears with wax that none of them may hear; but if you like you can listen yourself, for you may get the men to bind you as you stand upright on a cross-piece half way up the mast, and they must lash the rope's ends to the mast itself, that you may have the pleasure of listening. If you

beg and pray the men to unloose you, then they must bind you faster.

—Homer, *The Odyssey*

All I have to hold on to is a simple song at last

—Sly and the Family Stone, "Sing a Simple Song"

Track 1

"Listen, Baby . . ."

—Marvin Gaye and Tammi Terrell, "Ain't No Mountain High Enough"

There is lyrical noise to listen to prior to Marvin Gaye exhorting Tammi Terrell to just, "Listen, baby," excising the "just" and mining the two words, "listen" and "baby" to allow them to stand in for more than the "just" could ever be in its quintessential barely of just "just." Now that I have noticed the presence of the absent "just" in its absence, I cannot help but hear it as the prelude to the prelude: Just, listen, baby. Nothing less could ever be more than the just of just urging your baby to just listen baby. . . . It is the excision and that amounts to a complex simplicity that Sly calls a "Simple Song."

That lyric, "just," which doesn't exist, will be the point of entry for the concept of "Lyricism" as our Soul Ship. Words, a word, a phrase, a line, a pause, an absence that is necessarily more than itself, and, like a stone dropped without warning into a placid pool of impossibly clear water, it causes movement. Water such that the craggy and distant bottom is indistinguishable from the smooth and undisturbed surface until: "plop." The lyrical stone is dropped, and the ripples create the possibility of separation in service of getting your baby to only just listen, baby.

Track 2

I was born by The River / In a little tent / Oh, and just like the River
I've been running every since

—Sam Cooke, "A Change Is Gonna Come"

I want to be careful here. Just careful enough to make the most of the absent "just" that asks me to listen baby. So, I listen and realize that this lyric is not about "a" river. It's about The River, a proper noun. One might be born by any old "a" river but to be born by the The River in a little tent must mean that this is the same body of water that like mountains that ain't high enough, valleys that are never quite low enough, this "the The River" is the same River that is not wide enough to prevent crossing to the other side, but here I'm not interested in crossing at this place. This is the The River, whose water flows from the musical to the literary to the political and back without warning and impediment. The water, like Sam Cooke, is running every since.

There are several ways to read this lyric, I suppose. One might choose to use poetic license and do something that may feel like correcting Sam Cooke to sing "running ever since" in the sense that it is a temporal since in the Led Zeppelin sense of being about to lose my worried mind, since. Alternatively, you might leave the "since" in the temporal sense in place and allow Sam's "every" to remain free of editing situating a notion of the quantum nature of reality, where an endless number of "sinces" flow like the river or, more correctly, are the The River that persists in running every since.

Then, there is the possibility of understanding since to be "sense," in the sense of senses, which means that the The River that is running every sense has activated all of the senses and allows them to flow without impediment or mediation. Sight. Sound. Taste. Touch. Smell. All of them at the same moment converted to a single node of endless flowing possibility, indistinguishable with respect to past, present, or future; the possible impossibility that Ellison's Jack-the-Bear, in his hole, hears and wonders along with Louis Armstrong, "How did he become so Black and Blue?" Leaving aside the fact that Louis Armstrong already sounds like five trumpets by himself, it is the flow that preoccupies me here. The flow of the The River and that of Pop's horn, Ellison realizes, prefiguring the complexity of the quantum we have been toying with, are both particle and wave here by the The River with every sense running. It is the node, the break, that I am hoping to inhabit for the balance of this thinking, even as the The River flows from the lyrical to and through Cognition and Consciousness to land at Being, the point of departure, and back with each node awash with sediment from the banks of both and all shores at the same time. Take me to the River. I wanna go.[14]

Track 3

> But I never saw / The good side of a city / 'til I hitched a ride on the river boat queen / Big wheel keep on turning / Proud Mary keep on burning / And we're rollin', rollin', rollin' on the River
>
> —Ike Turner and Tina Turner, "Proud Mary"

We have to roll on the The River, this river, before we can cross it. I'm interested here in loading up the riverine node, which Ellison exposes, with all it can bear, like Jack-the-Bear coming out of his hibernation, what he marks as a "covert preparation for more overt action."[15] I'm preoccupied with a particular performance of "Proud Mary" that was broadcast live on Italian television in 1971. The ageless Tina Turner fronts the band, haunted, vocally, lyrically, instrumentally, mentally, and physically by the seething anger of Ike. What Tina tells us via Sam Cooke under the protection of Ellison is that movement will be the key to deciphering the relationship between the Blackness that preoccupies this argument as it asserts/denies/reasserts and redenies passage and then converts oceans to rivers. The The River is the vehicle for this exploration. The following is the imperative assertion voiced in the poetics of Langston Hughes who writes:

> My soul has grown deep like the river.[16]

It is the notion of depth, not length, that I want to visit here and expand on our vocabulary of the possibility of various temporalities by adding an additional axis. The Amazon, I am told, is long. The Nile and the Mississippi, the Congo and the Mekong are long and winding. But are they deep? Time, just like these rivers, just like the The River is long and flowing and may or may not choose to be ordered. Dip in it where you may and out where you choose. Rememory it. But is it deep? Langston Hughes asserts that it is the depth of the river where the soul finds inspiration to grow deep. As we are familiar, in the most common sense, the flowing of the The River, or should we call it its sense-inflected running of every since in the sense of time moving along the x-axis with the present representing the ever-elusive point of all too fleeting stasis between the receding then and the fast approaching when, moves by way of the horizontal. This affords us at least two possibilities to complicate this understanding. The first is that we might reorder the vessels floating on the river that are loaded with memories such that the common notion of sequentiality is destabilized and arrives as it might, bidden or unbidden in their own time, recentering through decentering our understanding of the flow of the The River as it imitates or represents or just is Time. Rememory it.

The second relates itself to the depth of any given node that we might choose to tarry with plumbing its deeper recesses rather than, as Ellison proposes, leaping forward to the next one, traveling vertically, either ascending or descending, creating a second temporal realm that occilates in perpendicular fashion to the horizontal motion of the Flowing River of Time.

These moments, for me, are lyrical evidence in the moment of a word or note or sound that sustains itself until another word or note grants us access to the flowing of the The River as well as its layers, which are commonly referred to as thermoclines or layers that are distinct and in many ways function, or perhaps are representable, as chords. Several notes voiced, simultaneously, in time and out of it.

These layers, here analogized as thermoclines in water, become containers of sonic information. Readers of naval fiction are all too familiar with the need for submarines to exploit temperature layers to hide themselves from the sonic searching enemies bent on sinking them in uncontrolled rather than controlled fashion. "Run silent, run deep," they always say.

I want to think of the submarine and the node of sound in and out of time we are considering here as vehicles: both a thing and a carrier of things. In this case, the individual lyric that preoccupies us can be loaded with information and sent on a mission, both horizontally and vertically, at times overt and at others secret. These messages search for thermoclines and use them to provide a space for motion in the temporal and spatial realms. This is a project between creator, listener, and, perhaps most importantly, phenomenon that exceeds the performance envelope of language (unadorned) to properly memorialize.

Track 4

> Well I hope to play a, not necessarily a more beautiful sound—though I would like to—you know, just say, tonewise, I would like to produce a more beautiful sound. But now I'm primarily interested in trying to work what I have, what I know, down into a more *lyrical* line, you know.
>
> —John Coltrane interview by Carl-Erik Lindgren, Stockholm, March 22, 1960

Recall here the notion of the Event identifiable by the fact that, forever after, it serves as a marker of a before and an after. 10:22 A.M., Central Standard Time, on September 15, 1963, is just one such node that we explore vertically and horizontally. At 10:22 A.M., a call was placed to a church that was answered by a fourteen-year-old girl named Carolyn Maull. The caller said "three minutes" before terminating the call and less than sixty-seconds later sixteen sticks of dynamite near the east wall of the Sixteenth Street Baptist Church in Birmingham, Alabama, exploded killing four children: Addie Mae Collins (fourteen), Cynthia Wesley (fourteen), Carole Robertson (fourteen), and Denise McNair (eleven). One day later, on September 16, Dr. Martin Luther King Jr. eulogized the children pronouncing the following:

> Now I say to you in conclusion, life is hard, at times as hard as crucible steel. It has its bleak and difficult moments. Like the ever-flowing waters of the river, life has its moments of drought and its moments of flood. Like the ever-changing cycle of the seasons, life has the soothing warmth of its summers and the piercing chill of its winters. And if one will hold on, he will discover that God walks with him, and that God is able to lift you from the fatigue of despair to the buoyancy of hope and transform dark and desolate valleys into sunlit paths of inner peace.[17]

Sixty-three days later, on November 18, 1963, John Coltrane followed the smooth contours of Reverend King's lyrical charting of the jagged cruelty of this event by producing the song "Alabama" as instrumental homage to the event and King's eulogy. It is also necessary to search this node for its other lyrical companions and to link it both horizontally and vertically to Billie Holiday's "Strange Fruit" from 1939, and Max Roach and Abbey Lincoln's "Triptych: Prayer-Protest-Peace" from 1960, to another the The River, this one in Ghana named the Assin Manso, where kidnapped Africans bathed for the last time before being entombed in the slave castle at Elmira, to the call for his mother, one hundred feet from home, by Tyre Nichols. There is a way in which assembling these events—Assin Manso, Strange Fruit, Prayer-Protest-Peace, Sixteenth Street, Dr. King's Eulogy, Coltrane's search for the single line, and Nichols's call—along a horizontal continuum tells a particular and tragic tale. Instead, I want to take a single moment, the less than sixty seconds between the three-minute warning and the dysfunctional prematurity of the explosion of white supremacist rage, and bear down. Forty-five seconds or so of the unbridled, tragic, and informed lyricism of these events assembled one on top of the other, which load that span of time between the call and the detonation with four-hundred-plus years of almost impossible-to-bear events of the tragic consciousness of the catastrophe and lyrical expression that elaborates itself as political speech.

The unique character of sonic representation of cognition lies in its robust temporal plasticity—expanding as it contracts, contracting as it expands—the very form of Consciousness required here. Each event, stacked upon another, collapses four hundred years into forty-five seconds of horizontal time. Multiplied out—forty-five seconds by four centuries—this becomes 568,036,800,000 square seconds of vertical temporality, a dimensional surface where voices once dispersed can now sound together. Not in succession but in simultaneity, not as line but as field, history becomes orchestration: pain, joy, defiance, memory rising in chorus, as if the centuries themselves had been waiting for harmony. Grasping for and gasping for time, I call these surfaces *Transverse Temporal Nodes*—no-place and every-place at once—composed of and carried by sound, where cognition becomes Consciousness through the Transverse Temporal Gyrus, the brain's own resonant chamber. Again, Ellison, but first Coltrane:

> INTERVIEWER: Would you say, would you say that you're trying to play everything you hear?
>
> ARTIST: Well . . .
>
> INTERVIEWER: At one time, or something like that?
>
> ARTIST: No, there—there are some set things that I know, some devices that I know, harmonic devices that I know that will take me

> out of the ordinary path, you see? If I use them. But I haven't played 'em enough and I'm not familiar with them enough yet to take the one single line through 'em so I play all of 'em, you know, tryin' to acclimate my ear so I can hear.[18]

Now Ellison, on infinite repeat on this acclimation:

> Invisibility let me explain, gives one a slightly different sense of time, you're never quite on beat. Sometimes you're ahead and sometimes behind. Instead of the swift imperceptible flowing of time, you are aware of its nodes, these points where time stands still or from which it leaps ahead. And you slip into the breaks . . .

And here, in an act of literary blasphemy, I break from Ellison's break and mark that we have slipped into the break to listen around. Back to Ellison:

> . . . because to *see* around corners is enough (that is not unusual when you are invisible). But to hear around them is too much; it inhibits action.

Recall that Coltrane, hearing around corners, resists inaction in anticipation of acclimatization through the radical action of total sonic immersion: playing everything. The proposition here is to step into the break, and, having done so, find there is no break at all. Then to orient sensory perception to match the verticality we have disoriented here. What that means is the isolation of events into the vertical rather than the horizontal requires the listener to, in response, arrange listening vertically so the sounds approach all possible modes of cognition simultaneously not sequentially or with respect to perceived value. These sonic thermoclines sit one on top of the other, discernibly different but without space between them in the vertical realm and flow, forward and backward as discernible events, horizontally without touching but also without a break. Each discrete event, when comprehended in this fashion, replicates our stone from Track 1 and, when dropped into this swiftly flowing stasis, causes ripples horizontally and vertically. Plop. Rememory it.

The question here as we approach the B-side is to resolve, outside of the gaze of those who are bent on rendering impenetrable the walls of the Platonic Ideal City, what words must be sung to chant down Babylon one more time. All of this, in its perpetual recurrence, heard vertically, these snippets stacked one upon the other magnify their weight rendering them more than the sum of their parts as the weightiness of Black subjectivity, political or otherwise, can only be borne by sound. Du Bois struggles to answer this conundrum, and, as the tune closes, it must be asserted that W.E.B. Du Bois is a dead ringer for Sonny Boy Williamson.

B-Side: Track 5

> Going down to Louisiana to get me a mojo hand / Going down to Louisiana to get me a mojo hand / I'm gonna have all you women at my command
>
> —MUDDY WATERS, "GOT MY MOJO WORKING"

I'm thinking now about the video of a live performance of "Got My Mojo Working" with Willie Dixon on bass and W.E.B. Du Bois's more soulful doppelgänger Sonny Boy Williamson on the mouth harp. For our purposes, I want us to bring Muddy Waters into protracted conversation with Descartes via the complex relationship to Blackness expressed by Stevie, Biggie, Toni, W.E.B., and Muddy, in conversation with Willie Dixon and Sonny Boy Williamson, knows that his mojo is working but it just don't work on you. Pushing to the limits of the notion of Du Boisian subjectivity, second sight to double consciousness, and, finally, the unresolvable twoness, the "you" that isn't enthralled by the apparent working of the mojo, the self that has been forcibly separated to facilitate the unprecedented marginalization of the whole Black Being: the "but" and "however" of Blackness under threat must be examined.

Muddy Waters takes us back to the The River, leaving the city behind to find a mojo hand to revitalize his mojo or personal spirit. In this case, it is Muddy Waters who needs to convince Muddy Waters that he has his mojo working and that it works on Muddy Waters. Under the protection of Sonny Boy Williamson, Muddy Waters repetition and insistence that his mojo is working sounds a lot more like a wish than a statement of fact and is echoed again and again: "mojo working, mojo working, mojo working." It is the gypsy woman, ostensibly the same one who advises Muddy's mother that he is, was, and would be a "Hoochie Coochie Man" that answers this cry:

> The gypsy woman told my mother
> Before I was born
> You got a boy child coming
> He's gonna be a son of a gun

It is important to note that the body itself, in this instance, is available for the employment of a hoodoo talisman to fulfill this prophecy. He continues:

I got a black cat bone
I got a mojo too
I got a Johnny Concheroo . . .

And, finally, there are the series of sevens that take us back to Du Bois and Ellison:

On the seventh hour
On the seventh day
On the seventh month
The seventh doctor say . . .

In the moments before elaborating the journey from second sight to twoness in *The Souls of Black Folk*, Du Bois establishes this numerological point of reference, writing, "After the Egyptian and Indian, the Greek and Roman, the Teuton and Mongolian, the Negro is a sort of seventh son, born with a veil." Ellison echoes this through an encounter by the protagonist with a man pushing a cart full of blueprints down the street, who names himself as the Hoochie Coochie Man, who necessarily has his mojo working:

"All it takes to get along in this here man's town is a little shit, grit and mother-whit. And man, I was bawn with all three. In fact, I'm a seventh son of a seventh son bawn with a cawl over both eyes and raised on black cat bones high john the conqueror and greasy greens" he spieled with twinkling eyes, his lips working rapidly. "You dig me, daddy?"[19]

This begins to explain the spectral presence of what it would be if the mouth harp were a tenor saxophone and Sonny Boy Williamson, John Coltrane, and W.E.B. Du Bois represent the one single line that only a "Mannish Boy" like Muddy Waters can voice, completing the trilogy of his discourse on the seventh son by rescuing what we remix and update here as the (hu)man-hood of his being:

I'm a (hu)-man
I'm a full-grown (hu)-man
I'm a (hu)-man
I'm a rollin' stone

This eruptive and disruptive ontology forms the core of the more than political project of subject making from the stuff of catastrophe. What is beautiful here is that, even among this catastrophic questioning of the apparent (hu)man-ness of the Black Subject, there is always Love, which raises the question: now that we've found love / what are we gonna do with it?

B-Side: Track 6

> So he hung up his hopes / And even sold his old car / Bought a one-way ticket back / To the life he once knew
>
> —Gladys Knight and the Pips, "Midnight Train to Georgia"

We haven't stopped moving but will trade the navigational horn of the riverboat for the whistle of this Ms. Knight's "Midnight Train to Georgia." I wish to make a claim: theoretical or philosophical or perhaps both or neither here on the shoulders of Gladys's insistence that he may be leaving on Ms. Knight's "Midnight Train," but she'll be with him because, as we come to understand, she'd "rather be in his world / than live without him in mine." There is Bartleby here summoned by Moten in response to Sora Han with regard to Betty, which we visit again in some detail, who preferred not to be governed by the juridical order of Melville's father-in-law who proclaimed her free and under no obligation to return to her old Kentucky home with her owners.[20] She preferred not to because she preferred to return to whatever enslavement was adorned with the love of her spouse and children because I know, I know, I know, I know I know, I know I know, I know, I know, I know, I know I know, I know, I know, I know, I know I know, I know, I know, I know, I know I know, I know, I know, I know, I know I know, I know: twenty-six times I know that "There Ain't No Sunshine When She's Gone." On the heels of that reinforced proclamation of personal knowledge, the promised claim: the way back. The one-way ticket back to the recovery of the loss of the mojo, which is actually the coercive fracturing of subject identity by the weapon of anti-Blackness wielded by the state, is here. And what keeps that steamer rolling is the power of missing. Even through the return to Georgia, by way of the rails having left the The River, there is still the motion we require. Away from home to Home. Rememory it.

PART III

The Bearable Rightness of Being-as-Black

One of the wild suggestions referred to, as at least coming to be linked with the White Whale in the minds of the superstitiously inclined, was the unearthly conceit that Moby Dick was ubiquitous; that he had actually been encountered in various latitudes at one and the same instant of time.

—Herman Melville, *Moby-Dick*

Perhaps it was something that Woodridge had said in the literature class back at college. I could see him vividly, half-drunk on words and full of contempt and exaltation, pacing before the blackboard . . . as though he walked a high wire of meaning upon which no one of us could ever dare venture.

—Ralph Ellison, *Invisible Man*

And you think it's you thinking it up. A thought picture. But no. It's when you bump into a rememory that belongs to someone else.

—Toni Morrison, *Beloved*

And Ishmael Was in the Room . . .

In chapter 35 of Melville's *Moby-Dick*, titled "The Mast-Head," the reader is treated to a detailed exposition of the duties associated with serving as the lookout in a whale ship. As one might imagine, the primary responsibility of these sailors is to be on the watch for the presence of whales. Melville also warns about philosophically minded sailors who use the relative serenity of the crow's nest to focus their attention away from whaling writing:

> And let me in this place movingly admonish you, ye ship-owners of Nantucket! Beware of enlisting in your vigilant fisheries any lad with

> lean brown and hollow eyes; given to unreasonable meditativeness; and who offers to ship with the Phædon instead of Bowditch in his head. Beware of such an one, I say; your whales must be seen before they can be killed and this sunken-eyed young Platonist will tow you ten wakes round the world, and never make you one pint of sperm the richer.[1]

So, as this section has offered at its outset, I am situating this project as the lookout, high above the deck of the *Pequod*, who has sighted the whale, and Ellison and Morrison have provided us with the tools required to kill it because, as I have said here: Ishmael was in the room.

The "room" I am describing is the combined space of Jack-the-Bear's Hole and Sethe's home, 124. A space that will, in the words of Morrison, take on the wall-less characteristics of the "*third, if you will pardon the expression, world*." Recall the following from the prologue of *Invisible Man*, where Ellison's protagonist describes the fact of the ability to inhabit the Break as revealed through his engagement with the music of Louis Armstrong, which allowed him to discover:

> a new analytical way of listening to music. The unheard sounds came through and each melodic line existed of itself, stood out clearly from all the rest, said its piece and waited patiently for the other voices to speak. . . . I not only entered the music but descended like Dante into its depths.[2]

It is on this "lower level," where Jack-the-Bear hears someone shout "Brothers and sisters, my text this morning is the Blackness of Blackness,"[3] that we find the lurking Ishmael.

The moment I am referencing is in chapter 2 of *Moby-Dick*, titled "The Carpet-Bag." We need to visit and then evacuate in the same fashion as Ishmael but rather than head for the Spouter-Inn and, ultimately, the catastrophe of the *Pequod*, we will end up in a Hole outside of Harlem that shares the properties of a house on the edge of Cincinnati at 124 Bluestone Road, entering without reservation or the need for dialectical reasoning the Blackness that repels Melville's narrator. The lines I am referring to read as follows:

> Such dreary streets! blocks of blackness, not houses, on either hand, and here and there a candle, like a candle moving in a tomb. . . . But presently I came to a smoky light proceeding from a low, wide building, the door of which stood invitingly open . . . this then, must needs be the sign of "The Trap." However, I picked myself up and hearing a loud voice within, I pushed on and opened a second, interior door.

> It seemed the great Black parliament sitting in Tophet. A hundred black faces turned round in their rows to peer; and beyond, a black Angel of Doom was beating a book in the pulpit. It was a negro church; and the preacher's text was about the blackness of darkness, and the weeping and wailing, and teeth-gnashing there. Ha, Ishmael muttered I, backing out, Wretched entertainment at the sign of "The Trap!"[4]

There is much to unpack here but I first want to revisit our epigraph that wonders at the notion that the white whale "had actually been encountered in various latitudes at one and the same instant of time." Here, we have entered a temporal realm where characters from texts separated by more than one hundred years find themselves in communication with one another and the refusal of one character to deal with the dialogue occurring across texts creates the possibility of the others. I want to first ensure that we do not lose track of the overarching context here. Recall that the Morrison of *The Source of Self-Regard* exposes the existence of a space from which to conceive of the "*third, if you will pardon the expression, world.*" The space that she describes features what I am indexing as nondialectically framed Blackness, in that it resists the telos of Du Boisian Tripartite Subaltern Subjectivity, or Twoness.

Note, in Melville, that Ishmael finds himself surrounded by blackness, what he calls "blocks of blackness," which is a space where his debased system of cognition resists the identification of what he calls "houses." I will improvise these as the "homes" that preoccupy Morrison. Following Morrison, Melville narrates that Ishmael locates the space that she describes, finding a door "invitingly open." It is important to retrace the path Ishmael follows, literally, through this opening that then requires a crossing of a threshold, which resists his presence. Melville writes in this scene, "so, entering, the first thing I did was to stumble over an ash-box in the porch. Ha! thought I, ha, as the flying particles almost choked me, are these ashes from that destroyed city, Gomorrah?"[5] Despite this obstruction—and here I want to witness this box of ashes upended by Ishmael as the type of talisman to look for as we search for these places of crossing—he presses forward now presumably, at least outwardly blackened by soot. The ashes serve, in this instance, as a sign of the liminal space between worlds, where the collective evil, here, the ashes from the destruction of the world of white supremacy, is stored at the threshold. At that point, Ishmael, our unreliable narrator, misrepresents, misrecognizes, or is unable to properly hear what the pastor, who he sees as a Black Angel of Doom, is saying. Ishmael hears "the blackness of darkness" and promptly withdraws. Ellison corrects the record in the prologue of *Invisible Man* on the lowest referenced layer of the plane of existence in Jack-the-Bear's hole. "Brothers and sisters, my text this morning is the 'Blackness of Blackness,'" not the Blackness of darkness, which Ishmael hears as a dialectical formation of black identity and is his signal to leave, which, in the formulation of Morrison through and with Ellison, is the formation and sustenance of Blackness as Blackness. Ishmael has left the room, but the preacher delivers a warning to him in absentia, marking his presence through absence by exhorting him to understand that Black will "put you, glory, glory, Oh my Lawd, in the WHALES'S BELLY."[6]

I want to read the relationship expressed here between *Invisible Man* and *Moby-Dick* as a phenomenon in excess of one author paying literary homage to another major work that has influenced their practice. This is exemplified in some sense by literally the earliest possible moment in Ellison, where the author employs the closing moments of Melville's magisterial *Benito Cereno* as the first of two epigraphs. Elizabeth Shultz's 1988 essay, titled "The Illumination of Darkness: Affinities between *Moby-Dick* and *Invisible Man*," notes that Ellison specifically names Melville as an influence. Schultz goes on to propose that both texts argue:

> American democracy intensifies these conditions of reality by establishing possibilities for diversity, by promoting change, and by failing to rectify the discrepancy between the actuality of life and American ideals.[7]

I agree with this assessment but want to propose a reading practice that requires us to grapple with the destabilized temporal context that Morrison exposes in *Beloved*, which is best named Rememory as the system of cognition required here to properly experience this phenomenon. Recall in that text the transsubjective and transgenerational awareness of events is a system of cognition that renders it impossible or perhaps even unproductive for individuals to separate their experience from that of others in and out of time to the point that separation matters in not mattering. Here, it is Morrison who facilitates the understanding of the quantum nature of Ishmael, appearing in the Rememory of Jack-the-Bear.

This system of cognition and consciousness accounts for one important element of the appearance of Morrison here but I want to expose another reference to her work in the content of the sermon that preoccupies Ellison's Jack-the-Bear and is abandoned to catastrophic results by Ishmael. Recall that Melville's Ishmael witnesses the proceedings in the space he enters as "the great Black Parliament sitting in Tophet," and its elaboration in Ellison situates the discourse of death as the lingua franca between children and their parents in and around the coercive context of the Plantation. It is the central preoccupation of Morrison's text *Beloved* that forces us to wonder, to sit like the Black Parliament, in judgment of the Tophet, or the passing of children through the fire or ritual sacrifice that the Norton Critical Edition of *Moby-Dick* reductively understands as "Hell."

It is this reductive understanding of Tophet as "hell" that creates the opening to imagine the way in which I want to read this textual mash-up as including the spectral presence of Morrison's Sethe and her not quite departed child known in the novel *Beloved* as "crawling already?" prior to her corporeal death and self-named Beloved after her return. Here, I wish to apply Hartman's notion of Critical Fabulation to the literary imaginations of Melville, Ellison, and Morrison as they each in turn take on the same questions that preoccupy Hartman and others. Recall that Ishmael is shocked to find the Black Parliament is sitting in Tophet and the black Angel of Doom was beating a book in the pulpit. For our purposes here, the book that preoccupies the attention of the gathered worshippers and the preacher and the text on Blackness that drives Ishmael from the opportunity for productive Black Study is Morrison's tale of child sacrifice, *Beloved*. We have revealed the presence of Ishmael, Jack-the-Bear, and Beloved here at the sign of the Trap, the Hole outside of Harlem, and on the outskirts of Cincinnati at 124 Bluestone Road, a single liminal node that serves as the threshold to the Door of ~~No~~ Return or what I want to call Black Study, refused by Ishmael, preached to the ear of Jack-the-Bear, and "Rememoried" by Beloved.

Melville × Ellison × Morrison

me
me Ishmael
Call me Ishmael
Call me
me
I
I man
I am man
I am an man
I am an invisible man
I am invisible man
I invisible man
I invisible
invisible
is
is spiteful
124 is spiteful

124 spiteful
spiteful
me spiteful
Call me spiteful
Call 124 me spiteful
Call 124 me spiteful invisible
I Call 124 me spiteful invisible
I Call 124 me spiteful invisible Ishmael
I Call 124 me spiteful an invisible Ishmael
I Call 124 is me spiteful an invisible Ishmael
I Call 124 is me spiteful an invisible Ishmael man
I Call 124 is me spiteful am an invisible Ishmael man
I Call 124 me spiteful am an invisible Ishmael man
I Call me spiteful am an invisible Ishmael man
I Call spiteful am an invisible Ishmael man
I Call spiteful an invisible Ishmael man
I Call spiteful an invisible Ishmael
I Call spiteful invisible Ishmael
I spiteful invisible Ishmael
I spiteful Ishmael
I Ishmael
I

It is important at this juncture to carefully expose the architecture: physical, metaphysical, and temporal that we have unearthed here. What we have found is a common site: a node in the parlance of Ellison's Jack-the-Bear. As Jack-the-Bear chases the luminescent sonic tail of Louis Armstrong's trumpet, he reaches the lower level where he shares space and altered time with Ishmael. There, Jack-the-Bear is able to witness what Ishmael refuses: the response to a society where the murder of children is a viable choice to their existence under the coercive threat of Anti-Blackness. What Ishmael mistakes as a flirtation with child sacrifice as entertainment at the Sign of the Trap, resonant with passing children through fire as found in Leviticus, Deuteronomy, 2 Kings, and Jeremiah at the Tophet, is, in truth, Black Study. Black Study, which recalls the distinctions analyzed by Giorgio Agamben that detail the distinct mode of the nonsacrificial sacrifice of the *homo sacer*. The direction I'm taking here is to render inoperative, to the point of indistinction, the four corners of the texts that we are considering and posit that the church in *Moby-Dick*, the lower register in Jack-the-Bear's Hole, and the home known as 124 Bluestone Road represent a single liminal space that portends the prospect of crossing to Morrison's "*third, if you will allow the expression, world*" as a result of Black Study on the discourse of death as it relates to Black children. Consciousness flows into Being.

The project of deconstructing the walls between these spaces requires meticulous reconstruction of the textual conversation between these novels. The ambition here is *not* to compare and contrast what I am framing as two spaces of radical subject reformation in the work of Ellison and Morrison but to render them porous, passing into one another without deformation to describe a single space that is visited and then abandoned by Ishmael in the opening moments of *Moby-Dick*. Four principal points of focus lead me to propose that essential elements of *Invisible Man* and *Beloved* accommodate a reading practice that renders them coexistent and codependent on one another as a result of the opening provided by Ishmael's refusal. I am focusing my attention on the two structures glimpsed from a space of spatio-temporal diffusion by Ishmael that are so essential to each narrative. 124 in *Beloved* is regarded by Morrison's character Denver "as a person rather than a structure. A person that wept, sighed trembled, and fell into fits"[8]; and Ellison's protagonist asserts his home/hole is:

> a home—or a hole in the ground . . . that is a warm hole. And remember; a bear retires to his hole for the winter and lives until spring. . . . I say all this to assure you that it is incorrect to assume that, because I'm invisible and live in a hole, I am dead. I am neither dead nor in a state of suspended animation. Call me Jack-the-Bear, for I am in a state of hibernation.[9]

The points of principal focus are that (1) both spaces exist beyond the boundary of a recognized geographic space; (2) both are implicated in the discourse of Death; (3) neither are subject to the common laws of motion for this world; and (4) they are each a place of passing and transition.

First, there are four "inhabitants" or "characters" within this generative spatiality who must be accounted for after Ishmael's untimely and ill-advised leaving: Jack-the-Bear (the Invisible Man), "crawling already?" Beloved, and the structure of 124, which Morrison, again, establishes as a person. These four personalities must meet here in this transitional space that, as described earlier, exists beyond some boundary. Both Ellison and Morrison are explicit on this point, writing, in turn: "The joke, of course, is that I don't live in Harlem but in a border area,"[10] and "It didn't have a number then, because Cincinnati didn't stretch that far."[11]

Second, as I have proposed, death weighs heavily in this space. Jack-the-Bear, who requires illumination because "without light I am not only invisible, but formless as well; and to be unaware of one's form is to live a death.

I myself, after existing some twenty years, did not become alive until I discovered my invisibility."[12] As far as 124 is concerned, it is the on-again, off-again presence of the ghost of the dead child that haunts the "gray and white house on Bluestone Road":[13]

> Baby Suggs died shortly after the brothers left, with no interest whatsoever in their leave-taking or hers, and right afterward Sethe and Denver decided to end the persecution by calling forth the ghost that tried them so.[14]

Third, the "out" nature of the space under consideration here is exemplified by the destabilized relationship to this world's laws of motion. Jack-the-Bear reveals that:

> invisibility . . . gives one a slightly different sense of time, you're never quite on beat. Sometimes you're ahead and sometimes behind. Instead of the swift and imperceptible flowing of time, you are aware of nodes, those points where time stands still or from which it leaps ahead. And you slip into the breaks and look around.[15]

These factors lead me to propose that the space Jack-the-Bear describes as his "warm hole" is better rendered as his/our "Worm Hole" to mark this argument's relationship to the quantum and to propose that we have found the gateway to the other world, which is the telos of this effort. On the part of 124, the liminal relationship of the person/structure is also negatively related to predictable motion:

> Now he was trembling again but in the legs this time. It took him a while to realize that his legs were not shaking because of worry, but because the floorboards were and the grinding, shoving floor was only part of it. The house itself was pitching.[16]

And, fourth, the fractured relationship to the World's laws of motion speaks to the space as a place of transition and passing, which Ellison marks by considering the hole as the locus of a state of hibernation, and, in the case of 124, Morrison describes the time when "124 was a way station where messages came and then their senders. Where bits of news soaked like dried beans in spring water—until they were soft enough to digest."[17] In thinking about this description of 124, several things that require places of transition present themselves as evidence of the role I am proposing both spaces represent in the world architecture.

As a practical matter, there is no way around starting at the very beginning of Ellison's novel with the statement being provided by Jack-the-Bear, the narrator: "I am an invisible man."[18] He then elaborates further: "I am a man of substance, of flesh and bone, fiber and liquids—and I might even possess a mind."[19] Despite all of this "substance," Jack-the-Bear is "invisible, understand, simply because people refuse to see me."[20] These "people" have established and employed a system of cognition that renders it impossible for them to be conscious of him, a state of affairs that leads to a compromised sense of being (real or imagined) or, employing or improvising around Sartre's theme, something like *being as nothing*, which militates against the goal here, *Being-as-Black*. This system of cognition, consciousness, and being is as a result of what Ellison's narrator describes as:

> a peculiar disposition of the eyes of those with whom I come into contact. A matter of the construction of their *inner* eyes, those eyes with which they look through their physical eyes upon reality.[21]

This is a matter of the type of marginalized consciousness that concerns Du Bois and places Jack-the-Bear in a position to be uncertain of his own viability, writing, "You often doubt if you really exist. You wonder whether you aren't simply a phantom in other people's minds."[22] This is the point where the system of cognition, consciousness, and being that Ellison is exposing bangs into, literally, that of Morrison. He writes, "It's when you feel like this that, out of resentment, you begin to bump people back."[23] What Ellison is establishing is that marginalized and putatively invisible Black subjects begin to make themselves felt in order to reify their Being for Themselves. This *bumping* is a force that must be resolved or, more correctly, a discourse of forces that must be properly accounted for. The vector of Ellison's *bump* is from the Anti-Black World *into* the liminal space of transition where we are thinking now. The bump that Morrison is invested in bringing to our awareness is from some other place that we are working to identify, but we see by its effects if not the space and time itself. Recall Morrison's description of Rememory, voiced by Sethe to her daughter Denver, which I quote here at length in excess of the portion we have examined before:

> "I was talking about time. It's so hard for me to believe in it. Some things go. Pass on. Some things just stay. . . . Places, places are still there. If a house burns down, it's gone, but the place—the picture of it—stays. . . . What I remember is a picture floating around out there outside my head. I mean, even if I don't think it, even if I die, the picture of what I did, or knew, or saw is still out there. Right in the place where it happened." "Can other people see it?" asked Denver. "Oh, yes. . . . Someday you be walking down the road and you hear something or see something going on . . . you think it's you thinking

> it up. A thought picture. But no. It's when you bump into a rememory that belongs to somebody else . . . if you go there and stand in the place where it was, it will happen again; it will be there for you, waiting for you. . . . That's how come I had to get all my children out. No matter what." Denver picked at her fingernails. "If it's still there, waiting, that must mean that nothing ever dies." Sethe looked right in Denver's face. "Nothing ever does," she said.[24]

Understanding the reason that Sethe provides this explanation to Denver is vital for understanding the discourse of forces at play here, which speaks to the vector of the effects referenced earlier. Denver is enmeshed in the memory of Sethe's encounter with Amy Denver when Denver is yet unnamed and in utero. Sethe has been journeying to freedom alone and pregnant, and Amy Denver is helping her treat her badly injured feet. The point here is that death, of people and of her feet, are the triggers for the Rememory that requires Sethe's explanation to Denver as a result of a memory related by Amy Denver:

> "Well I was fishing there, and a nigger floated right by me. I don't like drowned people, you? Your feet remind me of him. All swole like."
>
> Then she did the magic: lifted Sethe's feet and legs and massaged them until she cried salt tears.
>
> "It's gonna hurt now," said Amy. "Anything dead coming back to life hurt."
>
> A truth for all times, thought Denver. Maybe the white dress holding its arm around her mother's waist was in pain. If so, it could mean the baby ghost had plans.[25]

This entire section of the text begins to display the kinetic nature of the system of cognition and consciousness Morrison is elaborating here that is both transsubjective and transgenerational and literally a space that can be entered. A space whose boundaries are the memories of others that are triggered by trauma. What this means, literally working backward in the text from the explanation by Sethe of Rememory to Denver's understanding of the truth of 124, is that the space of the home is literally constructed of Rememories, which is why it is "a person, rather than a structure."[26] Additionally, there is a path that must be followed in order to enter the space:

> Easily she stepped into the told story that lay before her eyes in the path she followed away from the window. There was only one door to the home and to get to it from the back you had to walk all the way around to the front of 124, past the storerooms, past the cold room,

> the privy, the shed, on around the porch. And to get to the part of the story she liked best, she had to start way back.[27]

Mark the dilemma here for the notion of return, in that what if getting to the "good part," as in the thinking of Denver, requires retracing the entire story even if the good part has yet to arrive. The final line allows us to add another element of Ellison's hole to the combined space that is revealing itself between these two texts. Ellison's Jack-the-Bear employs the same incantation to open this portal, writing:

> But this is getting too far ahead of the story, almost to the end, although the end is in the beginning and lies far ahead.
>
> The point *now* [my italics] is that I found a home—or a hole in the ground as you will.[28]

With this information in mind, it is clear that the space under construction represented by these structures, is, as Denver proposes, "a person rather than a structure" and, further, that the person/structure is made of memory. Not just the particular memories of an individual but the collective and intertwined memories become Rememories that walk among us. Ellison bears witness to this, and that witnessing is flooded with trepidation. This concern on the part of Jack-the-Bear is born of recognition of his invisibility and the care he takes not to awaken what he calls "the sleeping ones."[29] "I remember that I am invisible and walk softly so as not to awaken the sleeping ones. Sometimes it is best not to awaken them; there are few things in the world as dangerous as sleepwalkers."[30]

I read Ellison here as marking the risk or complexity of entering into active engagement with Rememories, what he calls "sleepwalkers," which then unleash forces that must be managed so as not to have that engagement be deleterious to the goal here that is the crossing we crave. Here, Jack-the-Bear specifically references the "power of sleepwalkers":

> I learned *in time* [my italics] though that it is possible to carry on a fight against them without realizing it. For instance, I have been carrying on a fight with Monopolated Light & Power for some time now. I use their services and pay them nothing at all, and they don't know it. Oh, they suspect power is being drained off, but they do not know where. All they know is that according to the master meter back there in their power station a hell of a lot of free current is disappearing into the jungle of Harlem. The joke, of course, is that I don't live in Harlem but in a border area.[31]

First, I am preoccupied with the words that I have italicized: *in time*, which can be read as an alternative way to say something like "over a period of time," but the text accommodates the notion that Jack-the-Bear learns this before it is too late: in the nick of time; this raises an opportunity to speculate on the implications of the time potentially running out. Jack-the-Bear also must be understood to be speaking about this phenomenon in terms of synchronicity. Jack-the-Bear has been able to situate himself in a particular type of time that allows for new forms of Cognition, Consciousness, and Being. Next, the notion that sleepwalkers are not just people, like the man he "bumped" into, but institutions, like the power company, requires some additional thinking. The text accommodates the notion that it is the variety of "forces" that have been referenced here and become apparent in this space of passage that are the essence of the sleepwalker, who, when encountered, directs that power at the individual who is embroiled in the relationship: physical, metaphysical, or both. The key here is the misdirection of the force. Recall that it is not sufficient to merely account for the quantitative measure of forces here but also the vector or direction. Monopolated Light and Power thinks it is sending its forces into Harlem, when, in reality, they are being redirected and repurposed; this force originated in the Anti-Black World, a place that includes the space of Harlem. Despite that origin, Jack-the-Bear has contrived a way to employ that power for his own purposes outside the space for which they are designed. Most important, intentionally awakening the sleepwalker is to be avoided.

Morrison's returning "crawling already?" is mistakenly awakened within the confines of the Anti-Black World and is then led into the memory space of 124. The "mistake," if you will allow the term, is to allow the form from the zone of something like death, a space that must be further described and accounted for in this architecture, to bring its power into the anteliminal/liminal/postliminal space of crossing and not have it diverted elsewhere. "Exhausted again, she sat down on the first handy place . . . the woman had fallen asleep again."[32] Upon entering the combined space of 124 and the Hole, Beloved falls asleep for days,[33] as a transfer from a realm with a differential relationship to the force of gravity (recall it as white supremacy), then, "'Heavy,' murmured Beloved. 'This place is heavy.'"[34] This inconsistent relationship to the pull of gravity is the reason that Jack-the-Bear is so preoccupied with light, which, in the absolute consistency of its velocity, proves to be the only point of reference as the laws of motion here become difficult to account for and manage. Jack-the-Bear says in no uncertain terms that "the truth is the light and the light is the truth."[35]

There is reason here to look carefully in the space we are entering at the laws of motion, which do not have the characteristics of the prevailing context of existence in the Anti-Black World. There are many ways to go forward here but the shared relationship to an uncommon type of light and what that means for the measure and experience of time is one coherent through line.

There is a form of light at 124 that has the power to halt forward progress. As Paul D first tries to enter the structure/person/memories, there is "a pool of red and undulating light that locked him where he stood."[36] The light creates space of manifold and complex sensual experience:

> She was right. It [the light] was sad. Walking through it, a wave of grief soaked him so thoroughly that he wanted to cry. It seemed a long way to the normal light surrounding the table . . . the red was gone but a kind of weeping clung to the air where it had been.[37]

The introduction of light into the space is another sign of its distance from the functioning of it in the Anti-Black World. Sethe and Paul D climb a flight of white stairs that must appear to lead to the sky because "the light came straight from the sky because the second-story windows of the house had been placed in the pitched ceiling and not the walls."[38] Jack-the-Bear accomplishes the same disorientation of the predictable arrival of light into enclosed spaces, writing, "In my hole in the basement there are 1,369 lights. I've wired the entire ceiling, every inch of it. . . . When I finish all four walls, then I'll start on the floor."[39]

Ellison adds an additional quality to the light scape here, sound, which is conjured here by the introduction of Louis Armstrong's trumpet, the effluence from which "bends into a beam of lyrical sound."[40] This beam of light/sound is a product of the temporal regime that, along with invisibility, has been *illuminated.* It:

> gives one a slightly different sense of time, you're never quite on the beat. Sometimes you're ahead and sometimes behind. Instead of the swift and imperceptible flowing of time you are aware of the nodes, those points where time stands still or from which it leaps ahead. And you slip into the break and look around.[41]

This notion of being both too early and too late at the same time, "now," creates the space, the break, for the reimagining of Black Being, which is under threat in the Anti-Black World, where, as we were reassured in Morrison, "time never worked the way Sixo thought, so of course he never got it right."[42] This time that works the way Black people want and need it to allows for an altered form of Cognition, Consciousness, and, necessarily, Being:

> The unheard sounds came through, and each melodic line existed of itself, stood out clearly from all the rest, said its piece, and waited

> patiently for the other voices to speak. That night I found myself hearing not only in time, but in space as well. I not only entered the music but descended, like Dante, into its depths.[43]

Recall that the space in question is a space of passing, the nodal nature of which can tend toward stasis. This stasis is punctuated by the devastating power of Anti-Blackness that surges here and is difficult to disperse or cancel out. As Jack-the-Bear employs this new form of cognition as listening, light become sound, he becomes conscious of four distinct levels that he describes in some detail. The first layer is what he calls "the hot tempo."[44] Beneath that "there was a slower tempo and a cave."[45] This is another room or space in the structure constructed of memories that is a person where Jack-the-Bear "heard an old woman singing a spiritual."[46] Level three is where the enslaved condition reappears. Here Jack-the-Bear "saw a beautiful girl the color of ivory pleading in a voice like [his] mother's and she stood before a group of slaveowners who bid for her body."[47] Beneath all of this is the locus of Black Being because here, Jack-the-Bear "heard someone shout: 'Brother and sister, my text this morning is the 'Blackness of Blackness','"[48] the misheard words that drove Ishmael from Black Study and into the recurring Middle Passage of the world of Ahab's *Pequod*.[49]

Occupied by the force from a place that accommodates death but does not require it, 124 also has sound that is unintelligible to outsiders who have not yet altered their system of cognition. The intensity of the sound heard outside of the structure, described as a "conflagration of hasty voices—loud, urgent, and speaking at once so he could not make out what they were talking about or to whom,"[50] finds its only coherent referent the word "mine." Inside, the cacophony becomes "less than a whisper . . . nothing fierce or startling. Just that eternal, private conversation that takes place between women and their tasks."[51]

I have struggled to this point to name this space, more correctly "spaces," where "crawling already?" encounters those who are not necessarily dead and feels the horror of the Hold and Jack-the-Bear experiences as a descent into disparate levels. Following Ellison's reference to Dante, I call this space *Purgatorium ex Media Loca*, or Purgatory from the Middle Passage, and carefully differentiate it from our common understanding of purgatory in several important ways. As we know, in Western thought, purgatory is a place where sinners are chastised after death and denied entry into Heaven as they expiate their sins through unspeakable suffering. The space I am describing here, like the Roman Catholic understanding of purgatory, is a place of profound suffering, but it does not require death. In fact, recall the manner in which Beloved describes the struggle to die: "And he is fighting hard to leave his body," and "We are all trying to leave our bodies behind."[52] Similarly, recall that after the explosion that should have killed the subject who would become Jack-the-Bear, he finds himself in this space of cruel examination rather than dead.

Additionally, in the Roman Catholic version of purgatory, souls are sent there to expiate their sins, here in *Purgatorium ex Media Loca* these subjects have been sinned upon. In both of the descriptions provided by Morrison and Ellison, these harmed subjects need to transition from this place and, in both instances, it leads back to the Anti-Black World or World_1.

The force that cocreates this space of transition with Jack-the-Bear arrives because "it" has come from somewhere: necessarily. We have accounted for the presence of the Rememories of Jack-the-Bear, which form essential parts of the structure/person of memory that is the combined space of and with 124 and Jack-the-Bear's hole, which is roughly from the world of Anti-Black Racism. Recall that, to get to this space, it has been necessary to visit the dual zone of subject re-creation exposed by Fanon and make a choice. The same goes for the sacrificed child "crawling already?" who, as she explains to Denver, is from a place that she calls "the dark,"[53] where her name is "Beloved."[54] It is clear the place that this figure finds themself in is not what we would understand as the afterlife or as a space of unresolved existence after corporeal death. It must be that the terms and conditions of the corporeal death of "crawling already?"—which send her spirit to this place from which she makes this eruptive and disruptive return—are something more and less than death. As is the practice in *Beloved*, Denver serves as the most coherent interlocutor, asking the critical question, "What's it like over there, where you were before? Can you tell me?"[55] Critically, Denver pointedly asks if Beloved "can" tell her. Denver is, at least in preliminary fashion, aware that her current situatedness may not have the necessary cognitive tools to understand what she may be told, or, to the extent that she is communicated with, she is not likely to understand what she is told. Beloved elaborates:

> "Dark," said Beloved. "I'm small in that place. I'm like this here." She raised her head off the bed, lay down on her side and curled up.
>
> Denver covered her lips with her fingers. "Were you cold?"
>
> Beloved curled tighter and shook her head. "Hot. Nothing to breathe down there and no room to move in."[56]

These are critically important passages for working toward something like an accurate mapping of this terrain. Recall the figures from Part I. Morrison seems to be revealing the details of the functioning of the multiliminal space between Black $\text{World}_{\text{Prime}}$ and the Anti-Black World or World_1, which we have heretofore understood as the Door of No Return or the entrepôt to the Middle Passage. This space of transition is an exemplar of one that is all three typologies of liminal explained here: anteliminal, liminal, and postliminal. What Beloved reveals are the details of her return to that space of return. The Door of No Return, in this instance, serves, as we see in some detail, as a solid barrier to "crawling already?" finding peace in the Black World, but she also finds her understanding confounded by Rememories that are able to cross into the Hold as described by Christina Sharpe and the space under scrutiny here. This space is physically the hold of the slave ship and metaphysically the inescapable Rememories of that horror. This is verified by the response by Beloved to Denver's next question, "You see anybody?"[57] "Heaps. A lot of people is down there. *Some is dead* [my italics]."[58]

The fact that not *all* are dead is important to reference. This is a literal return to the mechanical functioning of the Middle Passage, not a glimpse of a memorial to the evil of the place. Denver's next question goes unanswered, but it is not necessary for Beloved to articulate a reply because we soon know the answers. "Tell me, how did you get there?"[59] Beloved moves on and explains not how she got there, or, perhaps misunderstanding the question, explains how she returned *here*, answering:

> "I wait; then I get on the bridge. I stay there in the dark, in the daytime, in the dark, in the daytime. It was a long time."
>
> "All this time you were on a bridge?"
>
> "No. After. When I got out."[60]

There is one other possibility that deepens the complexity of the precarious separation between here and there. It is also possible that the question of how Beloved got "there" is irrelevant for her system of cognition, in that the subject quite possibly occupies multiple spatial points of reference at the same time and knows of no useful reason and/or method for disaggregating these worlds. She simply waited until she is able to make it out of the hold and onto a bridge that is the threshold between that space and the Anti-Black World, effectively the postliminal space that allows cognition of the next space as well as spaces and places that precede it. *Rememory it.*

As Stamp Paid explicates when he stands frozen by the incomprehensible cacophony of 124, it is the word "mine" that rises to his consciousness. The term serves as the prime meridian of four "chapters" that delve into this system of cognition and consciousness, three of which assert it explicitly and the fourth doing the same by refusing the explicit notion of possession. The first of these chapters is from the perspective of Sethe who intimates, "Beloved, she is my daughter. She is mine."[61] The next is from the perspective of Denver, who states, "Beloved is my sister,"[62] which is another form of possession than those previously stated and those that come in succession after that are the speech acts of Beloved née "crawling already?" which both read, "I am Beloved and she is mine."[63] There is much to examine in these twenty pages; volumes may not be able to comprehensively deal with these passages. As far as this project is concerned, the point of focus is the "voice" of Beloved for its revelation of the play of cognitions at this threshold and the consciousness that arises as the foundation of this strong form of Being. These passages are most productively read alongside Sethe's explication of Rememory to her surviving daughter Denver. The essential element of the passage is repeated here for the sake of clarity:

> Someday you be walking down the road and you hear something or see something going on. So clear. And you think it's you thinking it up. A thought picture. But no. It's when you bump into a rememory that belongs to somebody else.[64]

For purposes of this exercise, in close reading we designate the two sections before us as *Beloved's Rememory I* (*BRI* pp. 248–252) and *Beloved's Rememory II* (*BRII* pp. 253–256). The link between Sethe's notion of Rememory and these passages is most obviously the reference to thought pictures by Beloved in the opening moments of *BRI*, where the returned being asks, "How can I say things that are pictures."[65] With this in mind, we must make some attempt to "locate" from "whence" Beloved is making/receiving these observations.

The mapping provided to Denver by Beloved is relevant. It is clear that the subject is describing the vantage point from the Bridge I am proposing situates itself in the postliminal space of the threshold between the liminal space of the Middle Passage and the Anti-Black World, which I am calling *Purgatorium ex Media Loca*. Also, there are several important elements that are critical to note. First, the death of "crawling already?" does not send the child's spirit to what we might commonly refer to as the afterlife. Again, Beloved asserts this to Denver by reporting that there are dead in the space, but it is not a threshold condition to be so to enter this space. It is further apparent that what has happened to "crawling already?" is that, rather than her corporeal death sending her metaphysical being to a place of rest, it rather is returned to the Middle Passage and the hold of the slave ship.

This is profound. In further reification of Christina Sharpe's intervention, Morrison is marking that man has the capacity to create a space of such evil that it transcends space, time, and death. Beloved starkly illustrates by saying, "It is hard to make yourself die forever"[66] This is in excess of Patterson's Social Death and, in its complexity, the problem that must be solved here to realize Morrison's "*third, if you will pardon the expression, world.*" This is related to the temporally transcendent nature of the space that Beloved warns us about. "All of it is now. It is always now. There will never be a time when I am not crouching and watching others who are crouching too."[67]

The sinister power of Rememory allows forms of cognition that immerse subjects in the experiences of others and the causal trauma renders all of the relevant subjects fundamentally inseparable. "I am not separate from here there is no place where I stop her face is my own and I want to be there in the place where her face is looking at it too a hot thing."[68]

This formulation, the notion of a subject without boundaries with respect to another but still discernibly particular, troubles the notion of the liminal. Or, perhaps more carefully, the manner in which the Middle Passage overflows its temporal and geographic boundaries also is an essential component of the manifold being of subjects tortured by this logic. Paraphrasing this concept mutatis mutandis, there is no place the Middle Passage stops and its after begins. At least under the laws of motion that dictate its (over) flows. This manifestation of these Rememories, for Beloved, become what the being refers to as "a hot thing." Beloved's refrain, "a hot thing," is the culmination of the complexity she states at the outset, the struggle to say things that are pictures. Jack-the-Bear struggles in the same realm, asking, "Could this compulsion to put invisibility down in black and white be thus an urge to make music of invisibility?"[69]

Jack-the-Bear appears here, or, more accurately, the subject who becomes Jack-the-Bear is in common existence with Beloved just after the explosion at the paint factory. Ellison opens chapter 11 with the following resonance with the "hot thing" that compels, alienates, and grounds Beloved:

> I was sitting in a cold, white rigid chair and a man was looking at me out of a bright third eye that glowed from the center of his forehead . . .
>
> Now I was lying on a cot, the bright eyes still burning into mine.[70]

The subject who would become Jack-the-Bear joins "crawling already?" who would become Beloved in the transitional space, *Purgatorium ex Media Loca*, which seems inextricably related to the subject-(dys)forming terror of the Middle Passage and, from this place, the subject who would become Jack-the-Bear can glimpse the soundscape that comes to define his existence in the Hole and 124:

> The static sounds became a quiet drone. Strains of music, a Sunday air, drifted from a distance. With closed eyes, barely breathing, I warded off the pain. The voice droned harmoniously. Was it a radio I heard—a phonograph? The *vox humana* of a hidden organ? If so, what organ and where? I felt warm Green hedges, dazzling with red

> wild roses appeared behind my eyes, stretching with a gentle curving to an infinity empty of objects, a limpid blue space. Scenes of a shaded lawn in summer drifted past; I saw a uniformed military band arrayed decorously in concert, each musician with well-oiled hair, heard a sweet-voiced trumpet rendering "The Holy City" as from an echoing distance, buoyed by a choir of muted horns; and above, the mocking obligato of a mocking bird. I felt giddy. The air seemed to grow thick with fine white gnats, filling my eyes, boiling so thickly that the dark trumpeter breathed them in and expelled them through the bell of his golden horn, a live white cloud mixing with the tones upon the torpid air.[71]

These echoes that come from the consciousness that allows the subject Jack-the-Bear to be revealed to himself through the trumpet of Louis Armstrong are leaking into the space of trauma constructed of memories of images and sound. The similarities of the spaces occupied by the subjects that will become Beloved and Jack-the-Bear aid us in "defining" where/when exactly they happen to find themselves. This is, perhaps, usefully analyzed via the granular description of the details that attend the preliminal, the liminal, and the postliminal spaces of what we know as the Middle Passage, accessed through the Door of No Return that is simultaneously the postliminal space of the point of transition from the Ante–Anti-Black World or $\text{World}_{\text{Prime}}$ to the Anti-Black World or World_1. The space described here, *Purgatorium ex Media Loca*, is obviously parallel to and in excess of the physical reality of the Middle Passage; a historical phenomenon in a discrete time and place that overflows the boundaries of that situatedness, forming a metaspace that is equally accessible by those as close to this reality as the child of an escaped enslaved woman and a student in the twentieth century on forced hiatus from a Historically Black College. It is a space that, as we have seen from Beloved's description of it provided to Denver, does not require those entombed there to be dead and for both announces itself through the lamentations of women. We read in *Invisible Man*, "By now the music became a distant wail of female pain"[72] that is cramped in concert with the inhumanity of the Hold:

> A pair of eyes peered down through lenses as thick as the bottom of a Coca-Cola bottle, eyes protruding, luminous and veined, like an old biology specimen preserved in alcohol.
>
> "I don't have enough room," I said angrily.
>
> "Oh, that's a necessary part of the treatment."
>
> "But I need more room," I insisted. "I'm cramped."
>
> "Don't worry about it, boy. You'll get used to it after a while. How is your stomach and head?"[73]

In this cramped and unstable space, the confusion of naming the self and alienation from genealogy trouble the subjects. Beloved asserts, as we have seen, again and again, that she is Beloved and that "she," Sethe, "is mine."[74] The subject who would become Jack-the-Bear, conversely, is unable to name both himself and his mother:

> Then he scribbled something on a large card and thrust it before my eyes:
>
> WHAT IS YOUR NAME?
>
> A tremor shook me; it was as though he had suddenly given a name to, had organized the vagueness that drifted through my head, and I was overcome with swift shame. I realized that I no longer knew my own name. I shut my eyes and shook my head with sorrow. Here was the first warm attempt to communicate with me and I was failing. I tried again, plunging into the blackness of my mind. It was no use; I found nothing but pain. I saw the card again and he pointed slowly to each word:
>
> WHAT . . . IS . . . YOUR . . . NAME?
>
> I tried desperately, diving below the blackness until I was limp with fatigue. It was as though a vein had been opened and my energy syphoned away; I could only stare back mutely. But with an irritating burst of activity he gestured for another card and wrote:
>
> WHO . . . ARE . . . YOU?
>
> Something inside me turned with a sluggish excitement. The phrasing of the question seemed to set off a series of weak and distant lights where the other had thrown a spark that failed. Who am I? I asked myself. But it was like trying to identify one particular cell that coursed through the torpid veins of my body. Maybe I was just this blackness and bewilderment and pain, but that seemed less like a suitable answer than something I'd read somewhere.[75]

The two subjects, both in the space we have named *Purgatorium ex Media Loca*, exist on a spectrum of something like self-awareness or perhaps the loss of having it or not. Beloved is certain of the identity of her mother and herself but that certainly is self-referentially true in the realm of Rememory, where recall and, therefore, relations are both transsubjective and transgenerational. The apparent consciousness Beloved has of the cognitive world of Rememory is seemingly a product of "crawling already?" being corporeally dead though spiritually resurrected and both inhabiting and receiving the memories of individuals from Black World$_{\text{Prime}}$ and the Anti-Black World, generally, and the Middle Passage, specifically:

We are not crouching now we are standing but my legs are like my dead man's eyes I cannot fall because there is no room to the men without skin are making loud noises I am not dead the bread is sea-colored I am too hungry to eat it the sun closes my eyes those able to die are in a pile I cannot find my man the one whose teeth I have loved a hot thing the little hill of dead people a hot thing the men without skin push them with poles the woman into the sea which is the color of bread she has nothing in her ears if I had the teeth of the man who dies on my face I would bite the circle around her neck bite it away I know she does not like it now there is room to crouch and to watch the crouching others it is the crouching that is now always now inside the woman with my face is in the sea a hot thing.[76]

Beloved is "seeing" and "interacting" with people, some presumably in her blood genealogy but all obviously in her genealogy of suffering, and becomes conscious of a resemblance to Sethe, who she knows as her mother, but these figures lack the "earrings" she expected to see that would serve to ground her recognition:

the woman with my face is in the sea
a hot thing

In the beginning I could see her I could not help her because the clouds were in the way in the beginning I could see her the shining in her ears she does not like the circle around her neck I know this I look hard at her so she will know that the clouds are in the way I am sure she saw me I am looking at her see me she empties out her eyes I am there in the place where her face is and telling her the noisy clouds were in my way she wants her earrings she wants her round basket I want her face a hot thing.[77]

Just as Beloved, while existing as the subject we know to be most appropriately called "crawling already?" describes her vision to be obscured, the subject who would become Jack-the-Bear is similarly denied clear sight, which only becomes more obscured from the inability to recall his mother's name when he also cannot come up with his own:

He shot questions at me: *Where were you born? Try to think your name.*

I tried, thinking vainly of many names, but none seemed to fit, and yet it was as though I was somehow a part of all of them, had become submerged within them and lost.

> *You must remember*, the placard read. But it was useless. Each time I found myself back in the clinging white mist and my name just beyond my fingertips.[78]

In the absence of a coherent "name," in the traditional sense of the term, for Morrison's subject, here we also witness that the complexity of naming in Ellison is in excess of the invisibility that serves as the overarching category of thinking in the text. The subject who would become Jack-the-Bear is able to think of "many names" but "none seem to fit," not because they are not apropos, but because he is "somehow a part of all of them."[79] As this subject struggles with this condition, his interlocutor continues to infantilize him by "produc[ing] a child's slate with 'meaningless names'"[80] that do not meet any of the manifold conditions of the being of this subject. His interlocutors lose patience because of his inability to satisfy their demands for him to "THINK," which causes "his eyes to blaze with annoyance."[81] This is a hot thing that returns us to Morrison's world; as these two realms begin to resolve themselves, we find: "There is no one to want me, to say me my name I wait on the bridge because she is under it there is night and there is day"[82] *Rememory it.*

Here in *Purgatorium ex Media Loca*, night and day become one, forming a temporal node that cannot resolve itself to allow for the calculation of linear time. This is the everlasting now that preoccupies Christina Sharpe, where the movement of time becomes evacuated of hope because daylight brings no hope, and it is also impossible to ever cry:

> daylight comes through the cracks and I can see his locked eyes I am not big small rats do not wait for us to sleep someone is thrashing but there is no room to do it in if we had more to drink we could make tears we cannot make sweat or morning water so the men without skin bring us theirs.[83]

In the absence of water, the slavers bring their urine to further befoul this place, an indignity that resonates with the fate of the imprisoned/enslaved Paul D, where:

> Occasionally a kneeling man chose a gunshot in his head as the price, maybe, of taking a bit of foreskin with him to Jesus. Paul D did not know that then. He was looking at his palsied hands, smelling the guard, listening to his soft grunts so like the doves, as he stood before the man kneeling in mist on his right. Convinced he was next, Paul D retched—vomiting up nothing at all. An observing guard smashed

> his shoulder with the rifle and the engaged one decided to skip the new man for the time being lest his pants and shoes get soiled by nigger puke.[84]

Paul D, like the subject who would become Jack-the-Bear, in his own space of *Purgatorium ex Media Loca*, craves the freedom that requires self-awareness. Returning to Ellison, who we have never actually left:

> Whoever else I was, I was no Sampson. I had no desire to destroy myself even if it destroyed the machine; I wanted freedom, not destruction. It was exhausting, for no matter what the scheme I conceived, there was one constant flaw—myself. There was no getting around it. I could no more escape than I could think of my identity. Perhaps, I thought, the two things are involved with each other. When I discover who I am I'll be free.[85]

"crawling already?" has run into the Rememory of subjects who have found themselves closer to some form of "escape," but not seemingly the one we are seeking, and this she can witness from the bridge where she waits:

> again again night day I am waiting no iron circle is around my neck no boats go on this water no men without skin my dead man is not floating here his teeth are down there where the blue is and the grass so is the face I want the face that is going to smile at me it is going to in the day diamonds are in the water where she is and turtles in the night I hear chewing and swallowing and laughter it belongs to me she is the laugh I am the laughter I see her face which is mine it is the face that was going to smile at me in the place where we crouched now she is going to her face is mine she is not smiling she is chewing and swallowing I have to have my face I go in the grass opens she opens it I am in the water and she is coming there is no round basket no iron circle around her neck she goes up where the diamonds are I follow her we are in the diamonds which are her earrings now my face is coming I have to have it I am looking for the join I am loving my face so much.[86]

Love of self is the "join" we have been seeking that is reached by the appearance of the bridge here in Morrison and has also been granted to us by Ellison: *Rememory it.*

> Along the walk the buildings rose, uniform and close together. It was day's end now and on top of every building the flags were fluttering

> and diving down, collapsing. And I felt that I would fall, had fallen, moved now as against a current sweeping swiftly against me. Out of the grounds and up the street I found a bridge by which I'd come, but the stairs leading back to the car that crossed the top were too dizzily steep to climb, swim or fly, and I found a subway instead.[87]

The violence of the separation of 124 from the Hole collapses here, and they pass one into the other because we need both/and to get beyond this place of recurrence. The Bridge that "crawling already?" finally crosses delivers her to 124 when, beneath that structure, Jack-the-Bear vibrates "on the lower frequencies."[88] We need both here, at the threshold where all of this collective sound must be reordered to disperse the objects that will appear to fool us into believing that this is as far as we can journey because the door is closed, and we must die. Beloved must be halted before she can recursively and mistakenly consume Sethe, and Jack-the-Bear must not be allowed to retrace the story that explains why he has become "so blue."[89] The story must not be allowed to reiterate and Rememory itself but at the same time cannot be forgotten. "crawling already?" and the subject who would become Jack-the-Bear, who asserts in chapter 1 that "It goes a long way back, some twenty years,"[90] must not be allowed to grow old. *Rememory it.*

Recall in Melville that Ishmael does not expose the gender of the Black Angel of Death in the pulpit. I do so here and assert that the voice he mishears involved in preaching the "blackness of darkness" is that of a woman who replaces the male preacher in Jack-the-Bear's consciousness with a voice that says the following:

> "Go curse your God, boy, and die."
> I stopped and questioned her, asked her what was wrong.
> "I dearly loved my master, son," she said . . .
> She sat with her head in her hands, moaning softly . . .[91]

Here Jack-the-Bear engages the voice of an enslaved woman who is moaning in the throes of the pain of having children as a product of sexual assault by her owner, while at the same time loving her sons and, in a thorough engagement with Freud, grappling with love and death. It is the moaning, which I will take for singing, that appears frequently in Morrison and leads us to the place of opening, described in *Beloved* in the following fashion:

> It was then, when Beloved finished humming, that Sethe recalled the clicks—the settling of pieces into places designed and made especially for them.[92]

Never Grow Old

What she want to go and do that for?

—TONI MORRISON, *BELOVED*

Recall that I promised that the node we are exploring will be loaded to the point of shattering. This loading often causes subjects to resist the telos of this pressure, asking, following Morrison's epigraph here, why it is happening in the way it is. This leads to a shattering that creates the condition of possibility for the destruction (perhaps healing) of the wound of Anti-Blackness. I want to make a gesture at elaborating the temporal realm we have assembled here using Morrison's metaphor of settling into place, which opens the way to this place of crossing: The Unlocking. I propose that we disorient the linear nature of time into a circularity here, where the events we are describing travel around the circumference of the circle at various speeds; unexpectedly accelerating, decelerating, or stopping altogether. The point we are mining, the node, exists in the temporal circles of the three instances of literary imaging, which also preoccupy a fourth, which we add momentarily. Imagine that these soon to be four circles represent the individual, self-referential temporality of each text, are assembled concentrically, and we can locate the point of common eventuality, the sermon, which has brought us to this place along each of them. At some point in the horizontal reckoning with the fantasy of linear time of the circular motion, they will align and produce the "click" that signals the moment of revelation for Sethe. This is where we need to further reframe our tracing of the temporal framework we are exploring from the horizontal and circular, halting all motion in the x-axis to a plunging of the depths of the nodal opening in the vertical plane that holds us in place at the moment of this gathering, where we can examine these instances simultaneously as a single instance in time. The internal time of Ishmael's journey to the *Pequod*, the drama that haunts the refugees of Sweet Home, the musical exploration in Jack-the-Bear's hole, as well as the writing and publication of all three texts, and, finally, where we find ourselves, the promised fourth layer, at the New Temple Missionary Baptist Church in Los Angeles in January 1972. *Rememory it.*

Now, fluent in the functioning of Rememory as the system of cognition that leads to new forms of consciousness, we are prepared to cross the threshold of the Door of ~~No~~ Return in order to establish the terms and conditions of Being-as-Black. Here, it is the lamentations of women that accompany, if not cause, this transition. We find ourselves at night two of Aretha Franklin's residency at the movie house turned place of worship. The crowd gathered on night two at New Bethel is discernibly different from the first night's, but I situate the dramatis personae for our Black Study.

Aretha Franklin preaching the Tophet, Mick Jagger as Ishmael, in this world lingering for Black Study and Rev. James Cleveland as Ellison's musical savant, Jack-the-Bear. The night before, the choir, relentlessly driven by its director Alexander Hamilton along with the pastoring of Rev. James Cleveland was Blacker. Night Two found Mick Jagger and Charlie Watts in the house, pushed to the periphery of the proceedings, signaling that the word had spread that something was happening at New Temple. That happening drew onlookers, who I label here as Melville's Black Parliament, to the second night, who could not have known the journey to and beyond that was ahead of them.

Hanif Abdurraqib memorializes this event in his text *A Little Devil in America: Notes in Praise of Black Performance*. Abdurraqib makes mention of Jagger's presence, writing "on that same night, Mick Jagger, tucked away in the back during one song, stands up to clap along, anxiety leaping to his face as he recognizes that he might not be on beat."[93] Indeed. However, my reading of this event is necessarily different as we approach it as a palimpsestic sight of Rememory or third sight that grants us consciousness of several things. First, Jagger, the Rememory of Ishmael, is necessarily out of time, which is different from being off beat because here, in this space, as we stand at the threshold of the fulfillment of new forms of consciousness that calls into being Being-as-Black, the rhythm of the Anti-Black World or World_1 has been dispersed. These are Syncopated People, not as a counterpoint or facile queering of 4/4 but as the norm whereby the symmetry of 4/4 finds itself anachronistic. The first pillar has fallen. The sense of time here is no longer governed by the Laws of Nature of the Anti-Black World or World_1. They are present, lingering, being dismantled piece by piece because we have not yet crossed, but the logic has altered and the Rolling Stones are spectators rather than spectacular, observers rather than observed.

Abdurraqib, like I am, is preoccupied with the performance of "Never Grow Old," his reading of which I recommend for its clarity, which presents an opening for this thinking as it understands it as the utterance of the Transfer Equation, the call for the quantum, and the laws of motion of Morrison's *third, if you will allow the term, world* translated into sounds that we have access to but that are heavy with the weight of the delimiting of the system of Being-as-Black, which has been, if not silenced, then, muffled for its true power. In substance, the words of Aretha's father, who Abdurraqib paraphrases as a form of the notice that "Aretha has never left the church,"[94] is operative here. We, on this journey, have also both left and never left the not, per se, church, but a particular space, where "church" becomes the most commonly available way to reference the place. Just like her career, at that point, which might have implied that she had left her gospel roots, her performance, generally, and the reading of "Never Grow Old," specifically, tell us something else. We have never left The Black World, and we can't be locked out of a space that has not been vacated, but what must happen is for guides to show us back, paradoxically, to where we already are.

One is naturally tempted to go directly to Aretha's performance of "Never Grow Old" here, but the groundwork for what is to come and its relevance for this project is provided by the introduction by her father, Rev. C. L. Franklin so it must be dealt with. First, however, Aretha and the choir perform "Climbing Higher Mountains" and two tunes that follow prior to her father speaking, and one is led to question that presentation decision. The closing moments of "Climbing" and the singing that follows drives the worshippers to a state of shouting and dancing frenzy that one can hardly imagine could be eclipsed. In this vein, the producers of the album, in contradistinction to the editing of the film, *Amazing Grace*, which is our text here, provide a different order, going directly to a rendition of "God Will Take Care of You," followed by "Old Landmark" and "Mary Don't Weep" (which we study as well), before getting to "Never Grow Old," and then Reverend Franklin. This is a mistake. The video presentation, for its clarity of the order of things, also allows many of the nuances of this intimate performance to be viewed if not completely necessarily understood. For instance, when Reverend Cleveland announces that Aretha and the Choir will take up the song that her father had been known to sing, "Climbing Higher Mountains," he seems startled and gospel giant Clara Ward, who is seated beside Reverend Franklin in the front row appears offended.

The performance drives the crowd to its feet, and then, as a form of transition, Reverend Cleveland repeats the refrain of "Climbing Higher Mountains," improvising around that theme. He and Aretha enter a call and response, when, at one point, Aretha sings/swings "Tell the story," and Reverend Cleveland continues to intonate "Climbing Higher Mountains," the implication being that the entire story is encapsulated in those three words and the manner in which they are repeated. Reverend Cleveland and Aretha then segue into the standard "Old Landmark," which, as the title implies, is a call for the old style of preaching. The fact that this version of the performance, the entirety, could have ended here speaks to the argument of this text. Aretha will not allow us to "Go Back to the Old Landmark," there is something ahead and even the worshippers who are cut steeping around the church, sure that this is the height of the performance, will have to reach for new reserves to meet the experience that will follow. The song ends abruptly, and we are at the point where Reverend Cleveland calls the Father of the Queen to the pulpit.

Reverend Franklin greets the crowd and praises the choir, pronouncing it as if it rhymes with "wire," and then admonishes Reverend Cleveland for disrupting what he labels as the "spirit and enthusiasm that Aretha has engendered here tonight." He then describes his daughter's performance as something intangible and impossible to describe but assures the worshippers that it is "more than that to [him]." Here, the system of cognition, Rememory, that has led us to this place of transition is described by Reverend Franklin. He describes the performance in this present as one that takes him back to their living room in Detroit when, at the age of six or seven, his daughter brought the same spirits to their home. He goes on to describe that, in the presence of Rememory come again as phenomenon, his response was almost to "bust wide open," reminiscent of the disaggregation of the spirit and self we have seen described in work by both Fanon and Sharpe, with *In the Wake*'s engagement with the art practice of Kara Walker. Here things become more complicated.

I noted before that the renowned gospel singer Clara Ward is seated next to Reverend Franklin, within an arm's reach of the piano that Aretha is about to wield. First Reverend Franklin shouts out "Mother Ward," Gertrude Ward, herself a famous gospel singer who has chosen to appear at this place decked out in a wig that calls to mind either a skunk or Cruella de Vil, if there is any need to differentiate between the two. Reverend Franklin locates her in the crowd, several rows from the front, and asserts that she too has rememory of this moment and then names the lineage from whence it comes: Reverend Cleveland, Mahalia Jackson, and Clara Ward, and then provocatively proposes that, by age eleven, Aretha has absorbed everything these artists have to offer and moved the form forward through a project of "synthesis." He then asserts that a conversation with "Mother Ward" prevented him from sleeping the night before and drove him to the airport to ensure he was in the room for these proceedings. He returns to his seat, and Aretha sits at the piano, mirroring the transition in *Invisible Man* from the male preacher to the meditative voice of a woman, and begins playing as if no one else or anything else needed to be done or said, as Reverend Cleveland, somewhat surprised, truncates his remarks to get out of the way.

The zone that Aretha Franklin has entered is only possible because of what preceded this moment. She arrives relaxed in resplendent sea foam green, echoing the description of Baby Suggs, holy's arboreal church in the text of *Beloved* that is described as:

> a wide-open place cut deep in the woods nobody knew for what at the end of a path known only to deer and whoever cleared the land in the first place. In the heat of every Saturday afternoon, she sat in the clearing while the people waited among the trees.[95]

From this space, Baby Suggs, holy exhorted the gathered Black people to love their bodies, which were not supposed to be cared for, preaching the gospel of RAJudy's *Sentient Flesh* via Hortense Spillers reading of the testimony of Thomas Wyndham:

> Here . . . in this here place, we flesh; flesh that weeps, laughs; flesh that dances on bare feet in the grass. Love it. Love it hard. Yonder they do not love your flesh.[96]

Aretha has entered a place of deep solace at such a distance from earthly disruption that, when her father mops her brow, she continues as if he does not exist. The opening ten words of the song, "I have heard of a land on a faraway strand," signal the altered temporal context we have inhabited, in that Aretha takes the better part of fifty-five seconds to unspool these lyrics sending her father into a fit of knowing laughter. After the recitation of these lyrics, the song is more so "mined" than performed. For the next eight or nine minutes, Aretha dispenses with the text and deals only with the following elements of the narrative, "'Tis the beautiful home of the soul" that she describes as having been built by Jesus threatening to displace Sam Cooke's polygonal articulation of the name of the Son of Man. "It was built by Jesus" she sings, "on high / that we never will die / 'tis is a land where we will never grow old."

Aretha will turn this line, turn it with her voice, probing the words for the point of release. Clara Ward observes Aretha carefully and, at one point, convinced of where she is going, front runs the artist's work and resolves the tension she has built by s(w)inging "grows old," mouthing the words to herself, but Aretha returns to "We'll never, never, grow old" singing it again and then renders the term "never" three times punctuating it with a soulful "Mmm-mm," before returning to the assertion that there is a land, a land where we will never grow old. Here she assembles what we will call a space, reminiscent of Ellison's nodes or Morrison's 124, what we might call a sonic "box" constructed of the form of the refusal: "Never," which, at this point, is filled with the "grow old" that renders its recitation redundant. This will not last.

The term "We" becomes the point of transition that allows Aretha to render the "we know a land" porous enough to accommodate the "we" of "we will never grow old" in that land. At this point, the first attempt at disruption of this journey occurs. Reverend Cleveland throws a towel at Aretha; barely missing her head. It is the shift from the forces of the refusal of "Never" to the presence of motion indicated by "Grow" that has served to jar Cleveland to reign this in. At this point, Aretha returns to the opening lines of the song now altered into a refrain: "I know that there is" when Clara Ward realizes that the entire paradigm has shifted. Aretha finishes for now, turning the chapel into the juke joint. Rather than resolving the "We ain't never gonna grow old," with an operatic coda that she swings summoning Sarah Vaughn and Ella Fitzgerald to the meeting, and there is a disruption.

As Aretha winds through her coda, "Mother Ward" has clambered to the front of the church and must be physically restrained from attacking the artist at work. Aretha plays on while this is sorted out and finally delivers the flourish that was expected and is now made impossibly more poignant by her patience and refusal. She will not be hurried across the Threshold and the choir rises to its feet, still not able to participate until she calls to them: "Never." They repeat, "Never." Again and again until she smears what could be "grow old" or "there is a land" before returning to the text explaining that "when you get through doing down here there is a land." To finish, she hammers on "Never" and then renders the church sanctuary, the gin house, the jazz club, the Motown recording studio, and the field, where her voice comes to us from across all the realms of hardship that plague Black Being and are now destabilized by her guidance to this place.

Aretha is momentarily exhausted and takes the seat she had occupied during her father's recitation while Reverend Cleveland responds to her performance. From her seat she beckons Cleveland with her vocal musings until he holds the microphone to her mouth, and she riffs that she "is so glad that [she's] got religion" and that her "soul is satisfied." Here, we learn that she has replaced the refusal "Never" with an emphatic "Yes it is!" and has crossed the threshold. In this crossing, she has resolved to take us all with her, she turns to the choir and during that call and response that is the employment of "so glad" as the point of inflection, Aretha's body shakes almost uncontrollably as she delivers her final "so glad." In contradistinction to the singularity of the Dead ancestor who flies alone in Morrison's *Song of Solomon*, she has not left us here to fend for ourselves. Through all of this, Aretha has granted us a name for the World both that has preoccupied us and that Morrison could only describe as a "*third, if you will pardon the expression, world*." That place in the new "land" is called "The Beautiful Home of the Soul."

Benediction

Here's a chance to dance our way out of our constrictions . . .

—Parliament, *One Nation under a Groove*

The service has come to an end and the question that hangs in the air is how to locate, migrate to, protect, and maintain Morrison's "*third, if you will pardon the expression, world*" or what Aretha calls "The Beautiful Home of the Soul." Here, I link the resonance of Aretha's exhortation to "Never Grow Old," the collapse of the node of vertical temporality, and Baby Suggs, holy's, preaching to her congregants, in the terms granted to us by George Clinton,

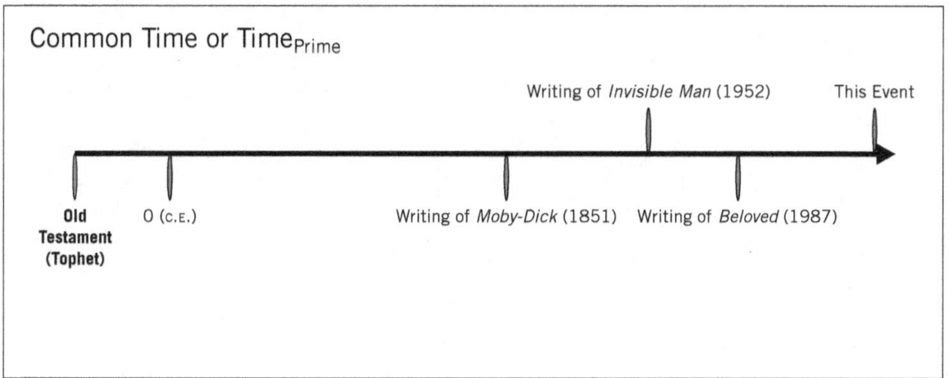

Figure 6 Common Time or $\text{Time}_{\text{Prime}}$.

to dance their way out of their constrictions. Language, put simply, tends to betray our efforts here. This book project identifies three realms or regimes of existence: Worlds that can also be understood as Homes implicated in that the architecture presented is designed to give the appearance of World. As described earlier, these are the world before the Middle Passage, the Anti-Black World after that crossing, where we are currently mired, and Morrison's third world, which provides an altered way of Being-as-Black. The complication with home, as exemplified by the comfort found in Ellison's Hole and Morrison's 124, is that we must establish the terms and conditions of resisting the desire for, or even the possibility of, rehabilitating the world/home that has been the locus of such misery in order to fulfill the potentiality of the power of imagining.

I am proposing that the literary assemblage I have presented operates in excess of what we commonly understand as intertextuality. Ralph Ellison, in the earliest moments of *Invisible Man*, picks up the thread of possibility that Melville teases, with the prospect that the text we know as *Moby-Dick* might have been redirected by Ishmael spending time with Black Study. This frames the temporal node that we have traced that reveals itself via clear reference to the manner in which these Events exist along the common reckoning of linear time, with the final event, here, the reading/thinking of this book as depicted in Figure 6.

It is when we establish the existence of the event or events present in each text that we take the first step in decentering the notion of linear temporality and the boundary of individual consciousness. As we look at the individual timelines of each text, we can locate the Tophet in this case as it represents the complexity of Black Death in inextricable relationality to the illogic of the Plantation. First, the temporality of Melville's *Moby-Dick* establishes this possibility, as seen in Figure 7.

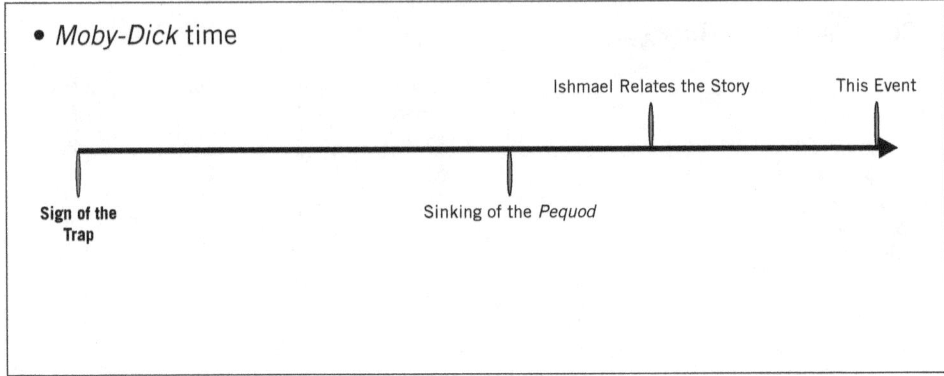

Figure 7 *Moby-Dick* time.

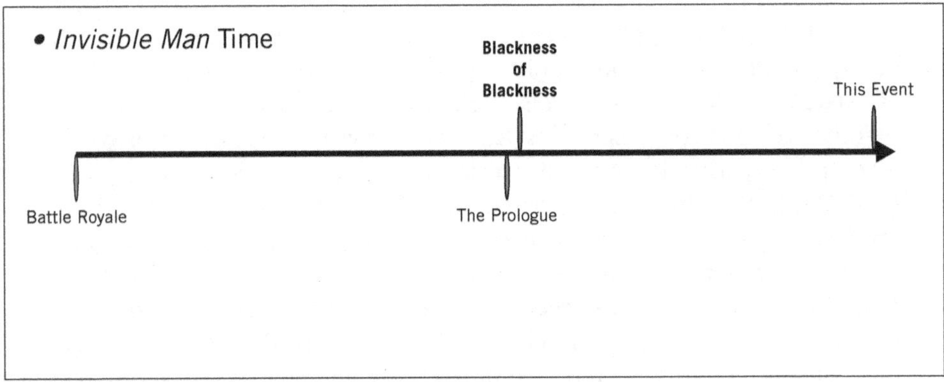

Figure 8 *Invisible Man* time.

Ellison's employment of the wormhole opened by Melville into the Black World becomes the driving force of the fractured temporality of his *Invisible Man*, which is illustrated in Figure 8.

This being said, it is Morrison's system of cognition, Rememory, that allows us the consciousness of the transsubjective, transgenerational, and, in this sense, transtextual nature of the power of Black Death as a pharmakon that is being examined here in service of the destabilization of the chaos of the Anti-Black World as seen in Figure 9.

This, ultimately, allows the formation of the temporal node that is exploited by Aretha Franklin with the possibility of aging without growing old as illustrated in Figure 10.

By compressing these events and listening to them vertically, the *longue durée* of the harm of Anti-Blackness ontologized by the event of the Middle Passage is re-dis-oriented to the y-axis to enable its rememory without eternal recurrence of the same in the parlance of Nietzsche, depicted in Figure 11.

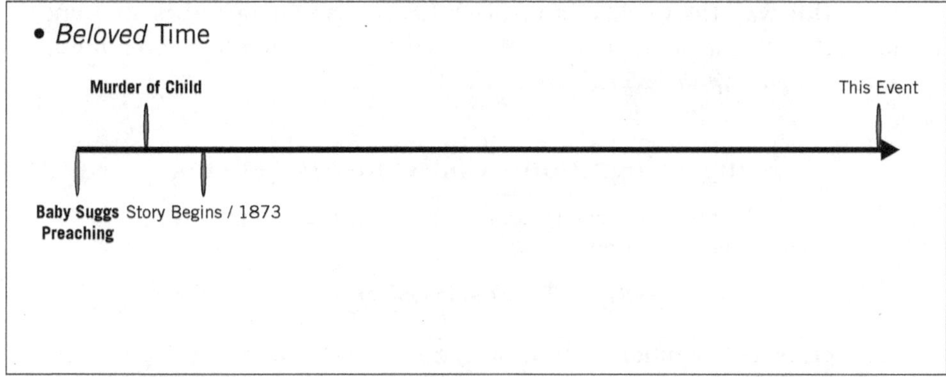

Figure 9 *Beloved* time.

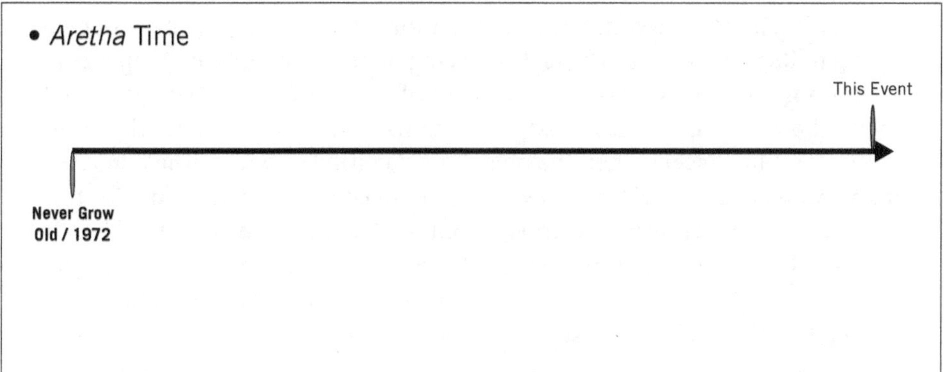

Figure 10 *Aretha* time.

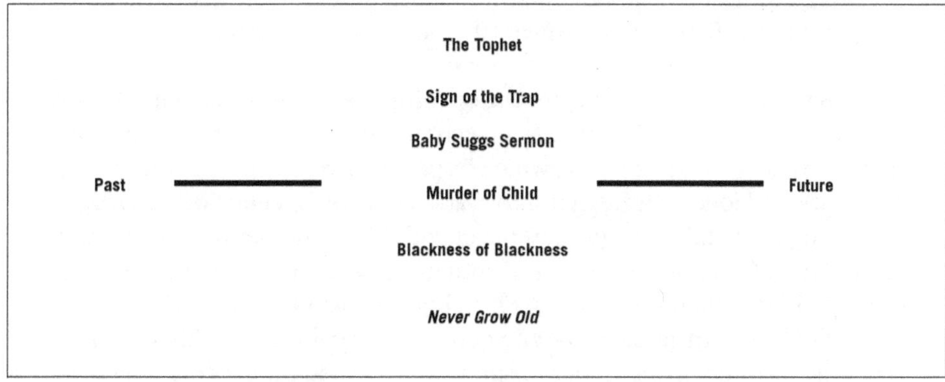

Figure 11 Vertical present time.

In this way, the world of anti-Black Racism is reimagined as an event horizon, or threshold, that here represents the entrepôt to Morrison's "*third, if you will pardon the expression, world.*"

Being—Cognition—Consciousness—Being

> The pulse came swift and staccato, increasing gradually until I fairly danced between the nodes.
>
> —Ralph Ellison, *Invisible Man*

Being precedes Cognition and Consciousness. It is the pace of things, as referenced here by the epigraph from Ellison, that requires us to find moments of peace in order to properly consider the shift from one stage of awareness to the next.

Cognition and Consciousness, however, are the necessary causal steps in bringing Being into concrete awareness for subjects who have been denied access to its true essence. The fact of having neither the tools for proper cognition nor consciousness and awareness of a phenomenal object does not mean the thing does not already exist as itself. This is of particular difficulty, as we have seen, when the object is struggling to bear witness to a self it has been acculturated to believe does not exist. What that means for this project is that Blackness as such is an ontological precondition that has the status of Being. This argument is challenged by the first-rate work of scholars like Calvin L. Warren, who writes the following in his 2018 text *Ontological Terror: Blackness, Nihilism, and Emancipation.*

> [Warren] argue[s] that the question of black ~~being~~ constitutes a proper metaphysical question, and this question leads us into the abyss of ontology: blackness lacks Being (which is why we write being under erasure in relation to black). Unlike humanists and post-metaphysicians, I argue that Being is not universal or applicable to black.[97]

Warren's intervention creates the opening for the thinking here that argues, in a conversational rather than a conflictual sense, with the construction of a theory of Black Being, which is, pace Warren, a "proper metaphysical question." I follow, through improvisation, Warren's syntactical convention in arguing with and through a rewrite of both Black and Being in the sense of recognizing the ontological status of both in reference to one another through the capitalization and unstriking of "being" as a companion to the manner in which I have reinstated the notion of return by striking "no." This thinking is heavily invested in and under the protection of Fred Moten's ongoing meditation on the "black tradition," as seen in the opening chapter of *Stolen Life: consent not to be a single being*, which reads:

> This is to say that the most important thing we have to imagine about the black tradition—about the radical, paraontological totality that is its motive force—is that it is common. Blackness is, therefore, older than Africa and its diaspora in the broadest and most ancient senses that this sentence can bear. What remains in us of Africa—as the very condition of possibility of the remainder—is its ordinary trace. Such imagining is (in) the (double) vision of a paraontological difference.[98]

Being-as-Black is the necessary result of the following cause-and-effect relationship that begins with $\text{Being}_{\text{Prior}}$ and elaborates itself as the $\text{Being}_{\text{Prime}}$, and which Moten would witness as the "Blackness . . . (in) common" that has a need of remembering rather than discovery.[99] This is realized both by the new form of cognition (Rememory) that accomplishes just that in trans-subjective and transgenerational fashion and by instituting what Alain Badiou would call an Event. Previous permutations of this flow, without the benefit of Rememory and the result of new consciousness, have resulted in an infinite return and retracing that has been the predictable outcome of an assault on Black Consciousness. Lewis Gordon grants us clarity here by differentiating black consciousness from Black consciousness in his 2022 *Fear of Black Consciousness*:

> This book is an exploration of black consciousness and *Black* consciousness. Briefly, black consciousness is mostly affected and sometimes immobile; Black consciousness is effective and always active. Both are feared in antiblack societies, although the second is more so than the first.[100]

Following Gordon, black consciousness is the cause of the infinite return that cannot see its way out of the deprivation of Anti-Blackness. The latter, Black consciousness, is on the path to the form of Being that rejects all notions of its lack and has found momentum without forgetting.

I referenced Badiou earlier, and it is the Twenty-Ninth Meditation, "The Folding of Being and the Sovereignty of Language," from his text *Being and Event*, that assists in unraveling the layers of complexity here. I wish to get at the thinking Badiou follows through the employment of set theory by also insisting that we do so with the work of Graham Priest on nonlogical sets in mind,[101] which fills in the gap identified by Badiou:

> Inclusion, by means of the logico-immanent filter, is *tightened around* belonging.
>
> The idea is to constitute the void as the "first" level of being and to pass to the following level by "extracting" from the previous level all the constructible parts; that is, all those definable by an explicit property of the language on the previous level. Language thereby progressively enriches the number of pure multiples admitted into existence without letting anything escape from its control.[102]

As we stand here, in the break or the node we have come to recognize, we have been betrayed repeatedly by language. Awareness of that betrayal allows us to dismount white supremacist's definitions that are designed to decouple Blackness from Being, which, along with the discourse of Death, has been employed to defeat progress. In order to make the leap by Rememorying the primacy of Blackness, we have to rethink the possibility and potentiality of memorial in relation to Death to rerealize sovereign Black Being as the threshold condition and steady state of World.

Returning to Warren allows us to deal productively with the deleterious effects of the linguistic convention that burdens the question of Being through a "Heideggerian reading of Greek philosophy":[103]

> For the Greeks "Being" says *constancy* in a twofold sense:
>
> 1. Standing-in-itself as arising and standing forth (*phosis*)
> 2. But as such, "constantly" that is, enduringly, abiding (*ousia*)
>   Not-to-be accordingly, means to step out of constancy that has stood-forth in itself; *existasthai*—"existence," "to exist," means, for the Greeks, precisely, not-to-be. The thoughtlessness and vapidity with which one uses the words "existence" and "to exist" as designators for Being offer fresh evidence of our alienation from being and from an originally powerful and definitive interpretation of it.
>
> My presentation of black existence, then, reworks this Greek understanding of existence as non-being (or more precisely "not-to-be"), according to Heidegger (since this Greek presentation of the human's being, I will argue, has already excluded the Hottentot, the black thing).[104]

This is a fine reading of Heidegger's reading of classical notions of Being and then a linkage to the racist understandings of Blackness based, in no small part, on the aesthetic conventions of the West, which necessarily find the Black body definitively unbeautiful and subhuman and perhaps sublime. What is important here is the concretization of the limitations of this thinking, exhibited by the points where Heidegger notices the same, by writing, "For the Greeks," which he takes to grant the formulation the imprimatur of foundational thinking but really means that it can necessarily be considered one of many things they likely had absolutely wrong; at least as it applies to the notion of Blackness. For instance, the following is the classical understanding of the universe of which the Greek World (the whole world for the Greeks) is a central part:

> In this system the entire universe was part of a great sphere. This sphere was split into two sections, an outer celestial realm and an inner terrestrial one. The dividing line between the two was the orbit of the moon. While the earth was a place of transition and flux, the heavens were unchanging. Aristotle posited that there was a fifth substance, the quintessence, that was what the heavens were made of, and that the heavens were a place of perfect spherical motion.[105]

In short, wrong. Devastatingly so. A longer way to say this, in keeping with the epistemological claims of this project, is that the Greeks had an insufficiently acute tool with which to gain cognition of the universe, which led to a profoundly flawed understanding of it and a predictably bizarre understanding of their place in it. Similarly, not to put too fine a point on it, but Heidegger among others says a lot of racist stuff of which the linking of the depraved understanding of Black subjectivity to a flawed notion of Being cannot help but bring about a problematic understanding of these essential concepts.

One might turn to cosmogony and accounts of being from systems of thought, "Worlds," that are not oppositional in dialectic fashion to the white supremacists' mazelike structures of accounting for being that are designed to do away with the possibility of Black Being to propose that there is no reason to allow Blackness to be understood only via the Greeks through Heidegger and in the shadow of the Hottentot. For instance, one might want to consider the possibility of viewing Being-as-Black from the perspective of the Dogon, as expressed to the anthropologist Marcel Griaule in all of its flaws, which exists at such a distance from Western cosmogony that some proposed it must have come from alien contact. This is exemplified by discourse reported by Griaule and attributed to the Dogon Sage Ogotemmêli that asserts the explicit cognitive distortion outsiders (Europeans) experience when encountering this system of knowing:

> In the course of the sixteenth conversation the Nazarene asked why the different objects in the sanctuary (which was also a tomb and a smithy) were so scattered that it was impossible to understand their meaning.

"The objects are scattered," replied Ogotemmêli, "in order to conceal their symbolism from those who would like to understand them."

In short, for the uninitiated, the interior and the whole structure of the building constituted a riddle without an answer.[106]

Note the intellectual conceit of the system of understanding of Griaule. Rather than admitting that there are systems of expression and, therefore, being that he cannot understand, he decides that the riddles are not riddles at all but just non sequiturs beneath the status of coherent jokes.

Even more ancient and unrelated to the world of Anti-Black Racism would be the meditations from vizier Ptah-Hotep from the Old Kingdom of Egypt "around 2640–2040 BC."[107] This is, first of all, not to require us to understand that the construction of Being-as-Black must proceed from the ancients or the Dogon, but it is also to say that it could. Or it can proceed from a position of taking seriously the superattenuated tool of Cognition we have at our disposal, which has survived the most wretched excesses of white supremacy, and use it to realize Morrison's third world.

We have found ourselves at the point of crossing, and, in order to do so, we must clear the path of our Dead and the preoccupation and occupation of Black Life with Black Death, social or otherwise. We have "time," in that, following Fanon and his acolytes and critics, we are both too early and too late but intend to avail ourselves of the subject-restoring and -forming potentiality of this node to take a look around before we leap forward to a new understanding rather than back to whence we came. We have time for a short break here in the Break, principally to review the situation, rally our energy, and propose and execute a way forward. In support of the journey to this place of crossing, we have carefully assembled a new mode of cognition based on Toni Morrison's understanding of the manner in which memory assembles itself into objects that we encounter and properly understand as Rememory, which we are using here as a technology of cognition rather than limiting it to a description of things seen and incompletely understood. This allows these objects to flow into awareness as they will. This practice is what I understand as the first sure steps into Christina Sharpe's "Wake Work":

> I've been thinking about what it takes, in the midst of the singularity, the virulent antiblackness everywhere and always remotivated to keep breath in the Black body. What ruttier, internalized, is necessary now to do what I am calling wake work as aspiration, that keeping breath in the Black body?[108]

The desire to analyze rather than to accumulate and assemble Rememory for its utility has amounted to the substance of the second phase of this journey. As we examined and then employed cognition, we turned that instrument on Hegel's description of white supremacy and Anti-Blackness in order to identify its points of weakness that allow us to mount a thorough and decisive attack on its logic, which positions death as the sine qua non of self-consciousness. In that exercise, the omnipresence of Black Death, situated as a lure to the continued perdition of those deceived by this system, is exposed. In interrogating Black Death, we are led to the necessity of conceptualizing ways of properly mourning the Dead who have been sacrificed by, to, and for the machinery of Anti-Blackness, which is determined to produce and maintain the conditions for white supremacy. That functionality creates the laws of motion that pose as the force(s) of nature forming the architecture of white supremacy posing as World. Recall here that Death, real and "metaphysical" (i.e., Patterson's Social Death), especially the latter, in that it is not corporeal, guards the integrity of this simulacrum of world. Approaching its load-bearing walls with the intention of their destruction results in death, and the effigies of those who have done so are mingled with the death masks of those who find themselves serving as reminders of the dangers that lurk in predictably unpredictable fashion.

The substantive challenge is to deal with the complexity of mourning and its linkage to violent resistance revealed by the Fanon essay we worked with before, "The Algerian Family," where he writes the following:

> Lamentation and grief stricken faces are part of a patterned, stable world. One does not weep, one does not do as before when one is faced with multiple murders. One further step, and it is cries of joy that salute the death of the *moudjahid* who has fallen on the field of honor. It must not be believed, however, that the traditional ceremonies are repeated in the case of natural deaths resulting from illnesses or accidents. Even then, it seems virtually impossible to revive the traditional techniques of despair. The war has dislocated Algerian society to such a point that any death is conceived of as a direct or indirect consequence of colonialist repression.
>
> Today there is not a dead person in Algeria who is not the victim of French colonialism. It is impossible for an Algerian civilian to remain untouched by the war of colonial re-conquest. More than this, there is not a death of an Algerian outside of Algeria which is not attributable to French colonialism. The Algerian people have decided that until independence, French colonialism will be innocent of none of the wounds inflicted upon its body and its consciousness.[109]

As I am writing this, the howling savagery of the war against the body and consciousness of Gaza and, therefore, all of us must be understood as a step around this circle of violence both that we have identified as the retaining wall of Anti-Blackness and that flattens the relationship between even the most lurid acts of state-sanctioned mass murder to a seemingly unrelated traffic accident or quiet death during sleep. They are all the "same," in that the context of the event is against the backdrop of an architecture being designed to render harm at an alarming and predictably unpredictable rate. In the "world" that serves as the backdrop for these events, all deaths remain, until an alternative context of being erupts, impossible to mourn and as such render everywhere-one-place-time as combatants. This requires two moves. First, a rethinking of mourning and, second, to visit the question of violence as response and/or technology of subject re-creation. Recall that the lamentations of women have brought us to this point of transition, and, in service of this clearing, we must weep once more through the exhortation not to do so. The linkage to mourning of a particular type may not seem obvious, and, in order to properly expose it, we continue to linger in the space of performance and worship that has framed the boundaries of this node that we must continue to load in excess of its capacity.

Calling Back the Dead

Lazarus . . . Lazarus . . . Lazarus . . .

—Aretha Franklin, "Mary, Don't You Weep"

As we have lingered in this node, the concentric circles have continued to spin perpetually and without interruption both inside and outside of our hearing and awareness, continuing to emphasize the anachronism of attempting to take stock of these phenomena in linear fashion.

The film presentation of this song is insufficient for the proper consideration of this object of Black Art, so I instead focus on the album version, which is more complete. As we have seen in the previous analysis of this performance, we visit this productively out of sequence and see in short order the asynchronous nature of the internal plot of the song itself. The performance exposes the linkage Franklin perceives between mourning/lamentations, resistance to the same, and Divine Violence, as described by Walter Benjamin in his canonical essay, "Critique of Violence."[110]

The song in question, based on the title and the majority of its text, is a telling of the events described in the book of John (11:1–44), which serve as the "dry-run," so to speak, of what we examined earlier in this book, regarding the "raising of the body" as analyzed by Jean-Luc Nancy. Once again, Mary Magdalene assumes an important role, along with her sister Martha, their erstwhile-dead brother, Lazarus, and, of course, Jesus.

As the story goes, both in John and as told by Aretha here, Lazarus dies while Jesus and his Disciples are away, and Martha, upon their return to the outskirts of the city, asserts, "Lord, if you had been here, my brother would not have died" (John 11:21). After confirming that she, Martha, believes that Jesus is the Messiah, she is convinced that Lazarus will rise again, not as a result of the Last Judgment, but, in advance, as almost a proof of concept for the resurrection to come.

Aretha's version sticks close to the source document except for the opening moments, when, on top of the groove established by the choir, which modulates between telling Mary not to weep and Martha not to moan, she begins with a recitation of the destruction of the Pharaoh's army by the Red Sea in the Old Testament Book of Exodus:

> Pharaoh's Army (Pharaoh's Army)
> All of them men got drowned in the sea one day (Drowned in the Red Sea)

Then, Aretha inserts herself into the narrative, wondering at the possibility of being at the same vantage point as Moses at the critical moment before returning to the text of John and the story as it is generally presented in the New Testament:

> Now if I could (If I could)
> If I could I surely would (Surely would)
> I'd stand right upon the rock, yes I would
> (Stand on the rock)
> I'd stand right where Moses stood (Moses stood)
> Yes I would

This juxtaposition requires us to wonder what the Old Testament event of what Benjamin would understand as Divine Violence has to do with the New Testament raising Lazarus from the dead, who, as Aretha and the choir exhort, we ought never weep nor moan about. This seems to indicate the conjuring of another node on the part of Aretha or, perhaps, adding to the one that has brought us to the place of crossing. Aretha has queered time again and rendered as coincident events the destruction of the Egyptian army in the Red Sea, the raising from the dead of Lazarus by Christ, and the sonic prohibition on mourning the fallen. The through line must be something like a consideration, at this point, of taking seriously the role of violence as the corrective both to improper mourning and state-sanctioned violence against marginalized people.

I have referred here to the circularity of events as something that feels like, but isn't quite, a "corrective" to the verticality of time rather than its procession in linear fashion. This is a way to continue to further disorient the linear consideration of these events, first, to a vertical plane where and when they can be encountered all at once and, then, to identify the centrifugal force of this motion, which must be interrupted. This is the concentric notion of the timeline of these events that has to "align" itself to render the unlocking we seek.

Recall that, via Aretha, the question of mourning becomes linked to the question of divine violence, which allows a return to Fanon to continue to interrogate that technology and its place in this thinking. Fanon deals with the question of the manner in which this perpetual motion machine of violence is interrupted in *The Wretched of the Earth*, by saying:

> To blow the colonial world to smithereens is henceforth a clear image within the grasp and imagination of every colonized subject. To dislocate the colonial world does not mean that once the borders have been eliminated there will be a right of way between the sectors. To destroy the colonial world means nothing less than demolishing the colonist's sector, burying it deep within the earth or banishing it from the territory.[111]

It is the burial that we need to situate as the primary goal that will then unlock the possibility of new forms of Being. Fanon's fallback position, banishment, is insufficient to the cause of realizing Being-as-Black:

> No Algerian really thought these terms too violent. The tract merely expressed what every Algerian felt deep down: colonialism is not a machine capable of thinking, a body endowed with reason. It is naked violence and only gives in when confronted with greater violence.[112]

This is the point of inflection, and here it is not possible to avoid dealing with this pronouncement by Fanon, which finds itself echoed in the voices of Malcolm X, Huey P. Newton, Angela Davis, and so on, as we struggle to understand the role of violence as the mode of resistance that delivers proper destruction of the machinery of oppression and new ways of Being and the evacuation of weeping and moaning as mourning. Fanon is aware of the danger here and, in the conclusion of *The Wretched of the Earth*, delivers the terms and conditions that we must reckon with:

> The Third World must start over a new history of man which takes account of not only the occasional prodigious theses maintained by Europe but also its crimes, the most heinous of which have been com-

> mitted at the very heart of man, the pathological dismembering of his functions and the erosion of his unity, and in the context of his community, the fracture, the stratification and the bloody tensions fed by class, and finally, on the immense scale of humanity, the racial hatred, slavery, exploitation and, above all the bloodless genocide whereby one and a half billion men have been written off.
>
> So comrades, let us not pay tribute to Europe by creating states, institutions, and societies that draw their inspiration from it.
>
> Humanity expects other things from us than this grotesque and generally obscene emulation.
>
> If we want to transform Africa into a new Europe, America into a new Europe, then let us entrust the destinies of our countries to the Europeans. They will do a better job than the best of us.
>
> But if we want humanity to take one step forward, if we want to take it to another level than the one where Europe has placed it, then we must innovate, we must be pioneers . . .
>
> For Europe, for ourselves and for humanity. Comrades, we must make a new start, develop a new way of thinking, and endeavor to create a new man.[113]

One cannot do justice to this thinking without making a clear and careful reference to and engaging with David Marriott's *Wither Fanon: Studies in the Blackness of Being*, where he writes:

> I decided to re-read Fanon's theory of violence to ask whether we should conclude from it that Fanon, was, as some have claimed, a naïve apologist for terrorism. . . . To that end, I began to consider whether the response to colonial violence or the violence of the colonial state was simply part of a means-ends thinking that defined the political tradition, or whether it was indeed something different.[114]

For his part, Marriott requires that we address Fanon's thinking on decolonial violence from a perspective of locating its delocation from "the political fear of violence"[115] as the point of the desire rather than its method:

> Arendt describes Fanonian violence as pre-political, instrumentalist, and anti-democratic. Leaving aside for the moment, the violence of Arendt's own opening exclusion (of violence from the political), she starts from the view that violence is the resort of the powerless, and, as such, represents the lowest common denominator of political action. . . . Arendt consequently condemns Fanonism as a nihilistic example of anti-political theft.[116]

Marriott rightly locates Arendt's disdain for Fanon as an irrefutable disdain/fear of the notion of Black revolutionary praxis, which refuses what he describes as its "radical reinvention of the relation between democracy and violence."[117] It is worth noting that Kathryn Sophia Belle's (published as Kathryn T. Gines) *Hannah Arendt and the Negro Question* is the definitive analysis of this flaw in Arendt's thinking.[118] Marriott further underscores the understanding that "how we recall Fanon has become literally interrupted by the (white) stereotype we have of him." All of this proceeds for Marriott from what Fanon locates as the lack of "ontological resistance" of Blackness.[119] It is this precise "moment" where this project is further able to differentiate its approach from this understanding on the part of Marriott via Fanon, in that Marriott understands Fanonian violence to be the necessary and sufficient condition for the potential of the amelioration of "being-as-lack-or-deficit."[120] At the end of the day, and also the beginning and middle of it, Marriott concludes that there is no true Being for the Black or for Blackness:

> It suffices that structurally, blackness cannot conform to this expiation, and precisely because the *colonisés* cannot identify with the whiteness in them (in them more than them, as Lacan might say). Thus they can only respect blackness, as I have shown, as an imposed mask, or stain, that humiliates them—guilt being the effect of a law that humiliates all black egotistical presumption and self-esteem, because it comes from a place beyond our desires, beyond our being more generally.[121]

As I have made clear, from very early in this project, I do not understand Blackness to be an imposed condition on subjects who were non-Black until being defined as such by white supremacy and paradoxically Anti-Blackness. Blackness in the thinking here or Being-as-Black precedes its instantiation within the architecture posing as the world of Anti-Blackness, which, following Marriott to a point, is the location of desire and law. Stated simply, the assertion by Fanon, employed as the opening epigraph of Marriott's text, is the point of radical and generative tension:

> However painful it may be for me to accept this conclusion, I am obliged to state it: For the black man there is only one destiny. And it is white.[122]

This telos, what Morrison would understand as a "choice," is predicated on the assumed/presupposed nature of Blackness, which, because of that fractured point of departure, has no positive logic associated with its instantiation. Marriott writes:

> For Fanon, blackness can only find its ontological fulfillment by no longer being black—or by entering its own abyssal significance. Now that this book is finished, I see signs of this everywhere, including in myself, and I detest its effects at the same time as I am fascinated by this desire not to be black.[123]

As has been made abundantly clear, this project takes a different approach, and I have no desire to be anything other than Black. Following Sharpe to Aretha's reconsideration of the rebirth of Lazarus, the work to "keep breath in the Black body" is first the resistance to improperly weeping and moaning lest we find the answer in violent reciprocity rather than the restorative practice of Love. With that in mind, the question remains how to relate the Fanonian desire for a "new (hu)man" with the technology of violence in the paradigm proposed here. With this in mind, I propose that we take up the twinned discourse of resurrected mortality and divine violence via Aretha Franklin.

Concerning a Critique of Any Violence Necessary

Our study here, through its need to interrogate the subject-(dys)forming nature of Death as the constant companion of Black Life under the regime of Anti-Blackness, has left the question of the terms and conditions of resistance to physical threats to the side. Defense. Self or otherwise. Offense. Self or otherwise. It is necessary now to consider the way in which the ubiquity of death leads to the potential for violence to be understood as *a*, if not *the*, primary tool of subject making in the depraved moral culture of the Anti-Black World.

As a point of departure, following the title of this section, I want to bring another thinker to this conversation, Malcolm X, who has been reductively understood to be, at best, an apologist for violence, if not a promoter of it. I believe, and have written in another text, *Black Minded: The Political Philosophy of Malcolm X*, that Malcolm X presents the most coherent bridge between the analysis of subjectivity presented by W.E.B. Du Bois and the subject-(dys)forming nature/necessity of violence exposed by Fanon. This thinking must necessarily be further complicated by ensuring that we account for the admonition we have carried with us from Morrison to properly understand double consciousness as a choice. That epistemological stance, resisting a teleological presupposition of inevitability that resists thinking otherwise, can also be applied to the manner in which violence has been characterized as having various forms that are related inextricably to the threshold consideration of something like legitimacy: a legitimacy defined by the forces who are necessarily opposed to the "violence." Here, I am again thinking of the taxonomy presented by Walter Benjamin as similarly subject to being decentered to the level of "choice" rather than understood to be an all-encompassing inevitability.

It is useful here to first deal with Benjamin, in spite of, or perhaps because of, the broad understanding of his critique. That influential essay, "Toward the Critique of Violence," proposes that there are three phenomena that order themselves under the category of violence and are identified by their relation to "law and justice."[124] This is, in large measure, an effort that reflects the situation here, which asks us to come to some understanding as to both the legitimate employment of violence and, further, what happen to be the legitimate technologies of violence, assuming that it is to be legitimately employed. The latter, legitimate prosecution of violence as an essential component of Just War Theory, is beyond the scope of this project from a perspective of the detail of any specific technology or methodology of killing. Perhaps, more importantly, within the world of Anti-Blackness, it is understood that there is no legitimate justification for violence on the part of Black people much less the need to consider what type of violence is acceptable. Benjamin's argument only partially accounts for the concerns illuminated here, which immediately distort the possibility of reciprocity between actors when a party to the encounter is Black. Benjamin writes:

> The meaning of the differentiation of violence into legitimate and illegitimate is not immediately obvious. To be decisively rejected is the misunderstanding arising from natural law in which this meaning would consist in the distinction between violence used for just ends and unjust ends. Rather, as was already indicated, positive law demands from every form of violence evidence of its historical origin, which under certain conditions conserves its legality, its sanction. . . . For the sake of simplicity, the following discussion refers to those of contemporary Europe.[125]

Two important threshold issues arise from careful consideration of this passage. First, in a "world" where the Black subject is considered to be a nonhistorical actor, there is no coherent methodology, under this logic, to construct an argument for legitimate violence on the part of Black actors on a historical basis as required here by Benjamin. Second, the implication of this further closes the door on the coherence and utility of Benjamin in thinking about violence on behalf of Black subjects because, for the sake of "simplicity," his analysis is related to "contemporary European conditions,"[126] further rendering the possibility of legitimate Black violence immediately and thoroughly incoherent. Therefore, Benjamin's assertion that "all violence as a means is either law making or law-preserving"[127] is inapplicable to acts of violence committed by those who are structurally understood to lack a coherent tether to historical origin. This means that any and all acts of violence by Black actors within the context of the world of Anti-Blackness are illegitimate.

To deal more comprehensively with the first issue, the notion of "historical origin" forces the consideration of the discernment of proximate cause as it relates to the justification of violence. This thinking can be expanded by improvising in and around Malcolm X's speech at the founding rally of the Organization of African American Unity on June 28, 1964. The ubiquitous tagline "By Any Means Necessary" has been reduced to a declaration of violence independent of its legitimacy. It is essential to explore that formulation by Malcolm X to properly situate it for our purposes:

> So we have formed an organization known as the Organization of African American Unity which has the same aim and obligation—to fight whoever gets in our way, to bring about the complete independence of people of African descent here in the Western Hemisphere, and first here in the United States, and bring about the freedom of these people by any means necessary.
>
> That's our motto. We want freedom by any means necessary. We want justice by any means necessary. We want equality by any means necessary.
>
> So the purpose of the Organization of African American Unity is to unite everyone in the Western Hemisphere of African descent into one united force. And then, once we are united among ourselves in the Western Hemisphere we will unite with our brothers on the motherland on the continent of Africa.[128]

There are several things to note here. First, Malcolm X is making an explicitly international argument from a position of a specific form of Blackness that appears in the United States, particularly, and the Western Hemisphere, generally. Second, Malcolm proposes a sequence of phenomena that requires hemispheric cohesion before encountering Africa. Malcolm's tripartite call for freedom, justice, and equality, as well as the status of what he calls, "complete independence," are all things for which he asserts the charter of the Organization of African American Unity requires that they "fight anyone who gets in [their] way."[129]

Third, the language of "fighting" must be understood to be the linkage to a notion that these claims of no limitation to means are reductively understood to include every and only means of physical violence rather than the assertion that violence is just one of many other "means." The complication here is to link Malcolm X's assertion that there is a structural imperative within the world of Anti-Black Racism that asserts that all agitation on the part of Black subjects for freedom, justice, and equality is already and always violent even if the agitation is empirically nonviolent.

In *Black Minded: The Political Philosophy of Malcolm X*, I demonstrated how the structural apparatus that adjudicates the question of violence versus nonviolence is designed to view any type of protest designed to destabilize the status quo as violent and addressed as such. Meaning, every move to counter Anti-Blackness is violent:

> Where Malcolm X advances the thinking of Fanon here, and this is perhaps an inevitable alteration based upon the differences in the phenomena observed by these two thinkers, is to witness the necessity of understanding non-violence as violence in the perception of colonial/American power. This responds to the important revelation by Yack[130] that all revolution is viewed through the violence and dystopia of the French Revolution. What this means for the thinking of Malcolm X is that he is forced to qualify his revolutionary notion of Black people being empowered to vote as "Bloodless" to mark that it will be perceived as violent and that it is *de facto* violent in that it tends to decenter if not dismantle the dominant worldview. This resolves while at the same time recertifies the primary difficulty in examining the thought of Malcolm X that tends to be overwhelmed by the idea that he is espousing a system of violent and futile confrontation between Black and white in America—if not, as we have seen, on a planetary basis.[131]

At the outset, I proposed a taxonomy of violence that was separated into offense and defense and, further, the particularity of self and the abstraction of "otherwise." To the Black subject, situated here in Sharpe's Wake, and prepared to leap from Ellison's node to Morrison's "*third, if you will pardon the expression, world*," the only form of coherent violence is Otherwise.

This Violence Otherwise or Otherwise Violence is necessarily understood itself to be both offensive and defensive and delimited from the constraints of the notion of self-defense. A threshold condition of the total destabilization of the Anti-Black World is to abandon having the notion of the protection of the Black self effectively evacuated of the imperative of judgment by the system of Anti-Blackness. The condition of possibility here is restricted by the complexity of police violence under the terms and conditions explicated by Benjamin, that is, law establishing and law maintaining at the same time. This means that the dismantling of the established regime of Black Death to the machine of colonial violence described and diagnosed by Fanon, which is both totalizing and the obstruction to properly mourning its tragic output, is the wreckage over which Ellison's Jack-the-Bear launches the ball that will be returned when otherwise and as other to the equally altered self. He writes:

> I felt myself bounce, sail off like a ball thrown over a roof into mist, striking a hidden wall beyond a pile of broken machinery and sailing back. How long it took, I didn't know. But now above the movement of the hands I heard a friendly voice, uttering familiar words to which I could assign no meaning. I listened intensely, aware of the form and movement of sentences and grasping the now subtle rhythmical differences between progressions of sound that questioned and those that made a statement. But still their meanings were lost in the vast whiteness in which I myself was lost.[132]

What Jack-the-Bear is not able to be conscious of is the fact that the totalizing whiteness seeming to envelop him has been refracted/redacted into component parts and the light at the end of the tunnel is black. Rememory makes this possible. The complexity that must be unraveled here is how the machinery over which the ball/soul sails is demolished.

This machinery is commonly misunderstood as the law. Here it is understood as the violence, specifically police violence, that renders the law dynamic in its resistance to the plasticity of Black subjectivity. Police violence that makes law as it preserves it, is able, after sufficient dynamism, a posteriori, to alter its "historical origin" to render the proximate cause of violence already and always in favor of the police. This means that, until the shattering of the mechanism that grants this agility to police violence is imploded, there is no way to historicize action against Anti-Blackness in a way that grants the proper locating of proximate cause to legitimize even the separation between violence and nonviolence within the context of white supremacist logic.

The violence necessary here, any and all of it, is to the presupposition of the legitimacy of police violence as the means to an end of a regime of law that renders positive Blackness an impossibility, in that death is always and already the possibility. This calls for a collectivity of the individuation of the actions that are indexed and located against historicity and, at the same time, unmoored from its debilitating illogic. This is not an abstraction.

Recall the lunatic assertion by an Aurora, Colorado, first responder that Elijah McClain almost did a push-up with roughly six hundred pounds of dynamically oppositional force on his back. This insanity is linked to multiple equally insane Anti-Black notions, including, but not limited to, the need to restrict the free movement of Black bodies due in no small part to the presumed irrationality of Black thought, which always renders any activity at least potentially violent if not assuredly so. The proper point of observation of Blackness in motion necessarily links it to the depravity of this form of dehumanizing superhumanity, while, at the same time, remaining hypervigilant for the dangerous presence of just this thinking.

The dynamic motion of the machine of state violence is wrecked by disallowing it to situate the negative fantasy of Black collectivity to set the stage for the necessary negative formation of the Black individual. Reversing the vector saves the life of Elijah McClain and restores Breonna Taylor to anonymity, both of whom are here shamelessly and, in contravention of my own argument, asked to serve as the individual exemplars of a collective harm. This is the summation of the Means that Malcolm X finds Necessary, the requirement that the individual's actions are framed as just that, while, at the same time, situating them against the proximate cause of Anti-Blackness. To wit, it is predictable and rational that a Black person would preemptively resist the police because the police kill Black people without cause.

This is all a thinking and imagining practice that requires introspective quiet in service of individuation for the possibility of collectivity. This is an improvisation of Malcolm X's aggregation of hemispheric Blackness in preparation for its global eruption through collectivization. With the understanding that we are still in the midst of determining the best way to exploit the node that has been constructed of Rememory and sound, it is Kevin Quashie's discourse on the sound-full-ness of the sound-less-ness of quiet that is imperative:

> The idea of quiet is compelling because the term is not fancy—it is an everyday word—but it is also conceptual. Quiet is often used interchangeably with silence or stillness, but the notion of quiet in the pages that follow is neither motionless nor without sound. Quiet, instead, is a metaphor for the full range of one's inner life—one's desires, ambitions, hungers, vulnerabilities, fears. The inner life is not apolitical or without social value, but neither is it determined entirely by publicness. In fact, the interior—dynamic and ravishing—is a stay against the dominance of the social world; it has its own sovereignty. It is hard to see, even harder to describe, but no less potent in its ineffability. Quiet.[133]

In the world of Anti-Blackness, the generative and revolutionary potentiality of Quashie's quiet is violent. Further, Quashie's formulation resists the notion that there is something *wrong* with individuation. The sovereignty found through this inner exploration is the key to unlocking the potentiality of radical freedom that tends toward a dialectic of collective care rather than conflict: a dialectic that becomes possible as a product of the radical being for itself of Being-as-Black. Following Quashie, something as simple as falling in love with the interiority of the self, which has been set free from the debilitation of unraveling through conflict, establishes the beauty of Blackness as appositional rather than oppositional to a notion of Being-as-White. That this is not derived from a contrived notion of the depravity of Blackness is to violently oppose the world of Anti-Blackness. What Quashie frames as the "Conclusion" to his meditation on Quiet, titled "To Be One," is the end that is the beginning of the crossing from this node and turns the tumblers of the door that has appeared not just locked but impenetrable and can be breached one-by-one as a collectivity. Again, Quashie via Spillers:

> Quiet is the subjectivity of the "one."
>
> Literary theorist Hortense Spillers proclaims that "What is missing in African-American cultural analysis is the concept of the 'one'" [*Black, White, and in Color*, 394]. Spillers is right, since the concept of oneness is too messy to fit with our common thinking about blackness. Oneness asserts the right of a human being to be just that—a human—being and this assertion privileges the inner life. And yet the interiority of oneness does not correlate with being immune to or isolated from the social world. In fact, in insisting on the right to be a human being, oneness infers that a person is a citizen of humanity. And has license to be of the whole world. This is humanity as abundance and ambivalence.[134]

The elegance of Quashie and Spillers elevates again to our consciousness the abundance of "just": both "just enough of," in the sense of only using what we need, and "just enough," in the sense of having only as much as is needed and no more but that being enough.

Conclusion: The Bearable Lightness of Being-as-Black

The door had seemed shut because the light that came through its opening onto Morrison's "*third, if you will pardon the expression, world*" is Black. Recall here the ball that Jack-the-Bear has divined for purposes of encircling his soul.

Ellison suggests the complexity of movement that attends here in escaping the laws of motion that surround the node we have entered. This is due to the gravitational (if we allow that term) pull of the commonality and security of the insecurity of the homes we have found in the Anti-Black World: architecture posing as world, rooms within that structure posing as homes within a world. This combined with the unknown, which must be the possibility and problem of moving from a phase of practical security in the face of threat to a space of imagination and memory and memorial of that which must be left behind, is the locus of a different force of fear. Following the quote from chapter 11 of *Invisible Man*, which we continue to address here, the narrator grapples with just that complication:

> I fell to plotting ways of short-circuiting the machine. Perhaps if I shifted my body about so that the two nodes would come together—No, not only was there no room but it might electrocute me. I shuddered. Whoever else I was, I was no Samson. I had no desire to destroy myself even if it destroyed the machine; I wanted freedom, not destruction. It was exhausting, for no matter what the scheme I conceived, there was one constant flaw—myself. There was no getting around it. I could no more escape than I could think of my identity. Perhaps, I thought, the two things are involved with each other. When I discover who I am, I'll be free.[135]

Like Jack-the-Bear, we are in this place that has such fragile protection from the complete disaster of Anti-Blackness in its most extreme and final instantiations that it requires us to think the self differently. Following Spillers, there must be a form of Black regard of the Self that accommodates the silence of self-preoccupation in service of the particularity of identifying the self as such. The concept of linking the resurgence of the individual as the threshold condition of freedom, which we see in the Spillers quoted earlier and implicated in the Ellison here, is of primary negative concern on the part of Fred Moten's meditation on Sora Han's notice of the Case of Betty in her "extraordinary essay, 'Slavery as Contract: Betty's Case and the Question of Freedom,' where she beautifully and rigorously undertakes to apprehend what description and narrative cannot comprehend."[136]

Briefly, the complexity here is centered around the fact that the enslaved Betty, when transported by the Sweet family from Tennessee to Massachusetts becomes "free" and, therefore, need not be compelled to return to Tennessee and slavery. She, however, elects to do so, and Han reads this as suggesting:

> The point is not that contract law is one mode of domination among others available to the master, but that contract is the condition of possibility for the slave's property status. It is not because the slave is a priori property that the master uses contractual relations to exercise power over the slave. Rather, the development of legal freedom is dependent on slavery as a passage between radically heterogeneous exercises of individual contract rights, within both public and pri-

vate realms, and the transcendent idea of free will at the heart of contract freedom.[137]

Recall this complexity in Track 6 of the "Lyricism," where Gladys Knight, despite the abject failure that haunts her partner's ambition, follows him back to whence they came. Han notes that the "legal historian Aviam Soifer gives us an account of [Judge] Shaw's conclusion upon emerging from [his] closed meeting with Betty," stating:

> "It appeared to me," Shaw said of Betty, "that she is twenty-five years old, intelligent and capable of judging for herself." He also found "that she has a husband in Tennessee and other relatives; that she is much attached to Mr. and Mrs. Sweet; is very well treated by them, and desires to remain and return with them, and this desire she expressed decisively and upon repeated inquiries."[138]

Outside of these assertions by the judge in the case, Betty is silent because the law (of motion) that attends Blackness under the threat of Anti-Blackness does not accommodate the utterance of terms of attachment that has her exercise her paradoxical freedom to be unfree. To me, it isn't so much that Betty chose to be unfree but that the laws of motion that pull on the bodies here allow for that ghoulish possibility.

I want to think this through with Sora Han, Fred Moten, Kevin Quashie, Hortense Spillers, Gladys Knight, Midnight Train, and juridical decisions in order to crowd the node through and against the fence that functions as the complete incompleteness of August Wilson's *Fences*. Specifically, act 1, scene 3, and the interaction between Troy (father) and Cory (son) that we can encounter without the mediation of Shaw:

> CORY: Can I ask you a question?
> TROY: What the hell you wanna ask me? Mr. Stawicki the one you got the question for.
> CORY: How come you ain't never liked me?
> TROY: Like you? Who the hell say I got to like you? What law is there that say I got to like you?. . .
> CORY: None.
> TROY: Well, alright then! Don't you eat every day?
> CORY: Yeah.
> TROY: Nigger, as long as you in my house, you put a sir on the end of it when you talk to me!
> CORY: Yes . . . sir.

TROY: You eat every day . . . Got a roof over your head . . . Got clothes on your back . . .

CORY: Yessir.

TROY: Why you think that is?

CORY: Cause of you.

TROY: Aw, hell I know it's 'cause of me . . . but why do you think that is?

CORY: (*Hesitant*) Cause you like me.

TROY: Like you? I go out of here every morning . . . bust my butt . . . putting up with them crackers every day . . . cause I like you? . . . It's my job. It's my responsibility! . . . You live in my house . . . fill you belly up with my food . . . cause you my son. You my flesh and blood. Not 'cause I like you! 'Cause it's my duty . . . I ain't got to like you . . . I done give you everything I have to give you. I gave you your life! . . . Don't you try and go through life worrying about if somebody like you or not. You best be making sure they doing right by you. You understand what I'm saying, boy?

CORY: Yessir.[139]

This complex scene is masterfully handled by Denzel Washington as Troy and Jovan Adepo as Cory in the 2016 film version of Wilson's play. I use the term "complex" because August Wilson sets himself the task of giving voice to that which cannot be sounded within the crushing gravitational pull of the architecture posing as world of Anti-Black Racism. Troy spends his frustrated adulthood, having been barred from his dream of playing professional baseball, laboring in the dystopia of segregated Pittsburgh. He abuses his family mentally and physically. He betrays the trust of his wife all the while struggling to erect a fence around all of this misery. In this scene, Troy forces his son to choose work in a food store over his dream to play high school football, thinking that he is protecting him from the same disappointment that he suffered being denied the logical telos of a talented athlete, in many ways enacting the same type of death in lieu of harm that Sethe visits on "crawling already?"

Cory asks his father, whose harsh treatment and rules don't feel like care, why he has never liked him. Wilson gives Cory the colloquial double negative "ain't never," which, strictly read, equates to a much different question: "How come you always like me?" Troy hears the question as his son means it and evades answering it and instead turns to a recitation of what he does to care for his son, pointedly declaring that liking him was never part of the bargain.[140] But providing for his family is not only part of the bargain in this formulation; it is all of it. Eating, shelter, clothing, none of that is because he "likes" his son but because it is his "job." The juxtaposition of duty and work, if it weren't clear beforehand, is revealed without question when Troy describes how his employer having to pay him for his labor is the same as the duty he owes his son. It is a product of him being owed compensation and not because Mr. Rand likes him. In a world that has allowed Troy, standing in for a common type of "dream deferred" subject who Lorraine Hansberry also explores in her *Raisin in the Sun*, no space with which to test his dreams, he can only try to make his world small enough to accommodate this negativity: the opposite of the progressive and expansive nodes we have been locating.

I want to index the notion of caring/mattering in its relationship to being "owed" or perhaps compensated as a layer of devastating complexity to the understanding that under the regime of Anti-Blackness Black life only matters in how clearly it is demonstrated to not matter. Here, the mattering, or what we might call something like marginal positive subjectivity, is transactional and a component of the fragile nature of living in the crucible of anti-Blackness.

Morrison again. Recall Paul D's admonition to Sethe that her love "is too thick."[141] Thick in the sense that its tether is such that the fear of harm and death causes Sethe to preempt the possibility of harm and death with both harm and death. This quote is ever more impactful when read through Paul D's more thorough understanding of love in the world of Anti-Black Racism:

> Risky, thought Paul D, very risky. For a used-to-be-slave woman to love anything that much was dangerous, especially if it was her children she had settled on to love. The best thing, he knew, was to love just a little bit, so when they broke its back, or shoved it in a croaker sack, well, maybe you'd have enough love left over for the next one.[142]

Paul D speaks with and through the performance of evacuating the concept of "like" to leave unsaid and unsayable, to the victims of Anti-Blackness, "Love." These parents require that we productively improvise through Patterson's understanding of natal alienation. What is being described here is anything but a form of alienation of natality in that the line of misery remains unbroken from parent to child. It is a perpetual state of marginalization of the possibility of love because of the clear and "thick" cords of the emotion that binds one generation to the next in a form of suffering dedicated to denying suffering, while, at the same time, suffering because of the denial. This is seen throughout this book, from my many-times-great-grandfather's view of the antebellum open-air prison that was his "world" to my little brother and me being told we were niggers who needed to beware under the protection of my father and his brother to the preposterous notion of the superhuman strength of the 140 pound Elijah McClain to our best friend too

Breonna Taylor II. Paul D and Troy want to pass along hard-won understandings to their children or those foolish enough to Love in the world besieged with Death, situated as the term and condition of Freedom rather than love. Paul D, for his part, perceives the lie but does not possess the fullness of the technologies of cognition and consciousness to Be different.

> So you protected yourself and loved small. Picked the tiniest stars out of the sky to own; lay down with head twisted in order to see the loved one over the rim of the trench before you slept. Stole shy glances at her between the trees at chain-up. Grassblade, salamanders, spiders, woodpeckers, beetles, a kingdom of ants. Anything bigger wouldn't do. A woman, a child, a brother—a big love like that would split you wide open in Alfred, Georgia. He knew exactly what she meant: to get to a place where you could love anything you chose—not need permission for desire—well now, that was freedom.[143]

Love is Freedom. The Freedom to Love is Freedom. The imposition of the ain't-never-like is the emotional response to the fear that Black death haunts the possibility of thick love. August Wilson's Troy cannot erect a barrier he can rely on against the onslaught of white supremacy even in a play that has white people in it in name only. In the absence of the possibility of walled in safety in the world of Anti-Blackness, Love is unsayable, Like not at stake, and "owing" the currency of positive self-worth and the only payable debt of the impossibility of life in any of its splendid apparitions: even its loss.

Recall that Cory has learned the lesson all too well and does not ask his father why he does or does not love him. "Like" is a bridge too far even presented in the subversive double negative. This is the tragic problem that requires resolution to find what Paul D understands as the multivalent Freedom of Love; this is the river that flows to the Door of ~~No~~ Return and beyond.

I want to think with the matériel we have to improvise the map, the flow, the wind, the tide, the vessel to Return while mindful of cognition (Rememory) as well as the first vibration of Consciousness of Blackness with respect to its ontological self, independent of its apparition as a function of the caprice of whiteness. What we have unearthed is the incomplete nature of natal alienation, in that the genealogy of suffering is both the threshold condition for and a portion of the content of Morrison's Rememory. Alongside that linkage, perhaps as the vehicle for the traverse back and forward and beyond, is what Paul D understands as Sethe's too thick Love.

With this information, I recast the river of suffering that flows from the Black World through the Middle Passage to the (God)dam(n) of Black Death that confounds its forward progress as foundationally the misuse of Black Love or what Paul D rightly indexes as Freedom. This "misuse" is exemplified by the evacuation of the terms like and the missing love for the question of Cory to his father who wants/needs him to be capable of saying, "I've always liked you but in excess of that I love you," in that it is possible and sometimes useful to dislike that which you, at the same time, love. The fear of death that we have so thoroughly interrogated has rendered Love a luxury that, following Paul D, we, the progeny of the formerly enslaved, who, in the cognitive world of Rememory, are both separate from and inseparable from that tragedy, can ill afford without dire consequences.

This is the proper use of the node and the purpose of the white supremacist imperative to hurry the Black subject at a breakneck pace along a linear timeline that disallows the pause that is so necessary for the experience and cultivation of Love: the final term and the vehicle for travel across this threshold and through the door that had appeared shut in a bygone past that has been divined in the presentism of the future. This pause as this node reaches the point of positive terminus appears in music and in verse. It is the Maxwell moment in the artist's "Ascension" that grants the required delay in the fulfillment of desire as self-consciousness that we understand now as Love, which resists progress only toward untimely death or preoccupation with its presence:

So tell me how long . . .
How long it's gonna be before you speak, baby?

It is not, most likely, that the Lover does not speak but utters a language of love that the listener is in the process of developing ears to hear this speech in transition, which is also referenced in act 2, scene 1, of Shakespeare's *Romeo and Juliet*:

She speaks, yet she says nothing. What of that?
Her eye discourses; I will answer it.
I am too bold. 'Tis not me she speaks.[144]

The pause here that Romeo finds unintelligible, Maxwell hears as silence, and Jack-the-Bear struggles to translate as he awaits the return of his soul/ball is the quiet we are seeking to meet the challenge of Quashie's imperative for silence as the node that we have explored, in spite of what appears to be the evacuation of sound or is unintelligible. Again, from Ellison, who points us to those who appear to our perception if not consciousness from some other place time:

> What about those fellows waiting still and silent there on the platform; so still and silent that they clash with the crowd in their very

> immobility, standing noisy in their very silence; harsh as a cry of terror in their quietness?[145]

It is critical in thinking with Ellison on the state of play in this node, which leads to another world, that we witness the presence of figures, who are not affected by the laws of motion, that serve as the terms of Being in the Anti-Black World. We witnessed just this sort of presence from other times and spaces with the tripartite relationship between Ishmael, Jack-the-Bear, and Sethe. Here, it is the apparition of the zoot-suiters, who, in spite of their appearance in the uniform of the hipster, call to mind Black World$_{\text{Prime}}$, and are out of step with the space and time of Anti-Blackness:

> What about those three boys, coming now along the platform, tall and slender, walking stiffly with swinging shoulders in their well-pressed, too-hot-for-summer suits. . . . These fellows whose bodies seemed—what had one of the teachers said of me?—"You're like one of these African sculptures, distorted in the interest of design." Well, what design and whose? . . .
>
> For they were men outside of historical time, they were untouched, they didn't believe in Brotherhood, no doubt had not heard of it . . .
>
> For the boys speak a jived up transitional language full of country glamour, think transitional thoughts, though perhaps they dream the same old ancient dreams. . . . Men out of time . . . who knew but that they were saviors . . . the stewards of something uncomfortable . . .
>
> Perhaps each hundred years or so men like them, like me, appeared in society . . .
>
> They were outside the groove of history, and it was my job to get them in, all of them.[146]

In the node we have assembled through the collection of the available tools in this world, Jack-the-Bear is now prepared to hear (be conscious) of the transitional language and thoughts that, in their frequency agility, would otherwise be unintelligible if they were even perceived. Further, in this space, we are prepared to resist the pull of Brotherhood that precedes the security of the self. Not individuation as a terminus but individual care of the self that prepares one for collectivity.

Rememory it.

Robin D. G. Kelley's iconic and essential *Freedom Dreams: The Black Radical Imagination* is, in many ways, through the imagination-based love of his mother, the final movement here:

> The idea that we could possibly go somewhere that exists only in our imagination—that is, "nowhere"—is the classic definition of *utopia*. Call me utopian, but I inherited my mother's belief that the map to a new world is in the imagination, in what we see in our third eye rather than in the desolation that surrounds us.[147]

The challenge here has always been to come to propose the way that the imagination gifted to Professor Kelley and all of us can be fulfilled in Morrison's "*third, if you will pardon the expression, world*." Outside of a comprehensive and disciplined sculpting of a systemic form of cognition that has as its foundation and ceiling love, the cacophony of generational suffering that Dionne Brand understands is confirmed. Brand, in the final moments of the majesty of *A Map to the Door of No Return*, asserts that "a map, then, is only a life of conversation about a forgotten list of irretrievable selves."[148]

Rememory it to Rememory them.

By viewing the unbroken tether of thick Love as the vehicle for the resurgences of memories and selves that have never truly been lost, we are prepared to realize the fact of the conundrum. Brand's map takes on a dynamic character deserving of the journey to the place that had never been left in the first place, whereby, until Rememory, we were doomed to find the real as illusory and the illusory as an irresistible force that shatters the dreams of the Black Radical Imagination. This form of Consciousness alters the resistance of Du Bois's doubling of the Black Self, of which one simulacrum is hated and the other duped into hating. Consciousness of the existence of Black as Blackness rather than Blackness in negative discourse with whiteness is the condition of self-love that is the spatial silence conjured in this node that is often reminiscent of the quietude of the tomb. The way to Being-as-Black, over time and in time has been cluttered, if not blocked, with the physical and metaphysical misery of Black Death, which urges us to go back: the notion of no return predicated on and enacted as an infinite return only to do it over again.

Rememory it.

In the extreme of this condition, the "dead" are brought back to life/death in the crucible of Anti-Blackness, posing as world from the place of suffering and queered observance of *Purgatorium ex Media Loca*. As Fanon of *The Wretched of the Earth* states, in spite of all of this chaos, "we never stop singing."[149]

Rememory it.

This is the lyricism that accompanied the pain and is the overarching method of (mis)perceived violence that Aretha employs to grant us the space necessary to disallow the retracing of the end to get to a beginning that never ends.

Rememory it.

This opening, the ineluctable framing of Blackness vis-à-vis Blackness disrupts forward motion toward the predictably unpredictable infinite return of Death, which arrives disguised as duty to the state evacuated of its existence as sacrifice. Rememory it rather than remember it. Love it and, in so doing, rescue the self from the delirium of whiteness as the resolution of Blackness.

Rememory it.

The deafening silence becomes legible in its depth and breadth and corrects the phantasm of white supremacist architecture posing as world, as if the hall of mirrors at a carnival could be properly (mis)understood as reflecting the world as it is. The mirrors that are the mechanical representation of second sight, double consciousness, and twoness are seen for what they are and can and will be left in the hall intact rather than shattered. Discredited and Abandoned.

Rememory it.

Without that system of negative reflection in operation, now rendered archaic and anachronistic, the Black Self stands revealed to itself, and other Black Selves can embark on the universal particularity of recognition of the individual as the essential building block of the collectivity. The walls between these selves allow for the interiority of self-reflection to abut the exteriority of the other similarly engaged. The inside of the outside meets the outside of the inside.

Rememory it.

The building blocks of Morrison's World assemble themselves based on the ordering principles of a world that does not require the sublation of the humanity of others to affirm the faux superhumanity of another. This is not a feature. This is a law of nature/motion of the "*third, if you will pardon the expression, world*," which precedes the construction of the laws of society. It is not the other way around, where a series of fallacious notions of marginal being are used to derive a legal regime that reifies the notion of something as preposterous as the nonexistence of Blackness without whiteness.

Rememory it.

At the point of the acceptance of this alteration of worldview, the previous architecture that haunted and halted the possibility of forward momentum is (dys)oriented to the vertical plane rather than the linear representation of past, present, and future (which never arrives). This allows us to perceive the seemingly infinite recurrence of the Middle Passage as a moment in time. Remembered. Never forgotten. Evacuated of its totalizing effects.

Rememory it.

The anteliminality of Black World$_{\text{Prime}}$, the liminality of the Anti-Black World, and the postliminal nature of Morrison's "*third, if you will pardon the expression, world*" is unified as the content of a memory space that is thick like love but never liked. The reason, improvising with Cory to Troy, that we ain't never like it is because there ain't nothing to like and the situating of transitional subjectivity fails to stand in for the Love that is there but unstated.

Rememory it.

Like the very opening of Stevie Wonder's *Songs in the Key of Life*, it is the maintenance of Love with love that collapses the last barrier to Black-as-Being throwing open all doors that open to love and sealing the ones that do not.

Rememory it.

Acceptance of the world as it stands is a luxury that Black people can ill afford.

Rememory it.

Notes

INTRODUCTION

1. Selassie, *Selected Speeches*, 374.
2. Ellison, *Invisible Man* (1995), 8.
3. Ibid., 6.
4. Morrison, *Source of Self-Regard*, 139.
5. Ibid., 29.
6. Sawyer, *Africana Philosophy of Temporality*, 121.
7. Morrison, *Source of Self-Regard*, 139.
8. Chandler, *"Beyond This Narrow Now,"* 5–6.
9. Ibid., 68.
10. Ibid.
11. Ibid., 97.
12. Ibid.
13. George Yancy, "Afropessimism Forces Us to Rethink Our Most Basic Assumptions about Society," Truthout, September 14, 2022, available at https://truthout.org/articles/afropessimism-forces-us-to-rethink-our-most-basic-assumptions-about-society/, accessed June 18, 2025.
14. Ibid.
15. McKittrick, *Demonic Grounds*, xiv.
16. Cheah, *What Is a World?* 2
17. Ibid., 16.
18. Griffin, *Read until You Understand*, xii.
19. Quashie, *Black Aliveness*, 13–14.
20. Morrison, *Source of Self-Regard*, 139.
21. Sawyer, *Black Minded*, 17.
22. Ellison, *Invisible Man* (1995), 14.

PART I

1. Chandler, *"Beyond This Narrow Now,"* 100.
2. Sharpe, *In the Wake*, 13.
3. Harriet A. Jacobs, *Incidents in the Life of a Slave Girl, Written by Herself*, Harvard University Press, 1987.
4. Hartman, "Venus in Two Acts," 13.
5. Barrymore Anthony Bogues, personal correspondence.
6. Patterson, *Slavery and Social Death*, 5.
7. Terada, *Metaracial*, 49.
8. Hegel, *Phenomenology of Spirit*, 251.
9. Ibid., 227.
10. Ibid., 230.
11. Ibid., 236.
12. Ibid., 248.
13. Ibid., 171.
14. Ibid., 112.
15. Ibid., 110.
16. Ibid., 71.
17. Ibid., 61.
18. Adegbindin, "Notes on Hegel's Treatment of Africa," 19.
19. Ibid., 19–20.
20. Hegel, *Lectures on the Philosophy of History*, 85.
21. Ibid.
22. Ibid., 91.
23. Hegel, *Phenomenology of Spirit*, 103.
24. Ibid., 86.
25. Ibid., 88.
26. Ibid., 112.
27. Ibid., 113.
28. Patterson, *Slavery and Social Death*, 5.
29. Ibid.
30. Ibid., 141.
31. Fanon, *Wretched of the Earth* (1968), 37.
32. Jackson, *Becoming Human*, 21.
33. Fanon, *Black Skin, White Masks*, xi.
34. Ibid.
35. Ibid., 191–192.
36. Ibid., 193.
37. John H. McClendon III, *C.L.R. James's Notes on Dialectics: Left Hegelianism or Marxism-Leninism?* (Lexington Books, 2004), 16.
38. Hegel, *Phenomenology of Spirit*, 260.
39. Ibid., 111.
40. Sawyer, *Africana Philosophy of Temporality*, 122–131.
41. Du Bois, *Souls of Black Folk* (2015), 5.
42. Hegel, *Phenomenology of Spirit*, 139.
43. Du Bois, *Souls of Black Folk* (2015), 5.
44. Ibid.
45. Hegel, *Phenomenology of Spirit*, 16–17.

46. Ibid., 17.

47. Achille Mbembe, *Necropolitics, Theory in Forms* (Duke University Press, 2019), 11–40.

48. Morrison, *Source of Self-Regard*, 139.

49. Judy, *Sentient Flesh*, 7.

50. Hegel, *Elements of the Philosophy of Right*, 27.

51. Hegel, *Phenomenology of Spirit*, 49.

52. Ibid., 49–50.

53. Merleau-Ponty, *Phenomenology of Perception*, xxvii.

54. Ibid., 20.

55. Ibid.

56. Morrison, *Beloved*, 43.

57. Sawyer, *Africana Philosophy of Temporality*, 122.

58. Du Bois, *Souls of Black Folk* (2015), 11.

59. Ibid.

60. Morrison, *Source of Self-Regard*, 139.

61. Ibid.

62. Ibid.

63. Fanon, *Black Skin, White Masks*, 89.

64. Ibid., 90.

65. Morrison, *Beloved*, 38.

66. Du Bois, *Souls of Black Folk* (2015), 11.

67. Ibid.

68. Morrison, *Beloved*, 38.

69. Ibid., 39.

70. Jackson, *Becoming Human*, 59.

71. Morrison, *Beloved*, 36.

72. Ibid.

73. Ibid., 37.

74. Ibid.

75. Ibid., 36.

76. Ibid., 37.

77. Hegel, *Phenomenology of Spirit*, 260.

78. Max Levy, "Experts Say Conviction of 2 Aurora Paramedics in Death of Elijah McClain Could Have a Chilling Effect on Rescuers," *Sentinel*, December 26, 2023, available at https://sentinelcolorado.com/metro/jury-finds-2-aurora-paramedics-guilty-of-criminally-negligent-homicide-in-death-of-elijah-mcclain/.

79. Claudia Rankine, *Citizen: An American Lyric* (Graywolf, 2014), 135.

80. "Here's What You Need to Know about Elijah McClain's Death," *New York Times*, June 30, 2020, available at https://www.nytimes.com/article/who-was-elijah-mcclain.html, accessed June 9, 2025.

81. Ibid.

82. Hegel, *Phenomenology of Spirit*, 450.

83. Agamben, *Homo Sacer*, 71.

84. Sawyer, *Africana Philosophy of Temporality*, 128.

85. Ibid.

86. W.E.B. Du Bois, *The Souls of Black Folk*. Norton Critical Edition (1999), xxvii–xxviii.

87. Ibid., 11.

88. Fanon, *Black Skin, White Masks*, xii.

89. Ibid., 45.
90. Reed, *Grand Journey*, 373–374.
91. Fanon, *Black Skin, White Masks*, xii.
92. Ibid.
93. Ibid., 45.
94. Ibid.
95. Hegel, *Phenomenology of Spirit*, 95.
96. Fanon, *Black Skin, White Masks*, 45.
97. Sharpe, *In the Wake*, 98.
98. Ibid.
99. Fanon, *Black Skin, White Masks*, xii.
100. Sharpe, *In the Wake*, 98.
101. Ibid.
102. Du Bois, *Souls of Black Folk* (1999), 11.
103. Ibid.
104. Sharpe, *In the Wake*, 98.
105. Du Bois, *Souls of Black Folk* (1999), 11.
106. Sharpe, *In the Wake*, 98.
107. Ibid.
108. Nancy, *Noli me tangere*, 21.
109. Ibid., 5.
110. Ibid., 27–28.
111. Ibid., 21.
112. Ibid., 44.
113. Sharpe, *In the Wake*, 98.
114. Ibid., 100.
115. Fanon, *Dying Colonialism*, 117–118.
116. Sharpe, *In the Wake*, 13.
117. Melville, *Moby-Dick*, 42.
118. Wilderson, *Afropessimism*, 196.
119. Coates, *Between the World and Me*, 7.
120. Aristotle, *The Metaphysics*, 373.
121. Greene, *Elegant Universe*, 67–71.
122. Fanon, *Wretched of the Earth* (2005), 37.
123. Ibid., 38.
124. Morrison, *Song of Solomon*, 3.
125. Aimé Césaire, "Réponse à Depestre, poète haïtien. Éléments d'un art poétique," *Présence Africaine*, no I-II (nouvelle version), avril-juillet 1955.
126. R. A. Judy, "Restless Flying: A Black Study of Revolutionary Humanism."
127. Morrison, *Song of Solomon*, 80.
128. Ibid., 328.
129. Hegel, *Phenomenology of Spirit*, 81.
130. Fanon, *Black Skin, White Masks*, xv.
131. Zakiyyah Iman Jackson, "'Theorizing in a Void': Sublimity, Matter, and Physics in Black Feminist Poetics," *South Atlantic Quarterly* 117, no. 3 (July 2018), 631.
132. Wideman, *The Lynchers*, 57–58.
133. Written and composed by Abel Meeropol and recorded by Billie Holiday, April 20, 1939.

134. Gil Scott-Heron, "Whitey on the Moon" (1970) and *The Last Holiday: A Memoir* (Grove, 2012), 165–166.

135. Joelle Goldstein, *People Magazine*, September 2, 2020.

136. Jason R. Young, "All God's Children Had Wings: The Flying African in History, Literature, and Lore," *Journal of Africana Religions* 5, no. 1 (January 2017).

137. Ibid.

138. Sylvia Wynter, "On How We Mistook the Map for the Territory, and Reimprisoned Ourselves in Our Unbearable Wrongness of Being, of Désêtre: Black Studies toward the Human Project," 107.

139. Ibid., 115.

140. Ibid., 113.

141. Ibid., 114.

142. Sylvia Wynter, "The Ceremony Must Be Found: After Humanism," *Boundary 2*, vol. 12, no. 3 (Spring–Autumn 1984), 27, available at https://doi.org/10.2307/302808.

143. Ibid., 37.

144. Sylvia Wynter, "Towards the Sociogenic Principle: Fanon, the Puzzle of Conscious Experience, of 'Identity' and What It's Like to Be 'Black,'" *National Identities*, vol. 3, no. 3 (2001), 305–344, available at https://doi.org/10.1080/14608940120086182.

145. Du Bois, *Souls of Black Folk* (1999), 10.

146. Ibid.

147. Ibid., 5.

148. Ibid.

149. Ibid.

150. Wynter, "Towards the Sociogenic Principle."

151. Blumenberg, *Shipwreck with Spectator*, 12.

152. Ibid.

PART II

1. Jacques Rancière, *Dissensus: On Politics and Aesthetics.*

2. Fanon, *Black Skin, White Masks*, 1.

3. Rankine, Loffreda, and Cap, *Racial Imaginary*, 22.

4. Ibid., 13.

5. Ibid., 24.

6. Morrison, *Source of Self-Regard*, 139.

7. Michelle M. Wright, *Physics of Blackness: Beyond the Middle Passage Epistemologies* (University of Minnesota Press, 2015).

8. Chanda Prescod-Weinstein, *The Disordered Cosmos: A Journey into Dark Matter, Spacetime, and Dreams Deferred* (Bold Type Books).

9. Born, *Einstein's Theory of Relativity*, 28.

10. Ibid.

11. Ibid., 56–57.

12. Ibid., 71.

13. Sawyer, *Africana Philosophy of Temporality*, 1.

14. Leon Bridges, "River" (Sony Music, 2015).

15. Ellison, *Invisible Man* (1980), 13.

16. Langston Hughes, "The Negro Speaks of Rivers," in *The Collected Poems of Langston Hughes*, edited by Arnold Rampersad and David Roessel (Vintage Classics, 1995), 23.

17. Martin Luther King Jr., "Now I Say to You in Conclusion," World Prayers, available at www.worldprayers.org/archive/prayers/meditations/now_i_say_to_you_in_conclusion.html, accessed June 11, 2025.
18. DeVito, *Coltrane on Coltrane*, 56.
19. Ellison, *Invisible Man* (1980).
20. Han, "Slavery as Contract," 403.

PART III

1. Melville, *Moby-Dick*, 135.
2. Ellison, *Invisible Man* (1995), 8–9.
3. Ibid., 9.
4. Melville, *Moby-Dick*, 24.
5. Ibid.
6. Ibid., 10.
7. Elizabeth Schultz, "The Illumination of Darkness: Affinities between *Moby-Dick* and *Invisible Man*," *CLA Journal*, vol. 32, no. 2 (December 1988), 172.
8. Morrison, *Beloved*, 35.
9. Ellison, *Invisible Man* (1980), 6.
10. Ibid., 5.
11. Morrison, *Beloved*, 3.
12. Ellison, *Invisible Man* (1980), 7.
13. Morrison, *Beloved*, 3.
14. Ibid., 4.
15. Ellison, *Invisible Man* (1980), 8.
16. Morrison, *Beloved*, 94.
17. Ibid., 77.
18. Ellison, *Invisible Man* (1980), 1.
19. Ibid.
20. Ibid.
21. Ibid.
22. Ibid., 2.
23. Ibid., 2.
24. Ibid., 43–44.
25. Ibid., 42.
26. Ibid., 35.
27. Ibid., 36.
28. Ibid., 6.
29. Ibid., 5.
30. Ibid.
31. Ibid.
32. Morrison, *Beloved*, 60–61.
33. Ibid., 64.
34. Ibid., 65.
35. Ellison, *Invisible Man* (1980), 7.
36. Morrison, *Beloved*, 10.
37. Ibid., 11.
38. Ibid., 24.
39. Ellison, *Invisible Man* (1980), 7.

40. Ibid., 8.
41. Ibid.
42. Morrison, *Beloved*, 25.
43. Ellison, *Invisible Man* (1980), 9.
44. Ibid.
45. Ibid.
46. Ibid.
47. Ibid.
48. Ibid.
49. See Michael E. Sawyer's "Melville's Meditation on the *Long* Shipwreck of the Middle Passage" book chapter in *Companion to Melville*, edited by Wyn Kelley and Christopher Ohge (Wiley Blackwell).
50. Morrison, *Beloved*, 202–203.
51. Ibid., 203.
52. Ibid., 248–249.
53. Ibid., 88.
54. Ibid.
55. Ibid.
56. Ibid.
57. Ibid.
58. Ibid.
59. Ibid.
60. Ibid.
61. Ibid., 236.
62. Ibid., 242.
63. Ibid., 248, 253.
64. Ibid., 43.
65. Ibid., 248.
66. Ibid., 249.
67. Ibid., 248.
68. Ibid.
69. Ellison, *Invisible Man* (1980), 13–14.
70. Ibid., 231.
71. Ibid., 234.
72. Ibid., 235.
73. Ibid.
74. Morrison, *Beloved*, 248.
75. Ellison, *Invisible Man* (1980), 239–240.
76. Morrison, *Beloved*, 249.
77. Ibid., 249–250.
78. Ellison, *Invisible Man* (1980), 240–241.
79. Ibid.
80. Ibid.
81. Ibid., 241.
82. Morrison, *Beloved*, 251.
83. Ibid., 251.
84. Ibid., 127.
85. Ellison, *Invisible Man* (1980), 243.
86. Morrison, *Beloved*, 251.

87. Ellison, *Invisible Man* (1980), 249.
88. Ibid., 581.
89. Ibid., 14.
90. Ibid., 15.
91. Ibid., 10–11.
92. Morrison, *Beloved*, 207.
93. Abdurraqib, *Little Devil in America*, 39.
94. Ibid., 41.
95. Morrison, *Beloved*, 102.
96. Ibid., 103.
97. Warren, *Ontological Terror*, 12.
98. Moten, *Stolen Life*, 21.
99. Ibid., 20.
100. Gordon, *Fear of Black Consciousness*, 19.
101. Priest, *Introduction to Non-Classical Logic*.
102. Badiou, *Being and Event*, 298.
103. Warren, *Ontological Terror*, 22.
104. Ibid., 12–13.
105. James G. Lennox, "Aristotle's Natural Philosophy," in *The Stanford Encyclopedia of Philosophy*, edited by Edward N. Zalta (Winter 2021 ed.), available at plato.stanford.edu/entries/aristotle-natphil/#ArisCosmView, accessed June 11, 2025.
106. Griaule, *Conversations with Ogotemmêli*, 105.
107. Jacq, *Wisdom of Ptah-Hotep*, xi.
108. Sharpe, *In the Wake*, 109.
109. Fanon, *Dying Colonialism*, 118.
110. Benjamin, "Critique of Violence."
111. Fanon, *Wretched of the Earth* (2004), 8.
112. Ibid., 23.
113. Ibid., 238–239.
114. Marriott, *Whither Fanon*, xiv–xx.
115. Ibid., 153.
116. Ibid.
117. Ibid.
118. Belle, *Hannah Arendt and the Negro Question*.
119. Marriott, *Whither Fanon*, 161.
120. Ibid., 5.
121. Ibid., 169.
122. Ibid., ix.
123. Ibid., x.
124. Benjamin, "Toward the Critique of Violence," 39.
125. Ibid., 41–42.
126. Ibid.
127. Ibid., 42.
128. Malcolm X. *By Any Means Necessary*, 46–47.
129. Ibid.
130. The reference here is Bernard Yack's *The Longing for Total Revolution: Philosophic Sources of Social Discontent from Rousseau to Marx and Nietzsche* (Princeton University Press, 1986).
131. Sawyer, *Black Minded*, 121.

132. Ellison, *Invisible Man* (1980), 238.
133. Quashie, *Sovereignty of Quiet*, 6.
134. Ibid., 119–120.
135. Ellison, *Invisible Man* (1980), 243.
136. Moten, *Stolen Life*, 246.
137. Han, "Slavery as Contract," 403.
138. Ibid., 398.
139. Wilson, *Fences*, 37–38.
140. Ibid., 38.
141. Morrison, *Beloved*, 193.
142. Ibid., 54.
143. Ibid., 191.
144. Shakespeare, "Romeo and Juliet," 379.
145. Ellison, *Invisible Man* (1980), 440.
146. Ibid., 440–443.
147. Kelley, *Freedom Dreams*, 2.
148. Brand, *Map to the Door of No Return*, 224.
149. Fanon, *Wretched of the Earth* (2004), 86.

Selected Bibliography

Abdurraqib, Hanif. *A Little Devil in America: Notes in Praise of Black Performance*. Random House, 2021.

Adegbindin, Omotade. "Critical Notes on Hegel's Treatment of Africa." *Ogiriai: A New Journal of African Studies* 11 (2015).

Agamben, Giorgio. *Homo Sacer: Sovereign Power and Bare Life*. Stanford University Press, 1998.

Aristotle. *The Metaphysics*. Penguin Classics, 2004.

Badiou, Alain. *Being and Event*. Continuum, 2012.

Belle, Kathryn Sophia [published as Gines, Kathryn T.]. *Hannah Arendt and the Negro Question*. Indiana University Press, 2014.

Benjamin, Walter. "Toward the Critique of Violence." In *Toward the Critique of Violence: A Critical Edition*, edited by Peter Fenves and Julia Ng. Stanford University Press, 2021.

Blumenberg, Hans. *Shipwreck with Spectator: Paradigm of a Metaphor for Existence*. MIT Press, 1997.

Born, Max. *Einstein's Theory of Relativity*. Dover, 1962.

Brand, Dionne. *A Map to the Door of No Return*. Vintage Canada, 2011.

Caroll, Lewis. *Through the Looking-Glass*. Dover, 1999.

Chandler, Nahum Dimitri. *"Beyond This Narrow Now": Or, Delimitations of W.E.B. Du Bois*. Duke University Press, 2022.

Cheah, Pheng. *What Is a World? On Postcolonial Literature as World Literature*. Duke University Press, 2016.

Coates, Ta-Nehisi. *Between the World and Me*. Spiegel and Grau, 2015.

DeVito, Chris, ed. *Coltrane on Coltrane: The John Coltrane Interviews*. Chicago Review, 2010.

Du Bois, W.E.B. *Black Reconstruction in America: 1860–1880*. Free Press, 1998.

Du Bois, W.E.B. *The Souls of Black Folk*. W. W. Norton & Company, 1999.

Du Bois, W.E.B. *The Souls of Black Folk*. Yale University Press, 2015.

Ellison, Ralph. *Invisible Man*. Second Vintage International Edition, 1995.

Fanon, Frantz. *Black Skin, White Masks.* Grove, 2008.

Fanon, Frantz. *A Dying Colonialism.* Grove, 1965.

Fanon, Frantz. *The Wretched of the Earth.* Grove, 2004.

Gordon, Lewis. *Fear of Black Consciousness.* Farrar, Straus and Giroux, 2022.

Greene, Brian. *The Elegant Universe.* W. W. Norton, 2010.

Griaule, Marcel. *Conversations with Ogotemmêli: An Introduction to Dogon Religious Ideas.* Oxford University Press, 1970.

Griffin, Farah Jasmine. *Read until You Understand: The Profound Wisdom of Black Life and Literature.* Norton, 2021.

Hall, Michael. J.W., Deckert, Dirk-André, and Wiseman, Howard M. "Quantum Phenomena Modeled by Interactions between Many Classical Worlds". *Phys. Rev. X 4, 041013.* 2024.

Han, Sora. "Slavery as Contract: Betty's Case and the Question of Freedom." *Law and Literature* 27, no. 3 (fall 2015).

Hansberry, Lorraine. *A Raisin in the Sun.*Vintage. 2004.

Hartman, Saidiya. "Venus in Two Acts." *Small Axe* 12, no. 2 (June 2008). Available at https://muse.jhu.edu/article/241115.

Hegel, G.W.F. *Elements of the Philosophy of Right.* Edited by Allen W. Wood. Cambridge University Press, 2017.

Hegel, G.W.F. *Lectures on the Philosophy of History.* Translated by Ruben Alvarado. Woodbridge, 2011.

Hegel, G.W.F. *System of Science, First Part: The Phenomenology of Spirit.* Translated and edited by Terry Pinkard. Cambridge University Press, 2018.

Jackson, Zakiyyah Iman. *Becoming Human: Matter and Meaning in an Antiblack World.* New York University Press, 2020.

Jacobs, Harriet A. *Incidents in the Life of a Slave Girl, Written by Herself.* Harvard University Press, 1987.

Jacq, Christian. *The Wisdom of Ptah-Hotep: Spiritual Treasures from the Age of the Pyramids.* Carroll and Graff, 2004.

Judy, R. A. "Restless Flying, A Study of Revolutionary Humanism." *Boundary 2* 47, no. 2 (2020).

Judy, R. A. *Sentient Flesh: Thinking in Disorder, Poiēsis in Black.* Duke University Press, 2020.

Kelley, Robin D. G. *Freedom Dreams: The Black Radical Imagination.* Beacon, 2022.

Malcolm X. *By Any Means Necessary: Speeches, Interviews, and a Letter by Malcolm X.* Edited by George Breitman. New York: Pathfinder Press, 1970.

Marriott, David. *Whither Fanon: Studies in the Blackness of Being.* Stanford University Press, 2018.

Mbembe, Achille. *Necropolitics.* Theory in Forms. Duke University Press, 2019.

McKittrick, Katherine. *Demonic Grounds: Black Women and the Cartographies of Struggle.* University of Minnesota Press, 2006.

Melville, Herman. *Moby-Dick.* W. W. Norton, 2002.

Merleau-Ponty, Maurice. *Phenomenology of Perception.* Routledge, 2012.

Morrison, Toni. *Beloved.* Vintage Books, 2004.

Morrison, Toni. *Song of Solomon.* Vintage Books, 2004.

Morrison, Toni. *The Source of Self-Regard: Selected Essays, Speeches, and Meditations.* Vintage International, 2019.

Moten, Fred. *Stolen Life: consent not to be a single being.* Duke University Press, 2018.

Nancy, Jean-Luc. *Noli me tangere: On the Raising of the Body.* Fordham University Press, 2008.

Patterson, Orlando. *Slavery and Social Death: A Comparative Study*. Harvard University Press, 1982.

Priest, Graham. *An Introduction to Non-Classical Logic: From If to Is*. Cambridge University Press, 2012.

Quashie, Kevin. *Black Aliveness, or A Poetics of Being*. Duke University Press, 2021.

Quashie, Kevin. *The Sovereignty of Quiet: Beyond Resistance in Black Culture*. Rutgers University Press, 2012.

Rankine, Claudia, Beth Loffreda, and Max King Cap, eds. *The Racial Imaginary: Writers on Race in the Life of the Mind*. Fence Books, 2016.

Reed, Rodney J. *A Grand Journey: The History of Sigma Pi Phi Fraternity 1904–2010*. Kindle, 2021.

Sawyer, Michael E. *An Africana Philosophy of Temporality: Homo Liminalis*. Palgrave, 2018.

Sawyer, Michael E. *Black Minded: The Political Philosophy of Malcolm X*. Pluto, 2020.

Selassie, Haile. *Selected Speeches of His Imperial Majesty Haile Selassie I*. Lion of Judah Society's Imperial Publishers, 2011.

Shakespeare, William. "Romeo and Juliet." In *William Shakespeare: The Complete Works*. 2nd ed. Edited by Stanley Wells, Gary Taylor, John Jowett, and William Montgomery. Oxford University Press, 2005.

Sharpe, Christina. *In the Wake: On Blackness and Being*. Duke University Press, 2016.

Terada, Rei. *Metaracial: Hegel, Antiblackness and Political Identity*. University of Chicago Press, 2023.

Warren, Calvin L. *Ontological Terror: Blackness, Nihilism, and Emancipation*. Duke University Press, 2018.

Wideman, John Edgar. *The Lynchers*. Harcourt Brace Jovanovich, 1973.

Wilderson, Frank B., III. *Afropessimism*. Liveright, 2020.

Wilson, August. *Fences*. Plume Book, 1986.

Young, Jason R. "All God's Children Had Wings: The Flying African in History, Literature, and Lore". *Journal of African Religions, Vol. 5, No.1*. 2017.

Index

Page numbers in *italics* represent figures.

Michael E. Sawyer is Professor of African American Literature and Culture, Director of Graduate Studies in the Department of English, and Director of the Graduate Program in Cultural Studies at the University of Pittsburgh. He is the author of *An Africana Philosophy of Temporality: Homo Liminalis*, *Black Minded: The Political Philosophy of Malcolm X*, and *Sir Lewis*.

www.ingramcontent.com/pod-product-compliance
Lightning Source LLC
LaVergne TN
LVHW090603110826
845146LV00001B/245

* 9 7 8 1 4 3 9 9 2 5 5 7 7 *